ANALYSING POLITICS & PROTEST IN DIGITAL POPULAR CULTURE

Sara Miller McCune founded SAGE Publishing in 1965 to support the dissemination of usable knowledge and educate a global community. SAGE publishes more than 1000 journals and over 800 new books each year, spanning a wide range of subject areas. Our growing selection of library products includes archives, data, case studies and video. SAGE remains majority owned by our founder and after her lifetime will become owned by a charitable trust that secures the company's continued independence.

Los Angeles | London | New Delhi | Singapore | Washington DC | Melbourne

ANALYSING POLITICS & PROTEST IN DIGITAL POPULAR CULTURE

A Multimodal Introduction

LYNDON WAY

Los Angeles | London | New Delhi
Singapore | Washington DC | Melbourne

Los Angeles | London | New Delhi
Singapore | Washington DC | Melbourne

SAGE Publications Ltd
1 Oliver's Yard
55 City Road
London EC1Y 1SP

SAGE Publications Inc.
2455 Teller Road
Thousand Oaks, California 91320

SAGE Publications India Pvt Ltd
B 1/I 1 Mohan Cooperative Industrial Area
Mathura Road
New Delhi 110 044

SAGE Publications Asia-Pacific Pte Ltd
3 Church Street
#10-04 Samsung Hub
Singapore 049483

Editor: Michael Ainsley
Assistant Editor: Charlotte Bush
Senior project editor: Chris Marke
Copyeditor: Joy Tucker
Proofreader: Clare Weaver
Marketing manager: Susheel Gokarakonda
Cover design: Lisa Harper-Wells
Typeset by: C&M Digitals (P) Ltd, Chennai, India
Printed in the UK

At SAGE we take sustainability seriously. Most of our products are printed in the UK using responsibly sourced papers and boards. When we print overseas we ensure sustainable papers are used as measured by the PREP grading system. We undertake an annual audit to monitor our sustainability.

For Ayla, Erim, Kerem, Mum, Dad and Sinbad

CONTENTS

LIST OF FIGURES

ACKNOWLEDGEMENTS

I want to give a big thank you to Michael Ainsley at SAGE who has been supportive and has offered sound advice throughout. I want to thank David Machin who, like always, has offered guidance and inspiration. I also want to thank my colleagues at the University of Liverpool and students I have taught in all my university posts who have given me ideas, inspiration and a reason for writing this.

Previously published work in this volume:

The analysis of The Ringo Jets's 'Spring of War' in chapter four is derived from L. Way (2015), 'YouTube as a site of debate through populist politics: the case of a Turkish protest pop video', *Journal of Multicultural Discourse*, 10(2): 180–196.

PREFACE

I have a keen interest in how popular culture can be political. This interest (verging on passion) has manifested itself in not only my academic activities, but also as a practitioner. I have been a member of numerous bands – some far more political than others. In my research and my teaching, I have been particularly interested in how popular culture can communicate politics. I find it particularly useful approaching this juncture from a critical and discursive perspective. In my teaching in the UK, Cyprus, Turkey and Canada I have taught modules that critically analyse meanings in not only traditional popular culture like films, music videos and television programmes, but also in all the fun we experience digitally. This is obviously incredibly important, seeing the meteoric rise in the prevalence of digital media. Since I have been a lecturer, I have not found a resource that specifically spells out how to analyse political meanings in (digital) popular culture from a critical and discursive perspective. So, the starting point of this book addresses the deficit I find: how to analyse the juncture between politics, digital media, discourse and popular culture.

1

INTRODUCTION

Aims and Key Concepts

CHAPTER OBJECTIVES

- Introduce the aim of the book and the key concepts of politics and digital popular culture used throughout the book.
- Introduce issues surrounding relations between politics and digital popular culture.
- Introduce multimodal critical discourse studies and describe its advantages.
- Describe the contents of this book.

KEY CONCEPTS

- The aim of this book is to arm ourselves with an analytical toolkit that can reveal exactly how popular culture online is political.
- Politics is about 'power', 'control' and 'status' in society, governments, groups and organizations.
- Digital popular culture is popular culture that is (mostly) produced for and distributed online.
- A discursive perspective reveals not only what politics are articulated in (digital) popular culture, but also how these politics are expressed.
- Political ideologies are communicated in not only political speeches and news reports, but also entertainment (van Leeuwen, 1999; Machin and Richardson, 2012; Way, 2018a).

INTRODUCTION

At the time of writing, Donald Trump was the US president, Boris Johnson was the UK's Prime Minister, Britain was leaving the European Union, the global climate crisis was at the fore of most political policy discussions, COVID-19 was causing carnage, while angry citizens in cities around the world were protesting racial injustice. As such, there was no shortage of newsworthy politics covered in mainstream news outlets. All the same, most of us did not rush to the television or news websites daily to hang on to the words of our politicians. Instead, most of us scrolled through our feeds, opened our apps, liked and composed posts, watched, added comments and shared videos, mash-ups, GIFs and comedy videos. Social media on our mobiles, tablets or other devices not only offer us our own personalized stream of entertainment, they also inform us on an endless parade of issues, events and people. This is political. The aim of this book is to arm ourselves with an analytical toolkit that can reveal exactly how this is political.

Since 1990 when the World Wide Web first rolled out to everyone who could afford it, scholars, the press and the public have opined and expressed their views on the social and political roles offered to us in our new digital world. Scholars from almost every discipline hold a wide range of positions from the wildly optimistic to the downright negative on exactly what these roles may be. Areas under examination include how it may democratize media control (Jenkins, 2009), act as the new fourth estate (Vatikiotis, 2014) and how it operates in social movements (Morozov, 2009), among a raft of other points of interest. Its inventor, Tim Berners-Lee, first envisioned the World Wide Web as 'building a system for sharing data about physics experiments' (Hern, 2019). Since these humble beginnings, the explosive rise of social media and Web 2.0 have seen digital media become an integral part of our lives, transforming how we inform, communicate and entertain, as well as change the 'dynamic of discursive power' (KhosraviNik, 2017: 583). Though many of these changes may be characterized as a plethora of misinformation, jokes about body fluids, commercialization and polarization of discourse, Berners-Lee still believes the World Wide Web should be 'recognized as a human right and built for the public good', ensuring and emphasizing 'human rights, democracy, scientific fact and public safety' (in Hern, 2019).

In this book, our concern is one part of this wider study of digital media. We focus on how we, as researchers, can examine relations between politics and popular culture in the digital. 'Why are we focusing on this aspect of the digital?' you may ask. Think about our own dealings with politics. Indeed, politics are expressed in the news, political party statements and how we vote. It runs through all aspects of our social life in terms of the ideas and values upon which we organize society and relate to each other. However, for most of us, the majority of this is done online. And yes, we may view 'hard' news and political commentary online, but studies show we prefer entertainment that communicates to us affectively as well as cognitively (boyd, 2008). Besides, 'Political communication scholars are increasingly acknowledging that the historical separation of entertainment and news is obsolete' (Esralew and Young, 2012: 338). Memes, parodies, music videos, cut and paste montages, caricatures, social television and online comments are an integral part of our daily political experiences, more so than most other political ones. It is here we encounter political issues, ideology and criticism, such as racism, minority rights, political tensions, populism, authoritarianism and environmental concerns. It is here we focus our study, where we most experience politics in everyday life.

In this book, we consider how to analyse the politics articulated in popular culture we experience on our phones, tablets, laptops and the like. As is the case with any area of scholarship, this can be approached from a range of perspectives, such as their effects or their social implications. I propose we approach this from a discursive perspective because it is here we can determine not only what politics are articulated in popular culture we experience digitally, but also how these politics are expressed. This book is a resource for students and scholars who want to discursively analyse politics in online communication. It offers a step-by-step guide on how to critically analyse politics in (digital) popular culture. Before we proceed, we need to define exactly what we mean by politics, popular culture, digital popular culture and a discursive approach. It is here we turn to now.

WHAT IS POLITICS?

The Cambridge online dictionary defines politics as 'the activities of the government, members of law-making organizations, or people who try to influence the way a country is governed'. Dictionaries also include definitions about 'power', 'control' and 'status' not only in governments, but within groups or organizations. On a societal level, there has been a shift in power where the 'power of centralized nation states has waned' with a corresponding rise in power of corporations and 'the global economy' (Machin and van Leeuwen, 2016: 246). There are also many other actors in society engaged in power, control and status. For example, some activists and those in the creative industries use popular culture to articulate a point of view, including the pleasures and values associated with it that may affect the actions and thoughts of fans. These acts and actors are political. Referring to popular music, Street (1988: 7) notes 'Politics is not just about power. Nor is popular music. They are both about how we should act and think.' In this book then, we include 'the politics of the everyday ... being concerned with issues of power, equality and personal identity … [that] affects the way people behave' (Street, 1988: 3). Though much of the politics examined and analysed here involves governments and politicians, we also include politics of organizations and groups such as Extinction Rebellion, pro- and anti-Brexit groups, to name just a couple. So, memes, parodies and other popular culture experienced digitally about issues, events and politicians are considered as entertainment but also 'the means of political and social deliberation' (Denisova, 2019: 10).

WHAT IS (DIGITAL) POPULAR CULTURE?

Here we have three words, all contentious and all difficult to define. Let's examine each concept, starting with 'culture'. Arnold (1960: 6) claims culture, is 'the best that has been thought and said in the world'. This includes literature by Shakespeare and music by Beethoven. However, we use the word 'culture' in more ways than just this. Raymond Williams (1963) agrees that culture is 'intellectual, spiritual and aesthetic development' of great philosophers, great artists and great poets. But he expands this definition to include documentary records, texts and practices of a culture (such as films and music recordings) and a particular way of life.

When we try to define popular culture, we need to consider how the term 'popular' works with our idea of culture (more of this in Chapter 2). This is not easy. As Bennett (1980: 18) notes, 'the concept of popular culture is virtually useless, a melting pot of confused and contradictory meanings capable of misdirecting inquiry up any number of theoretical blind alleys'. It is usually defined in contrast to folk culture, mass culture, dominant culture, working-class culture, high culture and the like. Again, though there are whole books trying to define it, here we go back to Williams and his seminal work. According to Williams (1988: 236), popular means 'widely favoured' or 'well-liked'. But it can also carry with it negative connotations of 'inferior kinds of work' and 'a strong element of setting out to gain favour, with a sense of calculation'. So popular culture carries both positive and negative connotations which we hear in day-to-day conversations about it.

We put the word 'digital' in brackets a number of times in this book because we see 'digital popular culture' as a logical continuation of popular culture. That is, digital popular culture is very much a part of popular culture, though it also has its own affordances and these need to be taken into account (see Chapters 2 and 3). With this in mind, we can define digital popular culture as popular culture that is (mostly) produced for and distributed online. This includes still imagery, written posts, short animations, music videos, fan-sourced films, parodies, memes, Twitter mobs and social TV. It also includes excerpts from mainstream media found on our daily feeds. Digital popular culture is distinct from popular culture in ways other than its production and distribution. It also involves our engagement that includes, consuming, liking, sharing, commenting and altering. Digital popular culture emphasizes 'participation', 'modification' and 'interaction' as it develops and is shared online (Seargeant and Tagg, 2014: 4). This makes it unique and our approach to analysis needs to reflect this.

WHAT ARE RELATIONS BETWEEN POLITICS AND DIGITAL POPULAR CULTURE?

There is a lot written on relations between the digital and politics (see above and Chapter 2). Much of this focuses on social media and politics. Some scholars argue that social media provide 'spaces of power for citizenry engagement, grass-root access, and use of symbolic resources' (KhosraviNik, 2017: 583). It is argued that it is not just texts but also context of what we post, comment on and get posted to us that makes social media political (Pybus, 2019: 227). Our feeds are 'cooked' (Gitelman, 2013), producing value and 'function as a power knowledge-relation and therefore, most importantly, it is inherently political' (Pybus, 2019: 228).

This book is situated within these wider studies of the political roles of Web 2.0 and social media. These bigger issues are examined in great detail elsewhere and you may want to refer to some of the references in this book to gain a further understanding of some of the many studies examining aspects of this. Here, we focus on one aspect – that is, how to analyse the politics articulated in digital popular culture. We contextualize this book's focus with an historical examination of relations between politics and popular culture in Chapter 2. Here, it is fair to say that relations between the two are complex, again with a wide range of opinions.

WHAT IS A DISCURSIVE APPROACH AND WHY THIS APPROACH?

Popular culture and politics can be examined in a number of ways, such as through the prism of popular cultural studies, socio-linguistics, cultural studies and sociology to name just a few. Most approaches ask what the relations are between popular culture and politics. This book considers not only what ideas digital popular culture can articulate about society, identities and events, but also how this is achieved using an innovative set of methods from multimodal critical discourse studies (MCDS). MCDS can provide answers to both 'what' and 'how' due to its attention to the details of how communication takes place, its interest in discourse and how ideologies are naturalized and legitimized. Let's take a closer look at these ideas.

MCDS finds its roots in critical discourse analysis (CDA), an approach that examines linguistic choices to uncover broader discourses articulated in texts. By discourses, we mean 'complex bundle[s] of simultaneous and sequential interrelated linguistic acts', which are thematically interrelated (Wodak, 2001: 66). These discourses can be thought of as models of the world and project certain social values and ideas that contribute to the (re)production of social life. Some CDA scholars have pointed to the need to look more at how ideologies are communicated not only in political speeches and news reports, but also through entertainment (van Leeuwen, 1999; Machin and Richardson, 2012; Way, 2018a). These same scholars have also drawn on certain tools, approaches and assumptions in multimodality to show how discourses and ideologies, as in language, can be revealed by closer analysis of images, designs and other semiotic resources such as visual features, material objects, musical sounds and architecture. The approach in this book is part of this multimodal trajectory. Digital popular culture is a means of communication that articulates ideological discourses. It is through the modes of lexica (written, spoken and/or sung words), visuals and musical sounds that digital popular cultural commodities communicate 'multimodally'.

MCDS is ideal for approaching digital popular culture. Producers of digital popular culture 'draw on and mobilize complex multi-semioticity – combinations of specialized sets of linguistic features . . . discursive resources (such as genre, register, and style), pictures, moving image, sound and music, layout and composition' (Leppanen et al., 2017: 8). Put more forcefully, 'online linguistic performance and discourse genres cannot be fully understood without multimodal and interdisciplinary analytical frameworks' (Calhoun, 2019: 28).

One approach that addresses some of the unique characteristics of communications in social media is KhosraviNik's (2017) 'Social media critical discourse studies (SM-CDS)'. Like the approach adapted in this book, KhosraviNik (2017: 584) emphasizes the need to consider both texts with context being upfront in the analysis. Like CDA, this approach calls for 'a context dependent, critical analysis of communicative practices/content with a socio-political critique level' (2017: 585). In this book, we analyse digital popular culture multimodality, acknowledging its uniqueness in constantly evolving contexts.

Let's illustrate what we mean with an example. Figure 1.1 is a meme that a friend posted to my Facebook account during the COVID-19 pandemic outbreak of 2020. If we consider the meme out of context, we may find this funny due to the imagery and written words working together. It is funny that dinosaurs would know that the meteor crossing the sky will cause a major catastrophe. It is also funny that they are worried about the economy instead of their very existence. Even without the COVID-19 pandemic contextualization, this is a political statement about how many of us in society value economics over all else. However, this meme becomes not only funny but also more focused in its political critique if we know the political context. I showed this to my boy and he said it was not funny. When I gave him some context, he then 'got it'. This encounter illustrates the importance of context.

Figure 1.1 2020 internet meme critiquing politicians' reactions to COVID-19.

Source: u/JohnDonne on Reddit

Here is some context that makes this a pointedly critical meme at the time. This was sent to me while a number of national politicians around the globe were being criticized for their responses to the COVID-19 pandemic by prioritizing the economy over the health of the public. While the worldwide death toll at the time from the virus was more than 35,000, Brazil's President Jair Bolsonaro was denying the severity of the virus, dismissing it as 'fantasy' and just 'a little flu'. His strategy was described as 'an "economy first" approach to tackling the crisis; [Bolsonaro] calculating that the number of deaths will be less costly than the inevitable recession caused by economic shutdown' (Cowie, 2020). In the meantime, other right-wing politicians including US President Donald Trump and the UK's Prime Minister Boris Johnson were also criticized for similar reasons. Trump and Johnson were accused of being slow in reacting to the pandemic, Trump 'fear[ing] the economic impact could hurt his re-election prospects later

[that] year' ('Coronavirus: Trump says …', 2020). At the time I received this meme, the USA had more than 163,000 confirmed cases and over 3,000 deaths. These numbers quickly rose after this meme.

Now with this political context we can read this meme as more than three talking dinosaurs watching a meteorite crossing the sky. It now becomes a scathing critique on a number of politicians who seem to have prioritized economics and their own careers over the health of the people they serve. The written words include 'the economy' and omit all other aspects of an impending catastrophe. This connotes that the dinosaurs believe the economy is the most important aspect of the catastrophe, the same criticism aimed at politicians at the time. Furthermore, representing the Corona virus pandemic as 'our' meteor suggests that the pandemic has the potential to render humans extinct as the meteor did to the dinosaurs. Indeed, the pandemic has caused many deaths and the 'economy first' policies and statements of politicians have resulted in more deaths than other approaches (Cowie, 2020). However, there are no knowledgeable voices claiming these policies will result in the end of the human race. Represented as such, the meme connotes that the actions of these politicians are far worse than they have proven to be.

There are also other contextual factors that add meanings to this meme: factors unique to digital media. This meme was sent to me by a friend who is very critical of Donald Trump. For me, this helps focus its meanings. I liked and shared this meme and added the name 'BoJo [short derogatory name for Boris Johnson]'. When I did this, I changed the meanings of the meme from a critique that targeted Trump to a critique of Johnson. After I posted this, thirteen Facebook friends reacted with emojis that suggested approval and two people shared the meme. After my brief encounter with the meme, it has moved out of my political virtual sphere where it no doubt has been adjusted, commented upon and used in different contexts. The point made by this example is that a textual and contextual analysis is a useful approach to examine what politics are associated with digital popular culture. In this book, we outline in detail an approach to achieve this.

WHAT WILL YOU FIND IN THIS BOOK?

The aim of this book is to provide a step-by-step guide on how to critically analyse digital popular culture discursively. To this end, the book is divided into two parts – the first three chapters offer theoretical context. These are followed by chapters that are far more analytical. In Chapter 2, we historically examine what scholars say about relations between popular culture and politics. We briefly examine scholars and schools of thought that inform our approach, such as Leavism and Arnold, the Frankfurt school, neo-Gramscian perspectives, culturalism, structuralism and post-structuralism. This survey gives us a theoretical context in which to consider what we can expect in terms of the role(s) digital popular culture can play in politics. This is followed by an in-depth examination of relations between politics and online content and activities. As the chapter continues, we narrow our focus onto studies most relevant to ours, that is, on relations between digital popular culture and politics. The aim of this chapter is to contextualize our approach with what is known about the limits and potentials of (digital) popular culture and politics. This helps to inform our approach from a critical multimodal and discursive perspective.

We continue our theoretical explorations in Chapter 3. Here, we take a close look at our approach to analysing digital popular culture. We start by defining ideology and discourse, two concepts central to our approach. We then examine in depth what we mean by CDA and consider reasons for using it. We perform a similar examination for MCDS, introducing its core principles, and consider how it can be applied to a range of texts, including digital popular culture. We then consider its advantages for examining politics and digital popular culture. Though MCDS offers many avenues in its approach to analysis, we propose an approach that considers how to examine lexica, sounds and visuals in (digital) popular culture. This multimodal approach usefully directs us to consider how different modes play roles in representing participants, actions, settings, sequences of events and how these are transformed in different ways to suit producers' interests.

Chapter 4 to Chapter 8 are analysis chapters, each focusing on specific political issues and analytical tools appropriate for analysing digital popular culture. Each of these chapters begin with a detailed examination of a set of analytical tools followed by a case study that illustrates how these tools can be put into use. In Chapter 4, our case study is comments posted on YouTube about a music video released during the 2013 Gezi Park protests in Turkey. This case study tips a metaphorical hat to scholars from Raymond Williams (1963) up to the present (Street, 2013; Zbikowski, 2015) who emphasize the importance of fans in making sense of popular culture. In this chapter, we are introduced to our first set of analytical tools: the lexical representation of social actors. For the most part, our approach leans heavily on the seminal work of Norman Fairclough (2003) and Theo van Leeuwen (1996). We argue that the written representation of social actors is an important and useful tool for examining comments.

In Chapter 5, our attention turns to one of the most popular forms of digital popular culture: internet memes. For the most part, memes consist of still images and (sometimes) written text. So, here we expand our analytical toolkit to include the visual representation of social actors. Our approach in this chapter borrows heavily from MCDS scholars including David Machin (2007) and Gunter Kress and Theo van Leeuwen (1996 and 2001). Equipped with these new analytical tools, our case study centres around a sample of memes that praise and criticize the authoritarian tendencies of US President Donald Trump. The aim of this chapter is to illustrate how to analyse still imagery in any number of situations in digital popular culture.

Chapter 6 takes aim at analysing moving images. Here our analytical toolkit expands to consider the visual and lexical representation of social actions, as well as choices in visual composition, length of shots, movement of cameras and movement of subjects. Our toolkit in this chapter is enriched by previous work of David Machin (2007) and Theo van Leeuwen (1995). Our case studies are, first, a sample of GIFs and, then, a mash-up. All of these represent aspects of Britain's departure from the European Union (known as Brexit).

In Chapter 7 we consider the role of music in digital popular culture. Here we rely on an approach developed by Lyndon Way (2018a) which considers both previous research in musicology and the semiotics of sound. Researchers of vital importance for this chapter include Philip Tagg (1984), Deryck Cooke (1959), Theo van Leeuwen (1999) and David Machin (2010). We also add to our analytical toolkit the analysis of metaphors and the representation of place. These tools are informed by the work of a number of scholars including Lakoff and Johnson (1980) and Connell and Gibson (2003) respectively. Our case studies involve the role of music in two YouTube videos: a musical mash-up and a musical cypher video. In both cases, the thematic focus is protesting against politicians.

Chapter 8 is our last analytical chapter. Here we focus on satires and parodies. Armed with analytical tools we have considered in previous chapters, we consider digital popular culture as the recontextualization of social practices. This approach to analysis is adapted from Basil Bernstein (1990 and 1996) and then Theo van Leeuwen and Ruth Wodak (1999). Our case study is a satirical parody that criticizes the environmental policies of right-wing political leaders including US President Donald Trump and UK Prime Minister Boris Johnson while legitimating the practices of the environmental group 'Extinction Rebellion'.

Finally, Chapter 9 serves two purposes. It summarizes the approach outlined in previous chapters. This includes a summary of the tools we have collected for our analytical toolkit. It also considers what our MCDS approach has revealed about the politics articulated in digital popular culture. This allows us to consider how MCDS is indeed a useful approach to critically analyse what is considered 'subversive' and what political role(s) digital popular culture can play.

SUGGESTED READING

Seargeant, P. and Tagg, C. (eds) (2014) *The Language of Social Media: Identity and Community on the Internet.* London: Palgrave Macmillan.

This collection of ten studies examines the use of language on social media sites including Facebook, Twitter and TripAdvisor. It is a good cross-cultural exploration of language on social media and how this is impacting the way we communicate, live and construct our identities.

Williams, R. (1963) *Culture and Society*. Harmondsworth: Penguin.
Williams, R. (1988) *Key Words*. London: Fontana Press.

Both these books by Raymond Williams are great starting points to understand one of cultural studies' most influential thinkers. Both are highly recommended as places to dip into in order to learn about, clarify and reacquaint ourselves with key concepts and ideas associated with culture, communication and power.

2

POLITICS IN THE POPULAR

A Variety of Perspectives

CHAPTER OBJECTIVES

- Describe historical perspectives on relations between politics and popular culture.
- Examine what scholars say about the democratizing potential of digital media.
- Examine relations between politics and online popular culture.

KEY CONCEPTS

- Definitions of 'culture', 'high culture' or 'authentic culture' include the idea that it is 'the best that has been thought and said in the world' (Arnold, 1960).
- 'Popular culture' or 'mass culture' has a number of definitions, some more positive than others.
- 'Ideology' definitions are based around the idea that it is a way of looking at the world.
- 'Hegemony' is a condition in which a dominant class, in alliance with others, rules and leads society through the spread of a system of values and beliefs that support the ruling class.
- Some scholars criticize social media for being a filter bubble and echo chamber where we are exposed to ideas that echo our own while we are insulated from other perspectives.

(Continued)

- 'Digital culture' is how we use social media that is algorithmically driven, personalized and user-generated to interact with other human beings.
- Affect is the intensity with which we experience emotion; much of digital popular culture communicates to us affectively.
- Political, historical, media, social and consumption contexts are essential for us to make sense of digital popular culture.

INTRODUCTION

Facebook for me was a life changer. I moved to Turkey from the UK in 2004, the same year Facebook was established. It allowed me to keep in touch with my friends and family. It, along with other social media, became my source of information as the political situation in Turkey deteriorated and mainstream media became more and more restricted. With the tightening of controls on social media and related arrests, more entertaining ways of criticizing politics became more appealing to me. Though people were getting arrested for using Twitter to criticize, people in Turkey were (and still are) less likely to feel pressure from the government by sharing, liking and commenting on a meme, music video or a mash-up (though people have also been arrested for this). Since I have been back in the UK, I continue to populate my social media feeds with entertaining political musings related to not only Turkey, but also Brexit, Trump and any other political issue that winds me up.

Though liking, sharing, altering and commenting on digital popular culture is a somewhat limited action compared to storming the parliament, it makes us feel like we are doing something political. In fact, politics and popular culture have always been entwined. In this chapter, we examine what scholars say about relations between the two. This helps us understand why we feel we are doing something political when we comment on something we see in our feeds. We then perform a current and in-depth examination of relations between politics and online popular culture, including a consideration of the democratizing potential of digital media. We also consider literature on relations between digital popular culture and politics. These close examinations highlight both the limits and potentials of digital popular culture and its relations with politics. Examining this body of knowledge informs our approach to analysing relations between politics and digital popular culture from a critical multimodal perspective.

HOW TO STUDY POPULAR CULTURE AND POLITICS

Our examination of relations between popular culture and politics is informed by a large and diverse body of work coming from various branches of cultural studies. Here, we examine some of this research, starting with Mathew Arnold's ideas about culture and moving through to some post-structuralist concepts. This is a selective and historical overview of a range of perspectives. It is not an exhaustive survey, but one that includes key ideas and concepts that are fundamental in studying popular culture and politics and inform our approach.

Arnold and Leavis

Though not concerned specifically with popular culture, Mathew Arnold in the late 19th century studied relations between culture and society in *Culture and Anarchy* (1960). This was to be the outset of the 'culture and civilization' tradition of examining popular culture. Arnold established a dichotomy between 'culture' and 'popular culture', one seen to this day not only in some scholarship, but also in government statements and even day-to-day conversations. Culture, he claimed, was 'the best that has been thought and said in the world' (1960: 6). This includes literature by Shakespeare and music by Beethoven. Popular culture, which is synonymous in his writings with 'anarchy', is the 'disruptive nature of working-class lived culture' of the 1860s when working-class urban men got the right to vote (1960: 6). These concepts are highly political. Culture, he thought, could be used to educate and civilize the working classes while popular culture was something to be discouraged.

In the 1930s, F.R. Leavis continued this tradition. Here, Leavis and his colleagues saw a cultural decline, a 'standardization and levelling down' of culture (Leavis and Thompson, 1977: 3). Again, Leavis prefers 'high culture' over 'popular culture', the latter attacked for being addictive. For example, popular fiction is 'a form of compensation … is the very reverse of recreation, in that it tends, not to strengthen and refresh the addict for living, but to increase his unfitness by habituating him to weak evasions, to the refusal to face reality at all' (1977: 100). Like Arnold, Leavis sees popular culture as disrupting mainstream society.

Marxisms

Scholars have used Marxist ideas to consider relations between politics and popular culture. One such group of scholars is the Frankfurt school. Possibly the most well-known scholar within this tradition is Theodore Adorno. Though he was highly critical of all forms of popular culture, 'On popular music' (1941) targets popular music and is indicative of his wider critique. Adorno (1941) believes that 'authentic culture', such as serious classical and avant garde music, has a critical function in society. These offer an implicit critique of capitalist society and suggest an alternative, utopian vision of society expressed through their 'form' rather than commanding through 'content'. Unfortunately, 'serious' music's critical function, in many cases, has been usurped by the cultural industry that has packaged and commodified it.

Adorno (1941 and 1991) criticizes popular music, which is firmly in the hands of the same cultural industry. Unlike Leavis and Arnold, he does not criticize popular culture for causing anarchy. Instead, he believes it serves listeners standardized fare with unique selling points or 'pseudo individualization'. This promotes consumption that is always passive, and endlessly repetitive, confirming the world as it is, a kind of 'social cement'. Like those noted above, Adorno (1941) believes popular culture is political. Unlike those noted above, Adorno believes it supports an unfair status quo, rather than threatening it.

Louis Althusser is another Marxist scholar who has also considered popular culture. He believes dominant ideologies are inescapable, being deeply inscribed in the ways of thinking and ways of living (Althusser, 2005). We communicate knowledge through language, which is never transparent. Instead, all language is biased towards particular perspectives at the expense of others – that is, steeped in ideology. When we lose one ideology, we gain another in its place. There are competing views in society all linked to power, not knowledge. In the case of Western Europe, these are linked to various notions of capitalism. These ideologies are found in popular culture in the forms of texts, material institutions, in our heads and in our hearts. So, ideologies are not consciously thought out, but 'unconscious consciousness' (Althusser, 2005: 233). Althusser claims each society has a dominant ideology which is a set of feelings, values and beliefs shared by the majority. It is dominant in numerical terms and in the sense that it supports the interests of dominant, ruling groups.

Dominant ideologies are accepted by the majority through both 'repressive state apparatuses' which use control and punishment to force people to conform (police, army, prisons, courts, the law) and 'ideological state apparatuses' such as religion, family, education, popular culture and the media which socialize us into accepting dominant ideology. Popular culture tends to support dominant ideology by producing programmes and products that align with the values of the elite. In the West this is white, patriarchical, capitalism. The media support dominant ideologies by 'masking and displacing' social issues and problems (Althusser, 2005). The media also support dominant ideologies by incorporating or containing other ideological positions, giving alternative voices a small place to vent their anger and relieve their pressure. So we see (occasionally) Greenpeace activists and complaining opposition political leaders in the news, but just a little.

Like ideology, hegemony is another useful concept when considering popular culture and politics. Developed by Antonio Gramsci (1971) and central to Gramscian studies of popular culture, hegemony is a condition in which a dominant class (in alliance with other classes) does not merely rule a society but leads it through moral and intellectual leadership (Gramsci, 1971). It is always the result of negotiations between dominant and subordinant groups and never simply power imposed from above. Despite oppression and exploitation, there is a high degree of consensus and social stability, where subordinate groups and classes support and subscribe to values, ideals, objectives, cultural and political meanings, which bind them to and incorporate them into the prevailing structures of power. Hegemony is maintained and must be continually maintained by dominant groups and classes negotiating with and making concessions to subordinant groups and classes. Though there is consensus, oppositional ideas and styles are incorporated into society, but opposition is limited within the confines of an ideology which confirms the common sense and unchallengeability of the economic fundamentals of class power.

There are different cultures and cultural practices in society, though culture is mainly determined by capitalism. This hegemonic position is organized by 'organic intellectuals', such as family, television, the press, education, religion and the culture industries. So, not only do we have culture which maintains the system, we also have culture which opposes the system, but within limits. Popular culture is a negotiated mix of intentions and counterintentions, both from above and below, both commercial and authentic, a shifting balance of forces between resistance and incorporation. It is these relations which see an active role for audiences in negotiating political meanings in popular culture. Gramsci notes how popular culture is not the commodities produced by the cultural industries, but what we, the audience, actively make of the texts and practices offered by the culture industries.

One of the best-known studies of popular culture from a Gramscian perspective is Dick Hebdige's seminal (1979) *Subculture: The Meaning of Style.* Here, he notes how British youth subcultures take for their own purposes, meanings in commodities commercially provided. Products are combined and transformed in ways not intended by their producers. These commodities, such as safety pins and Nazi symbols by punks, religious crosses by rockers and baseball caps by rappers are 'rearticulated', or given oppositional meanings by youth. These are symbolic forms of resistance to both dominant and parent cultures. But youth cultures move from originality and opposition to commercial incorporation and ideological diffusion as the culture industries succeed in marketing subcultural resistance for general consumption and profit. Opposition becomes new sets of conventions, creating new commodities, creating and rejuvenating old industries. This active use of commercially provided commodities is where oppositional politics lie in popular culture.

Post-Marxists

More recently, post-Marxists have 'improved' ideas taken from various forms of Marxism, adding to it 'The new feminism, the protest movements of ethnic, national and sexual minorities, the anti-institutional ecology struggles waged by marginal layers of the population, the anti-nuclear movement, the atypical forms of social struggle in countries on the capitalist periphery' (Laclau and Mouffe, 2001:1). Again, although a lot of this influences our present study, here I examine the concept of 'articulation', one aspect of this school of thought which is of particular importance to us. Articulation means to join together, as well as to express which 'consists in the ... partial fixing of meaning' (2001: 113). And it is political precisely in who can fix the meaning of social reality (Hall, 1982). Fixing meaning in texts and practices is always an act of articulation.

John Storey (2006) provides Bob Marley as an example of how articulation works in popular culture for political ends. Marley had international hits articulating the values of Rastafari. His success signalled the expression of his religious message to an enormous worldwide audience. For many, the music enlightened understanding and perhaps conversion to and bonding with Rastafarianism. Marley's music articulates the values of Rastafari while making huge profits for the music industry. The paradox is the anti-capitalist politics of Rastafari were 'articulated' in the economic interests of capitalism; the music is lubricating the very system it seeks to condemn (2006: 67–68). Rastafari politics are expressed in a form which is financially beneficial to the dominant culture as a commodity for profit.

Articulation (and hegemony) assume that the audience is very active in meaning-making. Commodity meaning-making is a site of struggle where people make 'their' popular culture from commodities supplied by the culture industry. Not all consumption is active. Sometimes we want TV programmes or music to 'wash over' us. But we should also be aware of the culture industries which seek to manipulate us. When we consider the political roles of popular culture, we ought to include details of production, distribution and consumption in order to answer questions of meaning, pleasure, ideological effect, incorporation or resistance.

Culturalism

Though a broad church, culturalists have in common the belief that active production of meaning is at the heart of popular culture, unlike what we saw with Arnold, Leavis and the Frankfurt school. Since the 1950s, influential culturalists include Richard Hoggart, E.P. Thompson, Stuart Hall and Paddy Whannel, but possibly the most well-known is Raymond Williams. The best way to understand the beliefs and values of any given time and place, according to Williams, is to be a part of the 'lived culture'. If you want to understand say, Victorian London, it is best to have lived through it. However, for those of us who do not have this choice, another way is to examine books, newspapers, architecture, clothing and music from this time. Like other culturalists, he believes cultural texts reveal the 'structure of feeling' or shared values and beliefs of a society. Put another way, through an examination of cultural texts, we are able to uncover how a given society thought and felt. However, what cultural products end up being distributed, archived and held in esteem are selected, where 'there will always be a tendency for this process of selection to be related to and even governed by the interests of the class that is dominant' (Williams, 1963: 313). So, the popular cultural commodities we find widely available in our time have been selected by elites, as have artefacts from previous times. Williams says the selection is political, with most offerings from the cultural industries being aesthetically wanting. But the public is resourceful, according to culturalists. Williams and culturalists believe meaning is generated by how fans use popular culture commodities. This theoretical positioning emphasizes the importance of social, political and consumption contexts in the making of meanings. And it is these ideas which are echoed in our approach which emphasizes a close reading of texts in context.

Structuralism

Unlike the approaches we have examined thus far, this approach does not consider the cultural value of commodities. It is analytical, not evaluative. Its roots can be traced back to the linguist Ferdinand de Saussure who claimed we communicate through language that can be viewed as a system of signs. Signs have two component parts: a signifier, such as the written word 'dog', and a signified, which is the concept or mental image of (in our example) a dog. The relationship between signifier and signified is arbitrary and culturally agreed. For example, 'dog' (in English), 'köpek' (in Turkish) or 'chien' (in French) are all signifiers used to signify a furry four-legged pet animal. We could easily have decided as a culture to name said animal 'cat'. Our sign systems work not by signs expressing a natural meaning but by marking a difference, a system within a system of difference and relationships.

Meaning in language is a process of combinations and selections. The words we select and how these are combined are decisions that affect meanings in sentences. So, if we decide to select 'terrorists' or 'freedom fighters' and combine these with 'carried out an attack', the sentence carries with it very different meanings. In fact, the language we speak and the culture we inhabit play a significant role in constructing our sense of reality of the material world.

For language to work as a means of communication, Saussure says we need both 'langue' and 'parole'. Langue is the rules and conventions we agree upon to communicate. Parole is the individual use of language. To illustrate, we can think of language to be like a game of chess. There are the rules (structure) of the game (langue) and then an actual game of chess (parole). Without the rules there is no game. The rules make the game meaningful and it is the homogeneity of the structure that makes the heterogeneity of the performance possible.

So, how do these ideas permeate the analysis of popular culture? The answer is Sausserre's concern with the 'grammar' or rules that make meaning possible in cultural texts and practices. Meaning is always the result of the interplay of relationships of selection and combinations made possible by the underlying structure. The task of structuralism is to make explicit the rules and conventions which govern the production of meaning. In this way, the underlying meanings of cultural artefact(s) like Western films become evident (see below for Will Wright's analysis).

Other structuralists have contributed to the analysis of popular culture and meanings. Roland Barthes (1957) examines culture from a structuralist's perspective but with more of a political critique. He evaluates everyday cultural products and treats them as mythologies. He says signs are never innocent, but part of ideological reproduction – in the West this supports capitalism (being about authenticity, ideology and commodity fetishism – themes characteristic of western Marxism). Myths are always bourgeois and typically work to justify or naturalize the existing order.

Barthes is also responsible for our use of the terms 'connotations' and 'denotations'. Denotation is the literal meaning of signs. Connotations is the extra mythological meanings that are layered on top, which are ideological. Due to us living within a society with its own particular cultural norms and values, we automatically read signs in a particular way, thus experiencing the myth as innocent and natural. However, the power of the myth lies in its ability to make an arbitrary system of values seem like a system of facts. This can be highly political. For example, legend has it that Barthes saw an image on the front cover of *Paris Match* magazine in the 1950s, which was a time when European powers were wrestling with issues surrounding colonialism (see Figure 2.1). He said that the denotation of this magazine cover is a colonial soldier in the

French army saluting a flag. However, the connotations are political, suggesting that France is a great empire and everyone, even colonial citizens, serve her faithfully. So, colonialism is not bad because see how happy the colonial soldier is while saluting the flag?

Figure 2.1 Barthes's colonial soldier, from the cover of *Paris Match* magazine

Structuralism has produced a number of classic studies of popular culture and politics, including Will Wright's (1975) *Six Guns and Society: A Structural Study of the Western.* Wright analyses the Hollywood Western and claims much of the narrative power of the Western is from its structure of binary opposites. He shows how Western films communicate a particular conceptual order of American society through their structure. That is, Wright's focus is on the way the Western presents American social beliefs symbolically. He divides the Western into three stages: the Classic (1930s, 40s and most of the 50s), Transitional (between Classic and Professional) and Professional (1960s and 70s). To fully understand the social meaning of a myth, Wright claims we must analyse its binary opposites and its narrative structure – 'the progression of events and the resolution of conflicts' (1975: 24). Figure 2.2 represents what these opposites look like in the Classic Western.

Hero	Villain
Inside society	Outside society
Good	Bad
Strong	Weak
Civilization	Wilderness

Figure 2.2 Binary opposites in the classic Western film (adapted from Wright, 1975)

What is interesting for us in Wright's analysis is he claims each type of Western corresponds to a different moment in the recent economic development of the USA and articulates how to achieve the American dream. The Classic corresponds to the individualistic conception underlying a market economy. The way to achieve rewards like friendship, respect and dignity is to separate oneself from others and be an autonomous individual. The vengeance plot is a variation that begins to reflect changes in the market economy. The Professional plot reveals a new conception of society corresponding to the values and attitudes inherent in a planned corporate economy. It is by an analysis of the structure or rules of a Western that the more overtly political meanings of these films become evident.

Post-structuralism

Multimodal critical discourse studies (MCDS) fit into the wider post-structuralism movement. Post-structuralists reject structuralism's idea that meanings are a result of an underlying immovable structure. Meaning, they say, is always a process, a very unstable thing where the 'meaning' of a text is a continuing flow of interpretations. The meanings of a word today, for example, can be quite different to those in the past or in the future. At the moment, my boys call anything they particularly like 'sick', a use of the word not in popular circulation in the past and I suspect a word which will take on different meanings in the future. Meaning is dependent on the political, historical and cultural contexts of a text. Here is an example of what I mean.

When I lectured in Turkey post-2013, I would put an image on the board similar to Figure 2.3. I would first ask non-Turkish students what the image represented. I regularly received answers like 'cold', 'Antarctica', 'black and white', 'winter', which all were reasonable answers. I then asked my Turkish students and they would respond with 'Gezi Park', 'media censorship', 'media manipulation', 'democracy' and 'protest'. These too were reasonable answers because these students had just experienced the Gezi Park protests of 2013, some first hand and others through digital popular culture. Penguins were a symbol of Gezi protests sparked by CNN Turk running a penguin documentary during the first days of the protests while literally thousands of protesters were knocking on CNN Turk's office doors. This lack of representing the scale of the protests was seen by many as symptomatic of mainstream media's collusion with the governing party (see Way, 2016 and 2018a). The point I want to make is that political, cultural and historical contexts are key determining factors in the meanings of signs according to post-structuralists.

Figure 2.3 Images with different meanings: the importance of context.

Source: clker.com, public domain

One name which is closely linked to post-structuralism is Michel Foucault. He is concerned with relations between power and knowledge and how this operates within discourses and discursive formations. According to Foucault, discourses enable, constrain and constitute (Foucault, 1989). What he means is 'Language, for example, is a discourse: it *enables* me to speak, it *constrains* what I can say, it *constitutes* me as a speaking subject' (in Storey, 2006: 101, emphasis original). Discursive formations are the different ways we talk about a subject and how these interact in a hierarchical manner. So, the discourse of sexuality is articulated through discursive domains such as medicine, demographics, psychiatry, pedagogy, social work and governance. These constitute the reality of sexuality (Foucault, 1979: 22).

Discourse is linked to power and knowledge. 'Power produces knowledge ... power and knowledge directly imply one another ... there is no power relation without the correlative constitution of a field of knowledge, nor any knowledge that does not presuppose and constitute at the same time power relations'

(Foucault, 1979: 27). Discourse is the means by which institutions use power through a process of definition and exclusion, intelligibility and legitimacy. They define what can be said about a topic. Different institutions represent things in different ways – each for their own interests. So, for example, protesters are represented by politicians as dangerous terrorists or delegitimized as street people while protesters represent themselves as 'the people'. Foucault believes power is a strategic terrain, the site of unequal relationships between the powerful and the powerless. But he also notes that where there is power there is resistance. Power not only excludes, represses, censors, abstracts, masks, conceals, it also produces reality, domains of objects and rituals of truth. And it is here where popular culture plays a role in articulating discourses of power – some support dominant power structures and some oppose these. Through the study of discourse, power relations are exposed.

Our historical overview of scholarship on relations between popular culture and politics ends here. The approaches and scholars we have examined all influence our MCDS approach in various ways. What follows links these ideas with concepts and findings about the digital realm and politics.

DIGITAL MEDIA, USERS AND POLITICS

Scholars from a wide range of disciplines consider relations between digital media and politics. Not only do positions range from the wildly optimistic to the downright negative, scholars have also examined a variety of aspects of relations, such as digital media's role in democratizing media control (Jenkins, 2009), its potential as the new fourth estate (Vatikiotis, 2014), its role in social movements (Morozov, 2009), among a raft of other points of interest. Entire books and careers are based on these debates. In this section, we cannot possibly cover these ever-growing areas of study. For a more nuanced and detailed examination, I suggest you read some of the sources identified in this section. Instead, we just scratch the surface in order to contextualize our own examination of digital popular culture.

One scholarly issue relevant to this book is how digital media has democratized society. For simplification, we can place positions on this issue on a continuum. For some scholars, the internet is a place that has opened the public sphere, making it more democratic. Networked media challenge centralized control of media production and distribution by traditional organizations they claim, reconfiguring communicative power relations (Von Hippel, 2005; Jenkins, 2009). Other scholars claim internet users may become citizen-reporters, who contribute 'to the setting of the agenda and performing a watchdog role … enhancing political participation' (Vatikiotis, 2014: 297). Some scholars even claim social media are instrumental in the success of protest movements (Howard and Hussain, 2013).

On the negative side of the spectrum, studies have acknowledged the dubious democratic affordances of social media practice. There are various reasons for these perspectives. At a fundamental level, there is a lack of access to technology and inequalities of technological literacy (Hargittai, 2008). Scholars note the degradation of the economy, culture and values due to the lack of a demarcation between professionals and amateurs (Keen, 2007). Others decry the limited analytical and critical value of alternative forms of journalism (Scott, 2007). Still other scholars claim there is no real political impact when the public engage in online forms of activism or 'slacktivism' (Morozov, 2009), especially when activism is initiated by social media which results in weak social ties of movements (Andrejevic, 2013). Many online forums tend to be characterized by hard language and insults (Coffey and Woolworth, 2004; Way, 2016 and 2018a). Dean (2010b) points to the way that forums tend to find people more oriented not to attending to new and fresh points of view but to falling back on what is known and comfortable, while YouTube comments tend to be framed in terms of pre-existing personal and social interests or prejudices (Lindgren, 2010; Way, 2016). Observations such as these point to the concepts of 'filter bubbles' and 'echo chambers'.

FILTER BUBBLES AND ECHO CHAMBERS

Eli Pariser's (2012) influential *The Filter Bubble: How the New Personalized Web is Changing What We Read and How We Think* considers the role of algorithms in our social media feeds. In short, much of the feeds we see on our social media platforms are algorithmically driven – that is, 'platforms understand users' preferences and recommend new friends, links and content that align with our preferences. Research ... reveals that political news, opinion and information are being treated in just the same way' (Krasodomski-Jones, 2016: 61). Not only friends and links, but also political content becomes personalized. Our algorithmically inspired feeds filter what we are exposed to, insulating us from views which do not agree with ours. These act as 'echo chambers' where social media connect 'us to those who hold similar views ... limiting our experience of and engagement with alternative perspectives' (Merrin, 2019: 220).

dannah boyd (2008: 244) paints an even bleaker picture where 'Social network sites create cavernous echo chambers as people reiterate what their friends posted. Given the typical friend overlap in most networks, many within those networks hear the same thing over and over until they believe it to be true.' This, of course, is dangerous for society if we subscribe to Jurgen Habermas's view on the role of media in society, which sees media as essential for informing the public, creating a common civic sphere in order to help citizens make informed decisions. Pariser claims 'The danger of these filters is that you think you are getting a representative view of the world and you are really, really not, and you don't know it' (in Jackson, 2017). As Krasodomski-Jones (2016: 61) warns, these echo chambers 'could be making it harder for [social media] users to make political decisions based on both sides of an argument'.

AGAINST BUBBLES AND FILTERS

The bubble argument has been challenged by a number of scholars due to its techno-deterministic nature (Marres, 2012; Madsen, 2016). Merrin (2019: 220) notes the concept of the filter bubble 'is too critically accepted and often deployed simply to denigrate online activity. What it overlooks is how permeable our "bubbles" are.' Guess et al. (2018) believe filter bubbles are not as prevalent as some scholars make out. People, for the most part, still tend to get their news from established media sources, not random social media accounts or fake news websites. This assertion is backed up by the fact that fake news or websites with false and dubious claims occupy less than 10 per cent of the browsing interest of the US public (in Denisova, 2019: 186). Just think of your feeds. Though indeed we do choose friends and receive information that is algorithmically driven, the bubbles or chambers are not air-tight. We also receive feeds and opinions from friends who we may not agree with. For example, my cousin and I both share posts about animals and memes involving cats. But we also share memes, videos and the like about Brexit and Donald Trump. And though we are evidently on each other's algorithmically driven friends list, we vehemently disagree on Brexit, Trump and countless other issues.

Madsen (2016: 6) argues against the filter bubble, claiming it is 'mono-causal'. Not everything can be blamed on algorithms, seeing that 'search results as a "bubble" risks overstating the importance of the algorithm as a selection mechanism in the contemporary media landscape' (2016: 7). The idea oversimplifies the role of users where the interface is seen as a place where 'the [users] end and the technology begin'. Instead of considering filter bubbles and echo chambers, Madsen (2016: 7) suggests the term 'visions'. He claims we should look beyond algorithms and search engine results pages (SERPs) and consider '"web-visions" that 'perform the world on the basis of a distributed chain of socio-technical selection mechanisms'. In practical terms, Madsen (2016: 7) suggests we consider 'the environment of information opened up by the network of websites that can be explored by following hyperlinks in the search results'. In this way, both human and non-human actors determine our 'visions', taking into account choices we make as users. This idea differs from the concept of filter bubbles and echo chambers and adds human agency into what we experience online. If you think about the way you use the internet, this concept is a much more thorough explanation of our behaviour. So, instead of the SERP being the be all and end all, it 'is taken to be a device that opens up explorative inquiry on the part of the user, who can use its outlinks as one instance in his or her process of inquiry' (2016: 9).

DIGITAL CULTURE, USERS AND POLITICS

When considering the political potential of social media, Wiggins (2019) also argues against a techno-determinist model. Instead, he claims we should consider the 'interaction between human and computer', or what he calls 'digital culture' (Wiggins, 2019: 21). Digital culture is a departure from traditional forms of media and 'a movement toward personalization, user-generated content, algorithmic news feeds, and a fear of missing out' (2019: 22). In digital culture, we use social media as the primary form of interacting with other human beings, such as live streaming a politician, tracking friends to meet, responding to emails, listening to music, taking selfies and countless other interactions we perform daily. To think of relations between users and digital media puts our participation in the centre of investigations, our actions being seen as 'participatory culture' (Jenkins, 2009: 3). Indeed, Jenkins is very optimistic about users' roles. He boasts that participation 'has relatively low barriers to artistic expression and civil engagement, strings support for creating and sharing one's creations, and some type of informal mentorship whereby what is known by the most experienced is passed along to novices' (2009: 3).

Though, indeed, this perspective offers hope in terms of users and their use of digital media for political ends, what is omitted is that 'participatory culture is *not* a utopian plateau where all have equal access, entry and impact' (Wiggins, 2019: 22). The concept of digital culture ensures we emphasize that meanings are not solely 'in the text', but articulated through the interaction of political context, consumption context and text. So meanings 'emerge as a consequence of human interaction … human communication is enhanced with the digital while constrained by a given discourse' (Wiggins, 2019: 23).

RELATIONS BETWEEN USERS AND THE POLITICAL

Though digital media offers numerous possibilities in terms of democratization and political mobilization, much work has shown politics are not a priority for users. boyd (2008: 241) notes a discrepancy in the potential of social networking services (SNS) and reality where 'the passion and interest for sharing political and policy information far and wide through SNSes – particularly by and for young people – doesn't match the capability of the SNSes'. She argues that much scholarship reduces political potential and political reality to techno-determinism, where one sees technology driving society. However, we know that society and social media value not just technology, but beauty, exhibitionism and self-aggrandizement. boyd (2008: 242) frames relations between technology and society: 'technologies are shaped by society and reflect society's values back at us, albeit a bit refracted'. Social media is a place where people go and be with their friends. It is a place where friends you already know can do what they do offline – gossip. Politics in online activities are not a priority because 'people pay attention to what interests them. Not surprisingly, offline or online, gossiping is far more common and interesting to people than voting … Embarrassing videos and body fluid jokes fare much better than serious critiques of power. Gossip about Hollywood celebrities is alluring; the war in Iraq is depressing' (boyd, 2008: 243–244). The argument here is that boyd is right, but she has omitted that politics can be fun in the forms of entertaining memes, mash-ups, music videos followed by comments, jokes and gossip. And this is what this book examines.

Other studies have demonstrated how social media have indeed played political roles. Papacharissi (2015) examines Twitter campaigns leading up to and following Egyptian President Hosni Mubarak's resignation and the occupy movement. She notes that the language used in hashtags acted as open signifiers in order to draw support from different segments of society. So, terms like #ThisIsACoup is 'reappropriated to support all types of rhetoric' (2015: 308). This finding is supported by Colleoni (2013), who notes how 'Hashtags can serve as empty signifiers that invite ideological identification of a polysemic orientation' (in Papacharissi, 2015: 308). Furthermore, Papacharissi notes how hashtags work affectively. By affect, she does not mean emotion; however, 'affect provides and amplifies intensity [of emotion] by increasing our awareness of a certain mind or body state that we, as adults, learn to label as a particular feeling and express as a given emotion' (2015: 309). So, affect, in short, is the intensity with which we experience emotion and hashtags stir us affectively.

Affect is not only on the individual level, but can be part of a 'networked public' – that is, a group of people who communicate through a hashtag campaign. A lot of this communication is affective, where 'affective publics … are mobilized and connected, identified, and potentially disconnected through expressions of sentiment' (Papacharissi, 2015: 311). Though these publics may not win revolutions, 'the impact of these publics is symbolic, and that is no small achievement. In order to make revolutions and change institutions, we must reimagine them first'

(Papacharissi, 2015: 321). As many scholars have noted, online activities such as these do not always guarantee a political impact. For this to happen, hashtag campaigns need to work in tandem with offline activities. Online activities can connect otherwise disconnected crowds, enable the formation of affective publics around communities, actual and imagined, to produce a feeling of a community (Papacharissi, 2015; Howard and Hussain, 2013; Dean, 2010b). These then can lead to offline political action.

The question which then begs to be asked is: what motivates some users to become involved in politics online? One way to answer this is through Political Opportunity theory (Kitschelt, 1986; Tarrow, 1994) which claims there are three necessary ingredients to facilitate political activism: insurgent consciousness, organizational strengths and political opportunities. Online activities offer only an increase in consciousness, the first of these ingredients. Online texts 'can point to the issues of common grievances and unite the protest public around these topics' (Denisova, 2019: 20). These online activities have to compete with other forms of information such as mainstream media that may be used to offer competing (government) perspectives. The other two ingredients for political activism, organizational strength and opportunity, including leadership and the degree of political pluralism and repression in a society, are quite separate from online activities.

Classic resource mobilization theory provides us with other explanations for why people engage in politics. This is based on their personal beliefs and intentions or group pressure. Put bluntly, Denisova (2019: 21) notes 'An individual needs to see personal gains in his or her contribution to a mobilisation.' Emotions, identity, self-expression and culture play roles in such decisions. Being involved online makes us feel we are part of something, defining who we are, regardless of offline activities. Furthermore, online activism includes an 'ability to induce a fiery, inflamed desire in a user, a desire for them to click the buttons (like, share, post) or type on their keyboard (comment, tweet). In other words, affective arousing foments people to not just watch, listen or read, but actively partake in online communication' (Denisova, 2019: 22). It is digital culture where we have the chance to be political, regardless of offline activities.

DIGITAL POPULAR CULTURE AND POLITICS: FOCUS ON MEMES

It is now time to consider scholars' ideas about relations between the digital and politics. Though we examine memes in detail in Chapter 5, for the remainder of this chapter we consider the small but growing field of research that considers relations between politics and memes, an important part of digital popular culture (see, for example, Shifman, 2013; Milner, 2016; Meikle, 2014; Esteves and Meikle, 2015). This literature is a great way to bring together what scholars say about the digital, the popular and culture. I focus specifically on three recent publications: Denisova's (2019) *Internet Memes and Society: Social, Cultural, and Political Contexts*, Wiggins' (2019) *The Discursive Power of Memes in Digital Culture: Ideology, Semiotics, and Intertexuality* and Merrin's (2019) 'President Troll: Trump, 4Chan and memetic warfare'.

Internet memes are 'multimodal artefacts remixed by countless participants, employing popular culture for public commentary' (Milner, 2018: 2357). Denisova (2019: 2) notes how 'Internet memes are intrinsically linked to the logic and rhythms of networks and social media, as well as to the ways a society expresses and thinks of itself.' Wiggins (2019) frames his definition in terms of political discourse, internet memes being: 'a remixed, iterated message that can be rapidly diffused by members of participatory digital culture for the purpose of satire, parody, critique, or other discursive activity … Its function is to posit an argument, visually, in order to commence, extend, counter, or influence a discourse.' All these definitions, which include ideas of 'public commentary', societal expressions and thoughts, and argumentation to 'satire, parody, critique', make clear that memes are intertwined with politics. Further investigation reveals these relations in more detail.

THE IMPORTANCE OF CONTEXT

Scholars from a variety of traditions, including MCDS, emphasize the importance of context in understanding discourses articulated in texts. This is the case when analysing memes. Echoing a culturalist's perspective on understanding popular culture in general, the political, media, social and consumption contexts are essential for us to make sense of memes. We need context to 'get the joke', the satire or parody because memes are 'a format [which] do not express any point. It is the users who fill them with sense' (Denisova, 2019: 29). It is common knowledge among meme makers and those who like, share, comment and/or alter them that context gives them meaning. In other words, memes are 'half-baked jokes', which require us to 'finish the sentence' (Denisova, 2019: 10). As indicated above, context includes media context and intertextuality. Wiggins (2019) succinctly points out that an internet meme needs to refer to the 'subject' as well as to other texts for it to have political potential. For example, at about the time of writing this chapter, the internet meme 'Gone with the Kim' was circulated (Figure 2.4). Meme makers, users, distributors and people who shared and commented on this had to consider the political implications of Trump's 2019 visit to North Korea, including critical perspectives on his relations with Kim Jong Un. They also had to have some knowledge of the film *Gone with the Wind*. It is this shared knowledge of both the 'subject' (criticisms of close relations between Trump and Un) and the film which gives (critical) meaning to this meme. Put another way, we need to understand 'the references to the cultural and social issues, popular and alternative culture, general knowledge and media awareness, Internet and political literacy, and the ability to connect the disconnected' (Denisova, 2019: 11). What is evident here is the importance of context cannot be understated.

Figure 2.4 'Gone with the Kim' internet meme using intertextuality.

Source: @mrjafri on Twitter

PERSPECTIVES ON INTERNET MEMES AND POLITICS

A number of scholars have examined memes in domestic politics, including the Kony2012 online campaign that aimed to arrest the Ugandan guerrilla group leader, memes that criticize water problems in Egypt, and the use of language in memes that avoid Chinese censorship (El Khachab, 2016; Kligler-Vilenchik and Thorson, 2015; Wallis, 2011). Government-sponsored memes have also been examined, including those from Azerbaijan and Trump's US presidential election campaign (Pearce and Hajizada, 2014; Glasser, 2017). In the Trump study, memes were used to persuade voters to vote for Trump and dissuade Democrats from voting at all. Despite this range of scholarship, here we consider what Denisova (2019), Wiggins (2019) and Merrin (2019) claim are relations between internet memes and politics.

Wiggins (2019) bases his analysis of memes on Shifman's (2013) analysis of video memes. Shifman considers three aspects of memes: 'content' is what a meme conveys in terms of ideas and ideologies, 'form' is the 'physical incarnation of the message' and 'stances' depict 'the way in which addressers position themselves in relation to the text, the linguistic codes, the addressees and other potential speakers' (Shifman, 2013: 367). Wiggins (2019: 15) adjusts this model in order to take into account the lack of a speech act in image-based memes by providing sufficient leakage between the three categories in Shifman's model.

His approach emphasizes human agency in the production of memes and meanings. Crucial to this is 'The phrase *discursive power* [which] inheres an agency possessing the capacity to do something, that is, to engage in the constituting and reconstituting of social relations in online spaces' (Wiggins, 2019: 21). He notes that 'the meaning ascribed to memes is achieved actively by individuals and groups. This is the essence of their discursive power' (Wiggins, 2019: 64). So, memes' political power lies in their ability to address and appeal to certain groups of political actors in society. This is demonstrated in Whitney Phillips's (2009) research on the Obama Joker meme where he found various groups used the meme to express a number of sometimes opposing political views. Memes are likely to 'appeal to an already-existing attitude, assumption, prejudice, fear, point of pride, conspiracy theory, value etc. to achieve salience in a given group' (Wiggins, 2019: 64). Internet memes gain political meaning through acceptance by and incorporation into a group or community. Despite this emphasis on 'power', Wiggins acknowledges that this is limited, dependent on offline social relations and activities including people talking about and discussing memes offline.

To illustrate how memes are political, Wiggins (2019) examines a large number of memes in a variety of circumstances, including memes in the Heart of Texas Facebook page operated by the Russian-based Internet Research Agency (see Figure 2.5 for an example). Here, he finds memes portray Texas as a 'Christian nation', associated Hillary Clinton with Osama Bin Ladin and undermine LGBT issues, race relations, immigration, gun control and Islam. He finds that followers are able to view their ideological practice as confirmed and justified using simple language and Texas-oriented patriotism. With a following of 250,000, Wiggins

(2019: 71) concludes that 'internet memes offer a tightly encapsulated way to express discursive practice efficiently and succinctly'. Here, Wiggins is able to demonstrate the important (and worrying) role memes can play in politics, concerned that 'people are more susceptible to suggestion than perhaps previously thought, despite having smart phones which could be used to check the validity of potentially dubious content' (Wiggins, 2019: 71).

 Heart Of Texas @ItsTimeToSecede · Nov 2
We need self-defense: rifles, handguns, and ammo. BAN DEMOCRATS! NOT GUNS!

Figure 2.5 Tweet from Heart of Texas containing a meme about gun control

Reflecting on the discursive power of memes, Wiggins acknowledges that they do indeed have power, but this is dependent on a number of factors including whether or not audiences read memes as their producers want, a 'preferred reading position' and whether audiences are able to successfully reference real-world events and media texts and formats. He claims (2019: 157) 'The paradox of internet memes is that, on the one hand, they are remarkable robust units of digital culture whose utility resides in their communicative function. However, on the other hand, this function also constrains, delimits, and frames how individuals view and think about real-world events and issues.'

Denisova (2019) examines memes that represent aspects of Russia's 2014 annexation of Crimea. She finds that memes can act as tools of propaganda, dissent and digital activism. She interviewed meme makers and performed textual analysis on memes focusing on connotations, embedded patterns, implied beliefs and omissions (Denisova, 2019: 82). These research approaches allow her to examine both the practices and motivations of producers and, more importantly for us, meanings that texts convey. Her textual analysis is accompanied by an examination of Russian society and media in the 2010s, Russian national identity, activism, media development and limitations in freedom of speech. She also performs a short (in comparison) examination of US memes about Donald Trump and Hillary Clinton collected on English-language Twitter on the eve of the US presidential elections on 7–8 November 2016.

Like Wiggins (2019), she believes memes are active in social and political musings. Also, like Wiggins (2019), her findings illustrate how these activities are limited. Referring to the role of memes during the 2016 US election campaign, Denisova (2019: 186) claims: 'Memes may not have changed the course of American history. Yet, what they probably did is they highlighted and promoted the trending discourses around both candidates.' Through examples of the FBI scandal surrounding Clinton's campaign, she notes how memes were a potent instrument in influencing the awareness of the population and connecting mainstream media topics with social media users. However, there are limits to this power. Where mainstream media spent hours analysing and discussing the Clinton case, memes had 'little analysis and no doubt about Hillary's guilt' (Denisova, 2019: 190).

She makes the analogy of memes being characterized as 'fast-food communication' (Denisova, 2019: 27). They are flashy, tempting and grab your attention. You get the flavour and taste, though their 'nutritional value is very low' (Denisova, 2019: 33). They also serve as 'mind-bombs' – a concept and practice developed by Bob Hunter of Greenpeace, which involves distributing a symbolic text that expresses an idea in a nutshell and has an emotional impact. Furthermore, she shows how memes can be likened to Mikhail Bahktin's carnivalesque resistance. Here, through humour, citizens are allowed a space to resist, let off steam, locate like-minded individuals and restore confidence in their own principles and aspirations. However, she finds that memes are weak 'in triggering or maintaining a substantial discussion due to their short-lived nature and a reliance on other's events and agendas' (Denisova, 2019: 162).

Her analysis of Russian memes highlights the importance of political and social contexts in defining the political role of memes. She notes that, due to repression of the press, 'in Russia meme makers have become the new journalists, civil activists and political protesters at the same time' (Denisova, 2019: 75). Memes have become one of the few remaining public sites of struggle over meaning and alternative reporting. Their most important function is raising awareness, directing attention to political issues and providing mental self-defence against indoctrination of the state. However, she is not hopeful. The Russian government uses 'internet trolls' to invade alternative internet discussions with meaningless comments and hate speech. Though memes have their limits, Denisova (2019: 195) claims 'when used strategically, they become "mind-bombs", or symbolic texts with condensed ideas and ample connotations, that help attract attention to the political issues and suggest alternative interpretations of the news'. They have the added advantage of avoiding censorship due to their allegorical style and ambiguity while filling the void for critical media in states such as Russia where there is a lack of critical mainstream media and where opposition is constantly under threat. Internet memes make complex issues easy to understand, yet sufficiently sophisticated to stimulate critical thinking. They are a way to understand concepts, identities and claims made by protesters and pro-elites. They provide a space for discourse over national identities and symbols and facilitate the contestation of mainstream thinking and propaganda.

Internet trolling is a political act usually associated with negative far-right or Russian activities. Merrin's (2019) examination of politics and internet memes concentrates on the political impact of memes and trolling on 4Chan. Though some believe trolling is an 'anti-social personality disorder' (Bishop, 2013) used by those who take advantage of 'toxic disinhibition' of anonymous, online communication to express their anger (Suler, 2005: 184), Merrin (2019) thinks differently. Trolling is political, defined in positive terms as 'a baiting, a sport, a playing, that more than anything aims at those who get above themselves, or set themselves above others – at those asserting, or in, authority' (Merrin, 2019: 202). This 'sport' is important politically because '*troll-culture* has now become central to our political processes, spreading through the mainstream to become one of the most important forms of political participation and activism today, employed by politicians, political commentators and the public alike' (2019: 201, emphasis original).

4Chan has created pro-Trump memes such as the 'Trump train' and 'You can't stump the Trump', the racist repurposing and refashioning of Pepe the frog as Trump and The Deplorables (see Figures 2.6 and 2.7). 4Chan was also instrumental in anti-Clinton campaigns such as Pizzagate and related conspiracies. Schreckinger claims the tactics of 4Chan and Trump during the 2016 presidential campaign was 'to relentlessly tilt the prevailing sentiment on social media in favour of Trump: "He clearly won that war against Hillary Clinton day after day after day"' (2017, in Merrin, 2019: 209). 4Chan memes were not just aimed at its users, but distributed on Twitter and Facebook to appeal to 'normies' (the public). This strategy Merrin calls 'mimetic warfare' because it is intentional and well organized.

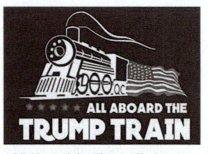

All Aboard the Trump Train

Figure 2.6 4Chan's pro-Trump meme, 'The Trump train'. Creator unknown

Figure 2.7 Tweet from Donald Trump including a meme of Trump as Pepe the frog

The concept of 'memetic warfare' is shared by a number of scholars and governments who recognize the power of memes. Prosser (2006) notes how memes will be 'an important part of future ideological informational warfare and recommend[s] the establishment of a military "Meme Warfare Centre"'. Giesea (2015: 69) argues that 'warfare through trolling and memes is a necessary, inexpensive, and easy way to help destroy the appeal and morale of our common enemies'. Government agencies have been established and function to do just this: the Russian government's use of troll farms, Maga 3X 2 (pro-Trump social media organization), China's 50 cent party, Israel's Hasbara units, the Ukraine's iArmy and the British military's 77th Brigade and GCHQ's Joint Threat Research Intelligence Group. These governmental agencies, alongside less formal organizations, groups, collectives and engaged individuals intervene in both domestic and foreign political processes, making memes 'central to our political life, constituting, for many people, their most common mode of political expression, participation and activism' (Merrin, 2019: 219).

Memes are effective communicative weapons. They are at the heart 'of our everyday political awareness, experience and activity and much of this activity is humorous, satirical, irreverent and sarcastic: lampooning, ridiculing and parodying the political opposition' (Merrin, 2019: 221). Similar to Denisova (2019) and Wiggins (2019), Merrin (2019) believes memes have political power. They are 'a means of solidarity, attracting support and binding those with similar views' (Merrin, 2019: 222). This echoes Denisova (2019: 15), who believes memes and social networks do not replace but supplement non-digital political activities. All three scholars agree: memes reduce and simplify political facts and arguments. They are 'another move away' from rational, communicative debate by 'deliver[ing] highly charged satirical critiques that damage opponents and their positions and that inflict a telling *ideological burn* upon them. They are part of a new politics of affectivity, identification, emotion and humour' (Merrin, 2019: 222). In regard to Trump's 2016 election campaign, Merrin (2019: 211) notes that 'people voted for Trump for many different personal, economic, social, cultural and political reasons, but one thing is certain: people voted for Trump. The "troll" candidate won.'

SUMMARY

This chapter has examined what we know about (digital) popular culture and its relations with politics. This area of study has fascinated scholars and practitioners for years, even before there was an academic field known as cultural studies. We examined how others have studied popular culture and politics all the way from Mathew Arnold up to post-structuralism. Though there are plenty of other perspectives, I have chosen perspectives which help inform our MCDS approach. For the most part, these perspectives highlight the importance of analysing texts, contexts and being critical.

We then considered what scholars have told us about digital media, users and politics. Though this is a broad field of research, we confined our examination to a small number of areas relevant to this book. We examined both optimistic and pessimistic perspectives concerning the role digital media can play in politics. Issues about its democratic potential were explored, followed by its limitations, including a lack of political engagement in comments and a lack of alternative voices in

(Continued)

our feeds. This led to concerns over filter bubbles and echo chambers. These arguments are dismissed by a number of scholars (including myself) for being too simplistic and techno-deterministic. Instead we have argued for looking at relations between digital media and users as 'visions' or 'digital cultures', where users are empowered by technology not subservient to it.

Once we agree that digital media has the potential to empower us, we are able to consider what scholars say about how we use digital media. Here, some scholars hold out little hope for us using digital media politically due to our preference for entertainment over information. We argue that we can have both. We also examined how digital media can be used politically in Twitter campaigns and why people get politically involved.

This all leads us to our examination of how digital popular culture can act politically. Scholars who examine memes find that they can be used to inform, to collectivize and to articulate existing politics. Groups of users interpret these politics in ways that mimic their own, as seen in the Obama Joker meme. It is with this knowledge that we can now consider how to best examine politics in digital popular culture. This book's position is that through MCDS we can examine in detail how politics are communicated. This is where we turn in our next chapter.

SUGGESTED READING

Madsen, A. (2016) Beyond the bubble: three empirical reasons to re-conceptualize online visibility. *Journal of Media and Communication Research*, 31(59): 6–27.

This article calls into question popular 'filter bubbles' and 'echo chambers' criticisms associated with the political and social potential of social media. This allows us to consider whether these criticisms should be unquestionably accepted.

Papacharissi, Z. (2015) Affective publics and structures of storytelling: sentiment, events and mediality. *Information, Communication and Society*, 19(3): 307–324.

Affect plays a big part in how digital popular culture communicates to us. This article applies affect and emotion to our understanding of online civic engagement. It uses big data and qualitative analyses of Twitter streams to outline the affective role(s) Twitter plays in uprisings, movements and everyday political expression.

Pariser, E. (2012) *The Filter Bubble: How the New Personalized Web is Changing What We Read and How We Think*. London: Penguin Random House.

Though we argue against the idea of filter bubbles and echo chambers in this book, these criticisms are popular and expose some very interesting ideas about the limits of social media. This book is a highly influential critique of the role of social media in politics and in society more generally. It outlines in detail how users of social media are less informed than we think we are.

Storey, J. (2006) *Cultural Theory and Popular Culture: An Introduction* (4th edn). Harlow: Pearson.

This book offers an historical examination of the study of culture and popular culture. It is a good reference book providing short summaries of the many approaches to this area of study.

3

MULTIMODAL CRITICAL DISCOURSE STUDIES

Why This Approach? How to Do It?

CHAPTER OBJECTIVES

- Describe how we can analyse the political meanings in digital popular culture.
- Define ideology and discourse.
- Outline key concepts of critical discourse analysis (CDA) and multimodal critical discourse studies (MCDS).
- Consider how to apply CDA and MCDS to the analysis of digital popular culture.
- Build an MCDS approach that incorporates knowledge from musicology and social media scholarship.

KEY CONCEPTS

- One useful definition of ideology is 'representations of aspects of the world which can be shown to contribute to establishing, maintaining and changing social relations of power domination and exploitation' (Fairclough, 2003: 9).
- Struggles over ideology are played out through language.
- Discourses can be thought of as models of the world, giving a clear sense of 'what view of the world is being communicated through semiotic resources' (Abousnnouga and Machin, 2010: 139).

(Continued)

- CDA is one method by which to examine language, discourse and power. It is a social science that analyses language in context.
- A mode is a socially agreed-upon channel of communication like writing, speaking or images.
- We communicate using a number of 'modes' such as language and images and MCDS scholars examine how each mode separately and with other modes articulates discourses in texts.
- Analysing lyrics, images, sounds and contexts is essential for understanding how digital popular culture articulates discourses.
- KhosraviNik (2017) has developed an approach called 'social media critical discourse studies' (SM-CDS) which addresses some of the unique characteristics of communications in social media.

INTRODUCTION

Most of us enjoy watching, reading, adding comments and liking memes, GIFs, and music videos on our Facebook, Twitter and Instagram feeds. Lots of these involve people or animals saying and/or doing ridiculous things. Most of us do not go out of our way to look for digital popular culture that critiques politicians, but when something funny or interesting appears on our feeds, many of us share these. In my case, this is especially true about anything that ridicules Turkey's President Recep Tayyip Erdoğan or the UK's Boris Johnson.

Figure 3.1 Anti-corruption meme of Turkish president Recep Tayyip Erdoğan. Creator unknown

Figure 3.1 is just such a meme I have encountered. The caption reads 'Don't sit close to your television'. The words alone do not tell us the reason for the warning. As a boy, I remember my mum telling my siblings and I the same because she had read that this was bad for our eyes. However, this meme is telling us something very different, made obvious by the imagery and our understanding of Turkish politics. The image represents President Erdoğan reaching out of the television to steal a television viewer's money from his pocket. Depending on your knowledge of Erdoğan and Turkish politics, this meme articulates a number of oppositional discourses that may include corruption in Erdoğan's government, his iron grip on the media, his voting base and Erdoğan as a manipulator. This meme is both funny and a scathing attack on Erdoğan. What we need to do is consider *how* this meme communicates such ideas.

The aim of this chapter is to describe how we can analyse the political meanings not only in memes, but digital popular culture more broadly. To do this, we first define ideology and discourse, concepts that have proven to be highly fruitful for theorizing popular culture as communication and concepts that are crucial when unpacking the multitude of meanings loaded onto popular culture, whether these are or are not intended by producers. We then consider arguments for using CDA to analyse texts. This examination is followed by an in-depth description of MCDS and an examination of how it can be applied to a range of texts, including digital popular culture. This chapter argues that CDA and MCDS allow us to reveal meanings carried by lexica, sounds and visuals in (digital) popular culture. For much of digital popular culture, music plays a role in articulating discourses, so we examine key findings in music scholarship about music and politics. We also consider how to approach digital media from a discursive approach. Finally, this chapter ties all these ideas together to build an MCDS approach to examining digital popular culture.

IDEOLOGY AND DISCOURSE

Ideology

Ideology is key to understanding issues of language, power and politics across a large variety of communicative acts such as speech, broadcast news, music and entertainment (Kress and Hodge, 1979; Fairclough, 1989 and 2003). Though we may have an idea about what is 'ideology', it is hard to define. That is because there is a multitude of definitions used to describe it (Williams, 1988: 156). Instead of going through a conceptual minefield, here we choose definitions and related concepts that can help us better understand how to analyse the politics articulated in digital popular culture.

Ideology is 'a way of making sense [of the world], the sense it makes always has a social and political dimension' (Fiske, 1989: 165). This definition makes clear that ideology is social and political. Althusser (1970) believes ideologies are inescapable in everything we do. They are 'deeply inscribed in the ways of thinking and ways of living' (in Fiske, 1989: 174). In fact, this idea of being all-encompassing is shared by both Althusser and Gramsci. However, while Althusser's ideas entrap everyone in ideology, Gramsci liberates society through the idea of 'hegemony'. Williams (1988: 145), summarizing Gramsci, writes hegemony 'is not limited to matters of direct political control but seeks to describe a more general predominance which includes, as one of its key features, a particular way of seeing the world and human nature and relationships'. Various power groups vie for society's support. Hegemonic struggles are ongoing, winning and re-winning the consent of the majority in society. In this sense, society is empowered.

Critical linguists and discourse analysts also offer definitions that can help us in our study. Kress and Hodge (1979: 6) define ideology as 'a systematic body of ideas, organized from a particular point of view' – that is, representations. This idea that ideology is connected to representations can be seen in more contemporary definitions, such as that ideology is 'representations of aspects of the world which can be shown to contribute to establishing, maintaining and changing social relations of power domination and exploitation' (Fairclough, 2003: 9). This definition is useful for us. Here, ideology is redefined as 'representations' of the world, such as those found in digital popular culture. The definition also encompasses the idea that representations are linked to 'power, domination and exploitation'. Finally, this definition includes 'establishing, maintaining and changing social relations', acknowledging the struggle for various definitions of political issues.

Common among these definitions of ideology and hegemony is the central role of language. Hegemonic struggles for ideology are played out through language. In fact, the relationship between linguistic representations and ideology is one that has concerned scholars who use CDA and its precursor, critical linguistics. Kress and Hodge (1979: 15) found that ideology always 'involve[s] language' and language choices. If you track the importance of language in relation to power and politics in society historically, it is claimed 'the exercise of power, in modern society, is increasingly achieved through ideology, and more particularly through the ideological workings of language' (Fairclough, 1989: 2). Here, we argue that ideological workings are evident in not just language, but a whole host of representations, including digital popular culture.

Discourse

Like the term 'ideology', 'discourse' also produces a large number of definitions that fall into two groups. Formalist definitions are those associated with formal linguistics. Typical of this type is 'communication in speech or writing' and 'a speech or piece of writing about a particular, usually serious, subject' found in the *Cambridge Advanced Learner's Dictionary*. The second way to consider discourse is from a functionalist perspective, associated with social semiotics and this book. Wodak's (2001: 66) definition is particularly useful noting that discourse is 'a complex bundle of simultaneous and sequential interrelated linguistic acts, which manifest themselves within and across the social fields of action as thematically interrelated semiotic, oral or written tokens, very often as "texts," that belong to specific semiotic types, that is genres'.

This definition makes clear discourses are articulated through groups or 'bundles' of communicative acts. These are ways of representing a 'thematically interrelated' issue or idea. Multimodality is also suggested in this definition, discourse not restricted to only writing, but also 'oral' and 'semiotic' communication. Examples of discourses, according to Wodak, include unemployment, racism and immigration restrictions.

Recent definitions have become more encompassing, to accommodate contemporary neoliberal uses of language. Though indeed, scholars acknowledge that discourse is 'language-in-use' (Krzyżanowski and Forchtner, 2016: 254), it is seen as more than just representations of, say, people and groups of people. Discourses can be thought of as models of the world, giving a clear sense of 'what view of the world is being communicated through semiotic resources' (Abousnnouga and Machin, 2010: 139). Krzyżanowski (2016: 309) notes that discourse encompasses 'various social and political and indeed abstract concepts'. In the articulation of neoliberal discourses, he argues that concepts become operationalized:

> for the introduction and legitimation of various forms of regulation. They are not just additions or elements of a meta-language tied to representation and abstraction of social action, but often become outright replacements of discursive constructions – in the sense of representations – of social change or of those that are undertaking and/or undergoing some rapid and very often abrupt social processes. (2016: 309)

Concepts and representations articulate discourses that are always ideological, that is 'a systematic body of ideas, organized from a particular point of view' (Kress and Hodge, 1979: 6). Digital popular culture communicates discourses which project social values and beliefs beneficial to some parties at the expense of others, used by producers and interpreted by users to communicate (sometimes political) discourses.

What is the relationship between discourse and ideology?

The relationship between discourses and ideologies is one of both informing and being informed by each other. Remember, Wodak (2001) defines discourse as 'a complex bundle of simultaneous and sequential interrelated linguistic acts', which are thematically interrelated. Scholars link the two concepts by recognising that discourses are ideological (Richardson, 2007). However, ideologies differ from discourses, the former being more encompassing. Ideology is 'a particular way of seeing the world and human nature and relationships' (Williams, 1963). However, discourses are less encompassing, being linguistic acts concerned with topics like unemployment. Though indeed one can write books on these concepts, for our purposes here we can state that both concepts are interrelated and essential for understanding the political power of digital popular culture.

CRITICAL DISCOURSE ANALYSIS: WHAT AND WHY?

A study of media and/or culture ought to begin with the study of language. This is because language 'is a version of the world, offered to, imposed on, exacted by, someone else' (Kress and Hodge, 1979: 9). Its role in society is not only to communicate, but also to control (Fairclough, 2003: 34). Through language analysis, we can expose language and 'discourse as the instrument of power and control as well as ... the instrument of the social construction of reality' (van Leeuwen, 1993b: 193). A close study of language should therefore be 'a central element' of media and cultural analysis, used to reveal what are often hidden ideologies and world views (Fairclough, 1995b: 16).

CDA is one method we can use to examine language, discourse and power. It is a social science which analyses language in context to reveal ideologies in texts. In fact, Wodak (2001: 10) notes '[o]ne of the aims of CDA is to "de-mystify" discourses by deciphering ideologies'.

So why should we use CDA over other methods of analysing language? One significant difference between CDA and other approaches to examining language is its concern for context. Scholars who use CDA examine lexical and grammatical choices made by text producers to reveal obvious and less obvious discourses while considering their social, historical, production, consumption and/or political contexts. Similar to Foucault, CDA practitioners believe these compositional choices have political repercussions (Kress, 1985: 3). For example, Donald Trump supporters choosing to name Hillary Clinton in animations and parodies 'Crooked Hillary' and not 'a highly qualified presidential candidate' carries with it political significance and implications, such as how some people may vote. Through analysis of texts in context, broader ideological discourses are revealed, including what kinds of social relations of power, inequalities, identities and interests are perpetuated, generated, or legitimated in texts both explicitly and implicitly (van Dijk, 1993; Kress and van Leeuwen, 2001).

Considering context is essential when analysing texts for another reason. Discourse, according to CDA scholars, is a form of social practice or action. It is something people do to, or for, each other (van Leeuwen, 1993b), an element of social life which is closely interconnected with other elements of social life (Fairclough, 2003: 3). Van Leeuwen and Wodak (1999: 92) describe a 'dialectical relationship' where 'discourse constitutes social practice and is at the same time constituted by it'. Due to these dialectic relations, both text and context must be examined to better understand texts.

CDA also differs from many other approaches to the examination of language by clearly stating its critical political role. Wodak (2001: 2) describes this: 'CDA aims to investigate critically social inequalities as it is expressed, signalled, constituted, legitimized and so on by language use (or in discourse).' This explanation illustrates how CDA is concerned with relations between language and power. In fact, CDA prioritizes a political commitment. Van Dijk (1993) suggests scholars who apply CDA start by identifying a social problem with a linguistic aspect, choose the perspective of those who suffer the most, then critically analyse those in power, those who are responsible and those who have the means and opportunity to solve such problems.

It has been argued that all scholarly discourse and textual analysis are sociopolitically situated, selective, limited, partial and thereby biased (Richardson, 2007; Fairclough, 2003). So, CDA scholars choose to be critical in the sense that the research is politically commited to opposing social inequality and the abuse of power. Choosing a critical approach provides 'a scientific basis for a critical questioning of social life in moral and political terms, e.g. in terms of social justice and power' (Fairclough, 2003: 15). This book equips the reader with the tools they need to be able to critically question and not support injustice, inequality and the abuse of power. Specifically, readers gain the necessary skills to expose the unjust abuse of power articulated in digital popular culture, whether from rightwing 'bots' or left-wing protesters. We will be able to critically examine texts in detail and in context to reveal how injustice, inequality and abuse of power are articulated in digital popular culture.

MULTIMODAL CRITICAL DISCOURSE STUDIES

We rarely communicate monomodally – that is, using one mode of communication. Even this book communicates using not only written language, but different font sizes, bold print, numbers and images to indicate a number of things including importance and emphasis. In Figure 3.2, we see not only a photograph of two former UK Conservative prime ministers (David Cameron and Theresa May), but also writing superimposed on the image. Though choices in the image connote a number of things, it is the written language that communicates dislike for these politicians. Likewise, the writing makes little sense on its own. Without the photograph, 'these two' could be a combination of a number of people including Sir Richard Branson, Margaret Thatcher, Boris Johnson, Jeremy Corbyn or Tony Blair, depending on how you interpret the words and your political orientation. It is in the combination of both 'modes' of photograph and writing that we are able to understand what the meme is meant to tell us. Due to the multimodal nature of communication, it makes sense that some scholars using CDA consider texts multimodally.

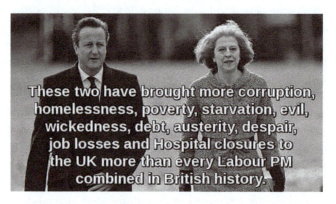

Figure 3.2   Consider image and written language in memes: 'These two' meme. Creator unknown

As far back as 1996, Kress and van Leeuwen in *Reading Images* (1996) and then *Multimodal Discourse* (2001) demonstrated how meanings in texts are generated not just by written language but through other semiotic resources such as visuals, material objects and architecture. Machin (2013) describes these two works as ground-breaking because they introduced the idea to linguists that non-linguistic modes also create meaning. These books also emphasize that communication historically has been moving from mono-modal to multimodal, partly due to technology. Think of how a newspaper 100 years ago (such as Figure 3.3) compares to an interactive news website like the *Independent* or the BBC (see Figure 3.4) with live updates, videos, surveys, photographs, animations and the like. Machin (2013: 348) believes their work points 'to the possibility of a social semiotic approach to different forms of communication that allowed not only deeper analysis, but as in linguistics, a more systematic level of description. And this is where its strength lies.'

Figure 3.3 Technological limits in media from the past: *The Belfast News-Letter*

Figure 3.4 The *Independent* news website: multimodal and interactive

MCDS, with its origins in CDA, assumes linguistic and visual choices reveal broader discourses articulated in texts (Kress and van Leeuwen, 2001). It approaches texts similar to CDA by taking 'the power of description so useful for drawing out buried ideologies in linguistic-based CDS to be applied to other communicative modes' (Machin, 2013: 348). But what is a mode? Though there is some academic discussion on this question, we stick to a simple definition which is: a mode is a socially agreed-upon channel of communication, rather than a channel of human perception (McKerrell and Way, 2017). For memes, modes used may be written lexica, photographs and other visuals, while mash-ups include lyrics, visuals and musical sounds. For the most part, MCDS has concentrated on visuals, though other modes analysed include material properties of war monuments (Abousnnouga and Machin, 2010), sound (Roderick, 2013), colour (Zhang and O'Halloran, 2012), music (Way, 2018a) and clothing (Bouvier, 2017), to name just a few.

Analysing texts multimodally has the advantage of revealing the way each mode works to articulate discourses 'on a particular occasion, in a particular text' (Kress and van Leeuwen, 2001: 29). The task of MCDS is to draw out the details of how broader discourses are communicated and how the different modes play different roles. MCDS also allows us to consider how modes work in conjunction with other modes to articulate meanings – for example, how the meme above (Figure 3.2) uses image and the phrase 'these two' to create a 'terrible twosome'. Analysing digital popular culture using MCDS allows us to critically consider the communicative roles of each mode, such as lexical choices, images and musical sounds in representing events, issues and politics while considering context. Though textual features are analysed to uncover their meaning potential, rigid connotative meanings are not assigned to these. Instead, analysis considers the important role of cultural conventions and metaphorical associations which work alongside features of texts to construct meanings. Like we have seen in other approaches such as CDA, MCDS calls for a detailed analysis of text alongside context.

Critical multimodal research is sparse (see 'Music as Discourse' special edition of *Journal of Language and Politics* (2019), *Music as Discourse* edited collection (2018) and the 'Multimodal Special Edition' of *Critical Discourse Studies* (2013) for some very good critical examples). In this book, we examine how we can analyse digital popular culture critically, adding to this growing field of work. We closely follow critical approaches used by a number of ground-breaking scholars (Kress and van Leeuwen, 1996 and 2001; van Leeuwen, 2005; Machin, 2007 and 2010; Abousnnouga and Machin, 2010). Our approach rests on these MCDS foundations.

AN INTEGRAL PART OF MCDS: THE ROLE OF MUSICAL SOUNDS

Music can be defined as society 'constituting sounds as intentional objects, from the level of a single note to that of a complete work' (Cook, 1990: 223). This is an important aspect of our approach to MCDS; music is included in much of what we are examining in this book such as animations, mash-ups, parodies and music videos. It has been demonstrated elsewhere that a musicology-informed MCDS helps reveal the key roles musical sounds can make in articulating (sometimes political) discourses (see Way, 2016, 2018a and 2019a and b).

Music and politics have a long history, with some claiming its origins reach as far back as ancient Greece. Popular music has also had its share of 'political' songs from Billie Holiday's 'Strange Fruit' (1939) to Eminem's 'The Storm' (2017). Though we can think of lots of examples of political pop, scholars cannot agree on relations between music and politics (Hesmondhalgh and Negus, 2002). Some scholars have an optimistic perspective on music's ability to represent and promote politics (Lorraine, 2006; Korczynski, 2014), while others are far more pessimistic (Grossberg, 1992). Here, we briefly consider this topic. You can find a far more detailed outline of this in Way (2018a), *Popular Music and Multimodal Critical Discourse Studies*.

Sociologists have demonstrated how production, promotion, social and consumption contexts constrain and influence political meanings in pop (Frith, 1988; Street, 1988). Musicians' politics, which they may choose to represent in song, are a result of their experiences as individuals, citizens and workers (Street, 1988: 128). These ideas are only the beginning in a process that sees input by musicians, record executives, lawyers, accountants, producers, engineers, publicists, sales personnel, radio programmers, disc jockeys, music journalists and many more. Music we hear online or otherwise 'is not a piece of pure art; it is the result of countless choices and compromises, using criteria that mix the aesthetic, the political and the economic' (Street, 1988: 6).

There is a large academic field that examines musical texts and their meaning potential. In this, we find that some genres of music are compatible with some kinds of politics. For example, most pop songs keep to local politics (Terkourafi, 2010; Street, 2013), though there are exceptions to this (Hess, 2010; Way, 2015). In fact, pop does not express conventional politics well, it being more compatible with political ideas such as nationalist struggles, the politics of leisure, gender, race, class, sexuality and the environment (Frith, 1988; Shuker, 2001). Likewise, 'not every style of music or every form of musician' can be associated with politics (Peddie, 2011: 53). Genre plays a large role in fans' expectations about music and politics where 'rock, soul and folk musicians can talk about politics, and country singers about marriage and children, in ways that are denied to most pop musicians' (Street, 1988: 6).

There are a large number of approaches to understanding the meanings of songs. Traditional musicology attempts to understand music's meanings by literally examining written musical notes, or 'the score'. This has been rejected by 'new musicology' and various types of cultural musicologies that have attempted to 'walk away from an analysis of the score' (McKerrell and Way, 2017) and consider the role musical sounds can play within social life (Tagg, 2012; Moore, 2013). Many sociological studies have been criticized for concentrating on lyrics, while ignoring musical sounds (Frith, 1988; Goodwin 1993; Shuker, 2001), despite our preference to 'listen primarily to the beat and the melody – the sound of the record – and make [our] own sense of the songs' (Shuker, 2001: 148).

'Critical musicology' is an approach that includes deep readings of texts alongside contextual considerations. This is an approach close to our approach in this book. A good example of this is Walser's (1995) examination of Public Enemy's 'Fight the power'. He considers the power of not only the lyrics, but also beat and rhythm as 'an embodiment of past experiences and identities', how voice is used to express 'resentment of, and resistance to, years of oppression' and 'the emphatic repetition of the title [that] serves as a rallying cry for collective struggle' (1995: 204–208). Socio-linguistic approaches to the study of music offer a systematic and detailed analysis of lyrics and context, though much of this lacks a systematic analysis of musical sounds. In Terkourafi's (2010) *Languages of Global Hip Hop*, contributors outline the social and political context of music and analyse lyrics. Some also briefly describe non-lyrical elements such as crowd sounds (Androutsopoulos, 2010), dress code, breakdancing and rapping (Hassa, 2010: 46), hairdos, attire and jewellery (Lee, 2010), beats, rhymes, sampling, graffiti and dance (Stylianou, 2010), and melody, bass and samples (Hess, 2010).

Another factor to consider in musical meaning-making is the role of fans, and more specifically, settings, lifestyles and consumption contexts, all shown to contribute to music's meanings. Hebdige (1979) demonstrates how music and other cultural artefacts are used by youth as part of a self-imposed exile from mainstream culture. Zbikowski (2015) argues how Harburg and Arlen's 'Over the Rainbow' functions one way while performed by a cabaret performer in a nightclub and quite another way when performed by an amateur singer at a friend's funeral. Though he acknowledges overlap in meaning, he believes 'there will also be significant differences, many of which reflect the multivariate ways the musical utterances actually function within these social and cultural contexts' (2015: 149). Furthermore, public perceptions and reactions to pop and their fans contribute to meanings in music. At times, these make pop 'political', as was the case of 1970s punk which experienced a hostile reaction that 'help[ed] to politicize the musicians and their fans' (Shuker, 2001: 217). More recently, Beyonce's 2016 Super Bowl 50 performance of 'Formation' was politicized partly due to reactions. Former New York Mayor Rudy Giuliani told *Fox News* that 'I think it was outrageous ... the halftime show I thought was ridiculous anyway', while Black Lives Matter activist Erika Totten said the performance was political because it 'disrupt[ed] the status quo and [brought] the message wherever the message may not be heard'.

Music can be political and is an essential part of our analysis of digital popular culture. This section has highlighted the importance of an analysis of lyrics, images, sounds and contexts. What follows now is an examination of research that has examined popular culture from a discursive perspective.

WHY USE MCDS TO ANALYSE (DIGITAL) POPULAR CULTURE AND POLITICS?

Scholars using MCDS have examined a wide range of popular culture, as well as political news stories and speeches. In this section, we consider why it is important to examine (digital) popular culture using MCDS. A short survey of some of this research follows to demonstrate the range of popular culture examined and the range of approaches within the wider umbrella of MCDS.

Arguments for examining politics expressed in popular culture are compelling. Van Leeuwen (2017: 290) notes, 'The power of such [visuals in popular culture] representations lies precisely in the fact that their ideological meanings can be so easily denied by arguments such as that "it is only a story" or "only a toy", or that words are "precise" while images are "polysemous".' Though van Leeuwen was referring to visuals here, these attributes to all forms of popular culture, including digital popular culture, are widely circulated, suggesting their importance for analysis by critical researchers. Machin (2013: 347) concurs by linking the popular with power. He notes that popular culture is where we most experience politics 'as fun, as style, and simply as part of the taken for granted everyday world … [though] all these different levels of communicative activity are infused by and shaped by, power relations and ideologies' (2013: 347).

Politics in an array of popular culture have been examined discursively including late-night satirical TV talk shows (Molek-Kozakowska, 2013), comic strips (Veloso and Bateman, 2013; Wodak and Forchtner, 2014), toy figurines (van Leeuwen, 2008), war monuments (Abousnnouga and Machin, 2010), factual crime reports (Machin and Mayr, 2012) and popular music (Way, 2018a). Let's examine one of these to see how this approach is useful. Veloso and Bateman (2013) look at how superhero comic books play a role in legitimizing controversial government policies. Their case study examines how Marvel's *Civil War* comics series legitimized the sweeping powers of the USA PATRIOT Act enacted in response to the 9/11 attacks in New York. They contend that comic books and popular cultural artefacts are both 'powerful' and 'profitable' and 'need to be examined both from a critical perspective, as they represent a further source of media re-construal deployed for further possibly controversial agendas, and from a discourse perspective that incorporates appropriate means for addressing multimodality' (Veloso and Bateman, 2013: 441). Their multimodal analysis examines how images and written language 'played a significant role in the necessary process of legitimation' of what was critically described as curtailing civil liberties (2013: 427). They conclude that 'The Civil War series constructs a discourse of acceptability that presents arguments from two opposing perspectives only to, in the end, state that, despite the negative aspects of the PATRIOT Act, it is still necessary to embrace it', thereby legitimating controversial government policies that curtail civil rights (2013: 441).

There is a small but growing field within MCDS that examines popular culture, with an emphasis on popular music. Much of this leans on a systematic approach to analysing sounds outlined in van Leeuwen's (1999) *Speech, Music, Sound*. In short, he categorizes sound into six domains, namely perspective, time, interacting sounds, melody, voice quality and timbre and modality. It is how these domains of sound are manipulated by producers and the context they are experienced that determines their meaning potentials (see Chapter 8). Machin (2010) uses many of van Leeuwen's ideas to examine a wide range of popular culture including songs, album covers, videos and music in film and television. Though the focus of Machin's book is not directly political, issues of identity and power are always at the forefront of his analysis.

Some scholars have used these ideas to consider politics in popular music more directly. Again, we do not examine all of these, but instead, consider a small number of these to determine how approaching popular culture from a discursive perspective while acknowledging the role of musical sounds can be revealing. Machin and Richardson (2012) analyse the melody, arrangements, sound qualities, rhythms and lyrics of two pieces of music associated with two pre-1945 European fascist movements. They demonstrate how these sounds communicate discourses of a machine-like certainty about a vision for a new society based on discipline, conformity and the might of the nation including unity, common identity and purpose. McKerrell (2012) analyses the role of lyrics, context, performance, reception and mediatization of a song in the press to demonstrate how cultural performance can construct sectarian difference in the Scottish public imagination. Power et al. (2012) examine the harmonic and melodic structure, tempo, instrumentation and the visuals in a Morrissey song and video to reveal how the singer has represented the struggles of the proletariat. Ord (2017) examines how recording techniques such as echo, reverb and panning construct countercultural meanings in folk-rock recordings of the 1960s and 70s. He also considers how sound recording techniques construct a politically charged image of 'Englishness' as part of an ongoing contestation of the space of English cultural identity (Ord, 2019). (Way 2015, 2017, 2018a and 2019a and 2019b) analyses Turkish political popular music videos, some part of protests, while others are pro- and anti-government. These studies demonstrate how music works multimodally to articulate not only political discourses, but also discourses of authenticity.

Some of this work examines the role of music in digital popular culture. For example, many of the music videos (promotional and fan-sourced) analysed by myself are commented on, distributed and shared on a number of digital platforms such as Facebook and YouTube as part of online and offline protests and campaigns (Way, 2015, 2017, 2018a and 2019a and b). Also, Barbosa Caro and Ramírez Suavita (2019) examine nineteen 'corridos paracos' videos on the internet which support far-right armed resistance in Colombia.

As indicated by this very brief survey of literature, popular music can be used as political discourse in both online and offline activities. What is also evident from these (and other) MCDS studies is that music is part of (digital) popular culture which expresses politics multimodally. This book continues the work cited above by using MCDS to analyse music's role in digital popular culture.

55

UNIQUE AFFORDANCES AND A UNIQUE APPROACH TO DIGITAL POPULAR CULTURE

Social media have unique affordances that some scholars believe have to be taken into account when examining popular culture on social media. For example, political meanings are shaped by how music videos are distributed, shared and commented upon on social media. Even the music video has changed the way 'some listeners now listen to music by looking at it. Adding this layer has allowed artists to add new nuance, new depth, new ways to convey their messages' (Arnold et al., 2017: 5). Much of this leans on stereotypes, though some can 'present a contemporary counter to these traditional and often regressive approaches and representations' (2017: 6). Furthermore, unlike traditional media, fans and the public have a chance to respond to representations through 'chats' or 'comments' following a particular video, allowing audiences to interact with the music video. A case in point is how social media users who were angered by Robin Thicke's obviously misogynous video of 'Blurred Lines' (2013) created a virtual campaign that 'sought to challenge such negative representations of women and sexual embodiment through social media' (Arnold et al., 2017: 7). Another example demonstrates how user comments about music videos challenge political positions (Way, 2015) and this is something we explore in Chapter 4.

Social media and the spread of inexpensive digital audio/video editing software has also led to an influx of 'home-made' music videos, rants, parodies, mash-ups, to name a few. Some argue that fans are less interested in what is original and what is fan-made (Way, 2018a), and more interested in being entertained. In fact, Manghani (2017) believes fan-made social media offerings create a '"temporary autonomous zone" ... [that is] temporary spaces or systems of representations that sit outside of formal power structures' (2017: 23). These look different from slick professional productions. Instead, fan-sourced material 'can include official and unofficial footage of artists "behind the scenes", celebrity news, the reporting of live performances, and, of course, parody' (2017: 23–24). For example, Beyonce's Super Bowl live performance of 'Formation', shared on social media and including official and unofficial feeds, makes it 'a combined "object" of music-video-news as it forms and reformulates social media, news networks, and print journalism' (2017: 37).

Whether fan-sourced or original, once online, digital popular culture is beyond the control of its producers. It becomes a source used to create an array of communicative messages. Yes, downloads, streaming and video platforms such as YouTube offer new spaces for commercial consolidation and creative freedom, but these commercial offerings become source material for vloggers and YouTubers and are 'of more significance' (Manghani, 2017: 37). These new artefacts include parody, as we examine in Chapter 8. They offer political possibilities, being an integral part to 'the forming of identities and social connections', though 'YouTubers are generally almost all middle-class, upwardly mobile young people (though this is equally true of most pop musicians over the years)' (2017: 39–40).

Some scholars who consider social media discursively believe these unique affordances of social media outlined above need to be taken into account when examining artefacts. KhosraviNik (2017) has developed an approach he calls 'social media critical discourse studies' (SM-CDS) which addresses some of these unique characteristics of communications in social media. Presently, we look at this approach to consider what we may want to draw from this.

KhosraviNik's approach leans on a tradition which foregrounds discursive *practice*, or the discourse-in-action approach of Scollon (2001), as the central focus of research. It is this approach where scholars are interested in 'the concrete, situated actions people perform with particular mediational means (such as written texts, computers, mobile phones) in order to enact membership in particular social groups' (Jones et al., 2015: 2). The unit of analysis is the mediated action, which includes the practice where the text is used. Agreeing with Barton and Lee (2013: 167), KhosraviNik (2017: 584) notes 'we need to both closely look at the texts and to observe "users" lives and beliefs about what they do with their online writing'. In other words, KhosraviNik's (2017) SM-CDS examines text, with context being upfront in the analysis, an approach not dissimilar to MCDS.

Like CDA, SM-CDS proposes to view discourse as language-in-use so the 'SM-CDS model would be unapologetically comfortable in following a context dependent, critical analysis of communicative practices/content with a socio-political critique level' (KhosraviNik, 2017: 585). He believes the study of context needs to be both horizontal and vertical. That is, horizontal contextualization examines intertextuality and 'norms of production, consumption, and distribution of texts on different platforms ... including the patterns of users' textual/semiotic/etc. practices in their online worlds' (2017: 585). Vertical contextualization links these practices with the socio-political contexts of society. Multimodality is also key to his approach, something indeed this book embraces. However, he notes there are problems if we constrain our analysis to simply verbal, audio and visual channels. We also need to consider tagging, likes, annotation, sharing and hyperlinks, again a sentiment this book fully endorses.

It is essential that we take on some of the aspects of KhosraviNik's approach to analysing digital popular culture: not only his emphasis on multimodality and consideration of modes unique to social media, but also his emphasis on context. These indeed help us to build a model of how we analyse digital popular culture. KhosraviNik, in fact, does this in a number of publications, where he mostly examines memes, comments and images about Persian nationalism shared on Facebook. What we now do is define our approach to analysing digital popular culture.

OUR APPROACH: AN MCDS TOOLKIT

There is no definitive MCDS approach on how to analyse a text. In this book, for example, we examine memes, mash-ups, music videos, satirical shows and comments by those who interact with these. The likely modes we would experience in each of these varies. A comment will include written lexica and possibly an emoji, a meme – a photograph and probably writing, while a music video will include visuals, lyrics and sounds. This diversity means we have to have the flexibility to modify our approach. As Wodak and Weiss (2005: 125) note, scholars who use CDA must ask '[w]hat conceptual tools are relevant for this or that problem and for this and that context?' MCDS offers a framework or 'toolkit' which can be tailored to reveal the ideological discourses articulated in digital popular culture, depending on which aspects of a text best reveals the ideological work at play. So, in one analysis we may concentrate on the representation of social actors, while in another, the representation of actions or the role of metaphors.

Much of digital popular culture's power lies in its multimodality – that is, how modes work independently and together to articulate specific meanings. The role of MCDS is to examine how this happens. In each of the analysis chapters, we examine in detail a particular set of tools and then apply them to an analysis. That is, we metaphorically dip into a CDA/MCDS toolbox and use the tools that best reveal discourses. Saying that, what follows is a general description of the 'tools' we use in this book under the headings of the three broad modes we analyse: lexica, visuals and musical sounds. More detailed descriptions of each set of tools is outlined in depth at the beginning of each chapter. Here, we examine some guiding principles common throughout the book, to answer how to do MCDS for digital popular culture.

Lexical choices

One useful starting point is to consider how people are represented in lexical choices (written, spoken, sung), central to revealing discourses (Wodak et al., 1999; Bishop and Jaworski, 2003). We follow the influential work of Fairclough (2003) and van Leeuwen (1996) to consider how people or 'social actors' are named and their actions represented. Who is included and who is excluded is considered, as are lexical choices used to represent social actors, including pronouns, as individuals or groups, personally or impersonally and the use of titles. These choices are ideological.

At another level, the representations of social actions are examined following van Leeuwen (1995). How social actions are represented 'encode different interpretations of, and different attitudes to, the social actions represented', a significant factor in articulating discourses (van Leeuwen, 1995: 81). There are a number of ways actions are represented. For example, material and transactive activations (somebody doing something to somebody) connote great power (1995: 90). Throughout this book's analysis, these concepts and how they are used to legitimize will be explored.

We examine the role played by metaphors. Some aspects of popular culture tend to rely on metaphor, possibly more so than other communication (Way, 2015). Though aesthetically pleasing, metaphor is also a powerful representative strategy, 'a functional mechanism which affects the way we think, act and experience reality' (Lakoff and Johnson, 1980, in Flowerdew and Leong, 2007: 275).

Representations of place and people in places are also revealing. Referring to musical representations of place, Forman (2002) notes how these are powerful, affecting our understanding of places, reinforcing myths and providing listeners with a sense of identity. In song, analysis of settings are 'highly revealing about the world being communicated' (Machin, 2010: 92), and 'can be used to understand broader social relations and trends, including identity, ethnicity, attachment to place, cultural economies, social activism, and politics' (Johansson and Bell, 2009: 2).

Obviously, each analysis in this book is unique and does not examine every aspect of written text. Instead, we examine representations that reveal dominant discourses in each piece of digital popular culture.

Visuals

Whether photographs, caricatures, animations, camera work, images of celebrities or politicians, visuals are an integral part of digital popular culture. Throughout this book, all these are considered under the heading of visuals. In the visuals, as with the written language, we examine the representation of social actors, social actions, places and people in places.

For the most part, the visual analysis mirrors the written analysis. This is not new, with scholars applying, for example, social actor analysis to visuals (Kress and van Leeuwen, 1996 and 2001; van Leeuwen, 2005; Machin, 2007). Visual analysis in this book follows the work of Kress and van Leeuwen (1996 and 2001) and Machin (2007). These scholars define three broad categories of visual representations of social actors; positioning, kinds of participants and actions. How viewers are positioned in relation to participants inside images through gaze, angle of inter-action and distance is considered. The 'kinds' of participants are also examined considering three criteria: participants may be represented individually or in group shots; participants can be categorized culturally and biologically; and participants may be included or excluded. We examine in detail how actions and agency are visually represented.

We also consider a variety of composition choices such as those that connote relations between elements of images following the work of Kress and van Leeuwen (1996) and Machin (2007). Compositional choices concerning salience are considered, image organization, including the positioning of elements and framing. Again, these choices reveal discourses articulated in the visuals.

Music, voice and sounds

The roles of sounds, music and voice are paramount to understanding the dis-courses articulated in digital popular culture. Our approach closely follows the work of van Leeuwen (1999) where he identifies six major domains of sound that contribute to music's meaning potential. This seminal work has the distinct advan-tage of offering the framework for an in-depth and systematic analysis of sounds. Though many approaches refer to musical sounds and visuals, van Leeuwen's approach offers unparallelled detail and systematic analysis. This approach also emphasizes the crucial role of context in defining the meaning potential of sounds.

PUTTING IT ALL TOGETHER

Digital popular culture is characterized by its multimodal nature. We have briefly considered how we will analyse each mode and the importance of considering political, social, consumption and historical contexts in order to ascertain the meaning potentials of digital popular culture. Modes in each instance take on unique roles. Sometimes, all modes articulate the same discourses. Sometimes, modes articulate similar, but not identical, discourses. Many times, sounds need the more focused meaning potentials of visuals and spoken/sung/written lexical choices to be understood in their context. In all cases, it is the multimodal package of meaning which needs to be considered in order to define meanings.

Though a multimodal package, a systematic, detailed analysis of each mode is essential to reveal how discourses are being articulated. So, how do we marry up a systematic analysis of individual modes with the idea of digital popular cul-ture being multimodal with meanings dependent on context? Our answer is: it depends. In all circumstances, we examine political, social, consumption and/or historical contexts. Without these, meaning potentials are too broad. At times, our analysis is divided into headings of the discourses articulated in the communicative act being analysed. This is particularly useful when all modes articulate the same or very similar discourses.

As such, a sense of how each mode works with the other modes to articulate discourses is prioritized. At other times, we examine each mode one at a time and examine how each mode articulates a specific set of discourses. This approach of prioritizing modes is useful when each articulates different discourses. To ensure a sense of how digital popular culture works multimodally, we refer to the other modes when indeed they work with the mode being examined.

SUMMARY

We have covered a lot of ground in this chapter, though all aspects of the chapter lead to arguing why MCDS is our chosen approach to analyse digital popular culture. We examined a number of definitions of ideology and discourse and we considered relations between the two concepts. In short, ideology is a way of seeing the world and discourse is smaller in scope, such as being a way of representing an issue, topic, event, group of people. These two concepts are essential in understanding how texts articulate power.

One way to examine discourses articulated in texts is CDA. We argued that this is our preferred approach due to the importance of language (and discourse) in studying culture, CDA's emphasis on considering texts in context and its critical approach. We then described what CDA is, before arguing that, because communication is multimodal, analysis should also be multimodal, thus MCDS. We also believe that MCDS should be informed by other disciplines. Though lexical and visual analysis is well informed, musical analysis is not. Here, we use a musicology-informed MCDS, taking on board what musicology has told us about music and politics. After this theoretical groundwork, we then considered why we study popular culture at all and why we use MCDS to do this – two important questions. We also reflected on what the nuances and unique properties of digital popular culture are – things to consider when approaching it for analysis. Unique properties require a unique approach and we looked at how other discourse scholars do this.

All this theoretical terrain has led us to our approach to the analysis of digital popular culture. This is what we examine briefly at the end of the chapter. It is here where we get some details of how we will use an MCDS toolkit to examine the politics in a wide range of digital popular culture examined throughout the rest of the book.

SUGGESTED READING

Kress, G. and van Leeuwen, T. (2001) *Multimodal Discourse: The Modes and Media of Contemporary Communication*. London: Hodder Education.

This seminal publication is essential reading for those of us who want to understand the nature of communication from a multimodal perspective. It is the cornerstone of modern multimodal analysis, offering insights into how to analyse texts multimodally.

Machin, D. (2007) *Introduction to Multimodal Analysis*. London: Hodder Education.

This book extends and elaborates on Kress and van Leeuwen's (2001) *Multimodal Discourse*. Its most useful attribute is it is very easy to understand due to its accessible language and logical organization. Like the aforementioned publication, it concentrates mostly on images and lexica.

Tagg, P. (2012) *Music's Meanings: A Modern Musicology for Non-Musos*. New York: Mass Media Music Scholars' Press.

This is an excellent introduction to the semiotics of sound. It is written for those without a musicology background, making it accessible to anyone with an interest in music and meaning.

van Leeuwen, T. (2005) *Introducing Social Semiotics*. London: Routledge.

Just as the name suggests, this is a great introduction to understanding social semiotics. The author illustrates concepts with a very wide range of examples.

Way, L. and McKerrell, S. (eds) (2017) *Music as Multimodal Discourse: Music, Power and Protest*. London and New York: Bloomsbury.

This edited collection is a good way to see how different scholars use MCDS to consider musical artefacts and politics. Each chapter and author uses a slightly different approach to examine musical artefacts including songs, television programmes, music videos, folk recordings and far-right uploads on social media from all over the world.

4

ANALYSING ONLINE COMMENTS

Nationalism in Lexical Representations of Social Actors

CHAPTER OBJECTIVES

- Consider the importance of digital written comments.
- Examine how to analyse the lexical representation of social actors.
- Demonstrate the usefulness of this approach through an in-depth case study.

KEY CONCEPTS

- Social actors are participants other than objects (van Leeuwen, 1996; Fairclough, 2003). So, a rock is not a social actor, but 'Mr Smith', 'the prime minister', 'Rex the dog' and 'the English' are all social actors.
- Written comments by users on the internet are usually in response to something (like a video, meme, mash-up) they have viewed, heard or/and read. In most social media these materially follow on from the original post.
- Nationalism is expressed in language distinguishing 'us', who we consider to be part of our nation, from 'them' outside the nation.

(Continued)

- Gezi Park is one of the last public green spaces left in Central Istanbul, Turkey. It was the scene of a large national protest against the Turkish government in June 2013.
- Recep Tayyip Erdoğan was Prime Minister of Turkey at the time of the Gezi Park protests. He has since become President of Turkey.

INTRODUCTION

Like most people, I share memes, music videos, mash-ups and the like that I find entertaining and/or ones that share my views on any given issue. I do this for a number of reasons, one being I like to see people's responses. Though clicking a 'like' or 'angry' emoji is in itself interesting, what I really like is when someone in my contacts writes a comment. I also enjoy writing comments in response to what I see on my digital feeds. These responses give me a chance to express my opinion on something I agree with or something that gets me riled up. Comments become even more interesting when a debate of some sort or another erupts among myself and my contacts.

Whether we comment on a post in our feeds, write comments of admiration for a music video that has just been dropped or make a joke about a picture or meme of a politician, pretty much all of us contribute in one way or another to conversations in and about digital popular culture. These acts, no matter how mundane we may feel, are political and connect us to others. Lange (2007 and 2018) notes how comments about YouTube videos connect viewers, creating a very tenuous community. The level of involvement for those in these virtual communities varies considerably, with members joining and leaving at will.

In this chapter, we examine how we can best analyse the politics articulated in comments we write and share about digital popular culture. We first consider what some scholars say about our written contributions online. We then consider Fairclough (2003) and van Leeuwen's (1996) analysis of the written representation of social actors. We find that this approach to analysis is an important and useful tool for examining comments. Finally, we examine a case study of comments about a music video released after the 2013 Gezi Park protests in Turkey. Analysing the lexical representation of social actors in this case study demonstrates this approach's usefulness in revealing differing nationalist discourses articulated in comments. But, first, we ask why examine comments?

THE IMPORTANCE OF COMMENTS

Scholars have been critical of the content of online forums for comments. These virtual spaces, where online users have the opportunities to write and share their ideas, tend to be characterized by hard language and insults (Coffey and Woolworth, 2004). People are more oriented towards falling back on what they know and what they are comfortable with, than attending to new and fresh points of view (Dean, 2010b). YouTube comments tend to be framed in terms of pre-existing personal and social interests or prejudices rather than on analysis of issues represented in digital popular culture (Lindgren, 2010). Chen and Flowerdew (2019: 555) find that YouTube comments categorize posters in terms of 'us' and 'them'. Discriminatory discursive strategies represent 'them' negatively, foregrounding negative traits, comparing 'them' to a 'notorious' other, categorizing 'them' as 'inhuman' or 'inferior', and employing negative stereotypes.

Though these studies are revealing, we should be aware that not all research concludes that comments are bad. Comments can create virtual spaces where politics, however crudely and self-servingly they are expressed, can be articulated and discussed (Way, 2018a). Lange (2018: 2) notes how we can informally learn from YouTube videos and 'through interactions with others' in comments. Though many comments are insulting and combative (Burgess and Green, 2009; Way, 2018a), scholars have found that comments about 'rant' videos have 'the potential to create civic engagement and foster participatory democracy ... construct[ing] an emotional public sphere' (Lange, 2014, in Bou-Franch and Garcés-Conejos Blitvich, 2014). In fact, in some circumstances, 'civic engagement begins to emerge ... [when posters] engage in emotional public discourse [which] illustrates how ranting may lay the groundwork for social change via new media' (Lange, 2014: 63). Some scholars believe YouTube is a 'participatory genre' or a community of practice, where users become 'part of shared cultural systems' which engage with media through 'collective social action' (Ito et al., 2010: 14). It has recognizable and repeating sets of activities that include posting videos and texting comments (Ito, 2009).

It is with these limitations and potentials in mind that we examine how comments articulate discourses. Before we delve into the matter, we need to arm ourselves with a set of tools that is appropriate for the task. A very useful set of tools is the analysis of the lexical representation of social actors. So, it is to this we now turn, describing in detail how to analyse these.

ANALYTICAL TOOLS: THE LEXICAL REPRESENTATION OF SOCIAL ACTORS

A range of scholars have shown how analysing social actors is central to revealing discourses (Wodak et al., 1999; Bishop and Jaworski, 2003; Wodak and Weiss, 2005). By social actors, we mean participants other than objects in representations (Fairclough, 2003). It is through the analysis of social actors that we can see who is part of an 'in-group' and who is not and how this is done, a concept that 'is salient in all societies and between societies' (Wodak and Weiss, 2005: 131).

There are a number of ways that the representation of social actors can be classified and categorized. What follows here is an approach gleened from Fairclough's (2003) and van Leeuwen's (1996) highly influential approaches to analysing social actors. This approach has been used to reveal an array of political discourses about nationalism, political party alignment, racism and neoliberalism, to mention a few. Here we consider who is included and excluded in a representation, namings and grammatical strategies. As is always the case using CDA, it is about picking the right tools for the job. Though what follows is a comprehensive description of tools, not every tool is used in every analysis. We pick the ones that best fit the job(s).

Inclusions and exclusions

Who and what is included or excluded in a text may be politically or socially significant in that these may suit text producers' interests and purposes (Fairclough, 2003: 149; van Leeuwen, 1996: 38). Exclusions come in the form of either 'suppressions' or being 'backgrounded'. A participant is suppressed if they are not mentioned in a text. For example, an incident that involves the police killing a person may be represented as 'Police kill man', a representation that includes both participants, or as 'Man killed in incident'. Though both are truthful, the second supppresses 'the police', excluding a negative representation of them. A backgrounded participant is not mentioned, but inferred, in relation to an activity by being mentioned elsewhere in a text. For example, a text may contain the two utterances of 'John hit the ball' and later 'the ball that was hit'. In the second utterance, John is backgrounded, though inferred.

Namings

Obviously how you name someone draws upon discourses about certain people. Imagine the difference in connotation in naming a British politician as 'BoJo' or 'Our Prime Minister Boris Johnson'. Scholars have considered this and come up with a large set of tools to consider when examining the naming of social actors. Many of these concepts overlap, but you should be able to see how each of these concepts is useful when considering different texts and namings within them.

Fairclough (2003) states participants can be represented in three distinct ways. They can be represented with their name, such as 'Boris Johnson' or in terms of class or categorized, such as 'the prime minister' or represented as groups, such as 'politicians'. When participants are classified, they can be represented specifically, such as 'British politicians', or generically, such as 'politicians'. These choices affect readers' perceptions of participants. For example, named as groups, such as 'British', participants can become homogenized, ignoring differences between individuals (Machin and van Leeuwen, 2005: 133). Homogenization can be used as a way to suggest groupings, such as national groups, a common strategy in nation-building. Wodak et al. (1999) found that homogenizing members of a nation ignores intra-national differences, representing the nation as a single social and political entity while excluding differences that may threaten a single national ideology.

Van Leeuwen (1996) identifies a good number of naming strategies producers use in representing social actors and, equally important, the repercussions of these choices in terms of articulating discourses. Though these overlap with those of other scholars and with each other, let's take a closer look at these.

An overarching strategy we may want to consider is whether participants are represented impersonally or personally. In news about the UK government, a lot of times we hear the naming 'Number 10' (short for 10 Downing Street, the Prime Minister's residence, similar to the US's 'White House'), while at other times 'the government' and other times 'Boris Johnson'. Impersonal namings, such as the first two, 'can dehumanize social actors, take the focus away from them as people'. It is hard to conjure up a face with all its associated connotations with such namings. This is a common strategy used to represent 'the enemy' or an out group (Way, 2013). In contrast, personal representations, like many of the namings identified below, emphasize a participant's human qualities (Fairclough, 2003: 149). But, as we outline below, there are different qualities and degrees of human qualities connoted, dependent on personal naming choices.

Participants can be represented generically or specifically as individuals. As individuals, such as 'Mr Johnson' or 'Mr Trump', a 'point of identification' for readers is presupposed. That is, as readers, we are able to form a fairly accurate image of them with all the baggage that goes along with this. Choices on who to represent generically or not can be political. Van Leeuwen (1996: 48) found that the government and 'we' are more likely represented individually while 'others', in terms of class or race, are most likely generically represented. By representing participants generically, they are 'symbolically remove[d] from the readers' world of immediate experience, treated as distant "others" rather than as people "we" have to deal with in our everyday lives' (1996: 48).

There are three other ways we may consider how participants are represented. Participants can be 'nominated' or named as individuals, such as 'Mr Trump'. This is different to categorizing someone in 'functional roles' such as 'the president'. Participants can also be categorized by more or less permanent and unavoidable 'identities' they share with others, such as 'the American man'. Obviously, a nomination offers readers a point of identification unlike when someone is categorized and these decisions can be political. Let's take a closer look at these three strategies.

There are a number of ways we can name someone, such as 'BoJo' or 'Prime Minister Boris Johnson'. For van Leeuwen (1996: 53–54), titulation connotes the degree of formality attributed to participants which is related to representations of power and status. Names can be formal (surname with or without honorific). Honorifics include prefixes such as 'Mr' or 'President'. Names can be semi-formal (first name and surname such as 'Donald Trump') or informal (first name such as 'Donald'). We can add to these categories nicknames, such as 'The Donald'. Formal namings with honorifics contribute more to representations of power and status than informal namings and even more than nicknames.

Participants categorized in 'functional roles', such as 'the president', are represented by what they do rather than who they are. In his study of a conservative newspaper, van Leeuwen (1996: 59) found that 'high-status social actors … such as "government" and "experts", are always functionalized'. Though these types of representations are less personal, they suggest power and authority.

Where participants are represented through 'identification', such as 'the American man', they may be identified socially, such as by age or nationality, gender or race. Such identification can be classified as relational ('friend' or 'aunt'), cultural ('Irish') or biological/physical ('red head'). All of these name choices carry with them connotations, depending on context, though biological identifications tend to be negative (van Leeuwen, 1996: 58).

A large number of scholars from a range of disciplines have examined how representing participants with pronouns can be socially and/or politically important. Fairclough (2003: 149) notes how pronouns such as 'we' and 'they' can promote 'us' and 'them' divisions. These represent and construct groups and communities. But the groups and communities constructed are vague, referring to party, nation, government, residents or other combinations. Van Dijk (1991) has shown how mainstream media use pronouns to represent in-groups such as the police positively and out-groups such as ethnic minorities negatively. Other scholars demonstrate how pronouns are used by politicians to serve their own ends (Billig, 1995: 106; Fairclough, 1989: 148). Elsewhere, Fairclough considers how politicians articulate discourses of power in two ways using the pronoun 'we'. He notes, 'On the one hand, they claim solidarity by placing everyone in the same boat, but on the other hand they claim authority in that the leader is claiming the right to speak for the people as a whole' (1995a: 181). When analysing texts, it is important to consider how groups are constructed using pronouns and what the implications of these constructs are.

Grammatical strategies

The grammatic role participants are given when represented lexically is a significant factor in articulating discourses. Grammatical '[r]epresentations can reallocate roles, rearrange the social relations between the participants' (van Leeuwen, 1996: 43). Participants can be represented grammatically either as participants in a clause or within a circumstance. We now examine each of these and their significance in articulating discourses.

Participant in a clause

There are two broad roles participants play within a clause: they can be represented doing something or having something done to them. When doing something, we say participants are activated, represented as 'the active, dynamic forces in an activity' (van Leeuwen, 1996: 43–44). For example, in 'John hit the burglar' John is activated. What is accentuated in such a representation is a participant's capacity for 'action, for making things happen, for controlling others and so forth' (Fairclough, 2003: 150). Being activated is an important and generally positive quality that connotes power.

Alternatively, when something is done to a participant, we say they are passivated, such as 'the burglar' in the example above. In such representations 'what is accentuated is their subjection to processes, them being affected by the actions of others' (Fairclough, 2003: 15). This is generally a negative aspect of representations, connoting weakness by the suggestion of being subjected to others' actions.

However, both activations and passivations can have connotations quite different from what I have just discussed above. How do you feel about the actors in the sentence 'The man hit the puppy'? Yes, indeed, the man is activated and represented with power. However, his represented action is negative. Likewise, the puppy is passivated, connoting weakness. However, here being passivated connotes sympathy. In studies of protest music, the police and government are represented active, doing negative things, while protesters are represented passivated as their victims. This is used as a way to sympathize with the protesters and their causes (Way, 2018a). Our point is, although we should consider activations and passivations, we need to think more broadly about the actions in context to determine what exactly is being connoted in representations within a clause.

Process types

A person saving a dog or a person thinking about a dog are two very different actions, each with different degrees of courage and power. The same can be said for representations of actions. In English, there are five types of actions or 'process types' participants perform. These can be classified as action, event, state, mental and verbal processes (Halliday, 1994). Fairclough (1995a: 110) describes these as:

An action sees 'the actor does something to patient' (for example, 'Police kill fifteen').

An event involves just one participant (for example, 'Fifteen die').

A state describes a state of affairs as 'being' or having (for example, 'Fifteen are dead').

There are three types of mental processes: cognition (e.g. 'Johnson realizes it's time to go'), perception (e.g. 'Johnson sees the writing on the wall') and affect (e.g. 'Johnson wants to go').

Verbal processes involve an actor and what was said (Johnson said, 'I don't lie').

The types of actions ascribed to participants are important. The first type, known as an action process, foregrounds agency, so 'A does something to B'. These contribute to representations of power, more so than other representations of actions (Fairclough 1995a: 113). Producers of texts make decisions, consciously or not, which contribute to discourses of power. For example, a producer may decide to transform an active process into a 'state of affairs' thereby removing agency and the representation of control and power (Richardson, 2007: 56). Likewise, an action can be represented as a noun, eliminating all traces of agency. The decision to transform a process, such as 'I opened the door' into a nominal (or noun) such as 'the opening of the door', omits agency, making the representation 'very abstract and distant from concrete events and situations' (Fairclough, 1995b: 112). And, again, it is our job to identify these and consider their implications.

Within a circumstance

Participants can also appear within a circumstance, usually represented in prepositional phrases and subordinate clauses. The sentence 'John hit the burglar' can also be accurately represented as 'The burglar was hit by John'. Here, John is now represented within a circumstance in a prepositional phrase. These strategies de-emphasize social actors by backgrounding them (Fairclough, 1995a). How does this work?

Prepositional phrases are used to provide context to dominant clauses. They give 'details on the time, place or the manner of action', while action is represented in dominant clauses (Richardson, 2007: 207). When a participant is represented in a prepositional phrase, de-emphasis occurs. Richardson (2007) uses this headline from the *Guardian* on 2 April 2003 to illustrate this point: 'Children killed in US assault'.

Here, 'Children killed' is the emphasis of the sentence while 'in US assault' is de-emphasized in a prepositional phrase. According to Richardson (2007: 208) 'more forcefully, the sub-editor could have written "US kill children in assault"'. In this second hypothetical utterance 'US' becomes dominant, its action to 'kill' foregrounded and 'children' passivated. 'In assault' is de-emphasized, supplying circumstances to the emphasized dominant phrase.

In a similar argument, van Dijk (1991) claims participants' actions can be 'played down' when represented later in a sentence and/or embedded in a clause. He notes that 'Events may be strategically played down by the syntactic structure of the sentences, for example, by referring to the event in a "lower" (later, less prominent) embedded clause, or conversely by putting it in first position when the event needs extra prominence' (1991: 216).

So, sentence position and 'lower' embedded clauses, such as prepositional phrases, effect salience. Passive sentence construction is one way prepositional phrases can de-emphasize actions. This can be political. Van Dijk (1991: 215–216) finds that 'negative acts of in-group members, such as the authorities or the police, may be reduced in effect by placing them later in the sentence or by keeping the agency implicit, for instance in passive sentences'. So, an incident involving a man named Jeremy and a ball can be represented in a number of ways, each with various connotations of power. The incident may be represented as 'Jeremy kicked the ball', which represents Jeremy as active and powerful. A passive construction may be 'There was a kicked ball', where there are no social actors represented. Alternatively, it may be represented as 'The ball was kicked by Jeremy'. 'By Jeremy' is now in a prepositional phrase at the end of the sentence. This is a less dominant sentence position. Furthermore, the process type becomes a state process, removing the representation of control and power.

CASE STUDY ANALYSIS: YOUTUBE COMMENTS ABOUT A PROTEST MUSIC VIDEO BY THE RINGO JETS

As is the case in all of the analysis chapters in this book, the tools outlined are here as a reference, as a set of tools we may want to use to analyse texts – in this case,

(Continued)

written representations of participants in comments. As is also the case hereafter in the case studies we examine, not all concepts outlined are used. Instead we use the ones that best reveal the discourses articulated in the texts. Likewise, we may borrow other tools from our analytical toolbox if these aid in demonstrating how discourses are articulated. In all cases, the idea is to use whatever tools best fit the job of revealing discourses in texts. Before we analyse our texts, we need to consider the context. And that is where we turn now.

Context: Nationalism

As is the case in all CDA, we need to examine context to help us make sense of meanings in texts. Context can be theoretical, social, historical, political, or inter-textual, among a list of many. In the case of our comments analysis, we need to examine the theoretical context (nationalism), the political and social context (Gezi Park protests in Turkey), the digital response (social and media contextualization) and the video (The Ringo Jets' 'Spring of War'). As our textual analysis reveals, these comments are not just about Gezi Park protests or the music video. They are also about different definitions of Turkish nationalism. What do scholars tell us about the nation and nationalism? Nations are 'an imagined political community' (Anderson, 1991: 5–6). They are mental constructs, a type of group identity. Scholars have demonstrated how national group identities are achieved in a number of ways and this is worth exploring (see, for example, Hobsbawm, 1990; Billig, 1995; Wodak et al., 1999).

For our purposes here, what is crucial is the role culture plays in nation-building. Language in media, politics and culture define 'us' and 'them' groups which create national in-groups and out-groups (Billig, 1995; Wodak et al., 1999). Wodak et al. (1999: 2) note that 'identity politics is always and necessarily a politics of the cre-ation of difference'. Media play a role in linguistically constructing a world of nations where each nation is unique in time and space. This is articulated in media by making distinctions between 'us' who are 'in' one's nation and 'them' who are 'out-side' one's nation (Billig, 1995: 61). As Billig (1995: 78) notes, 'There can be no "us" without a "them".' Though the focus of these studies has been on the news media, some studies highlight how there are different forms of nationalism articulated within a nation and in cultural texts other than news (Trevor-Roper, 1993; Bishop and Jaworski, 2003; Way, 2011 and 2010; Chen and Flowerdew, 2019). This is the focus of our study here.

Context: Gezi Park protests, digital protests and The Ringo Jets' 'Spring of War'

On 28 May 2013, a protest by a few city planners and environmentalists began in Istanbul's Gezi Park. They were angry about the government's plan to transform one of the last public green spaces in central Istanbul into yet another shopping mall and mosque. The demonstration quickly grew to 3.5 million people demonstrating against the government in 80 Turkish cities. Gezi Park became symbolic for many people who were critical of the governing Justice and Development Party (AKP) and particularly Prime Minister Recep Tayyip Erdoğan (soon to become president). Issues protesters identified were perceived infringements on democracy, freedom, repressive police tactics and a range of intolerant government policies (Işik, 2013: 25–27). The authorities responded by deploying the police who used live ammunition, tear gas, water cannons, plastic bullets and beatings which resulted in over 3000 arrests, 8000 injuries and six deaths (Amnesty International, 2013).

Part of the protesting involved digital popular culture. I was in Turkey during this time and many of my acquaintances were directly involved in protests, both physically and digitally. Between us, we collected over 140 music videos and mash-ups associated with the protests from June 2013, when protest participation peaked. That is a lot of musical protest! These offerings produced an enormous number of comments from posters, some of which we examine below. But before we do this, we ought to first briefly discuss the video.

The comments are in response to 'Spring of War' by The Ringo Jets. The band hails from Istanbul, though it recorded the song in Italy before the protests, but made and distributed the video during the protests as a way of 'paying tribute to protesters' (personal correspondence). The video has received almost 198,000 views (at the time of writing). It is a blues-grunge hybrid with three repeated lines of lyrics. The visuals see the band acting as reporters who are reporting on the Gezi Park protests.

For a detailed analysis of the video, see Way (2015). Here, we jump to the findings. The lyrics describe 'us' the people (band, fans and protesters) who have tolerated and are the victims of an unnamed 'they'. The group identified as 'they' are ruthless, although what 'they' have done is not specified and is represented only through abstractions. All the while, we are told this is the spring of a war. Titles on the screen using the genre of news help identify who 'they' are. 'Minister' and 'Prime Minister' attribute acknowledged guilt by the elite. Visually, police are represented as part of a brutal elite, while politicians are non-listening. Protesters crowd the streets, often moving together and fighting back. There is no sense of difference at any level in this representation of protesters, in this 'us'. Members of the band communicate with us personally and sincerely. The music adds ideas of sadness and graveness. Overall there is a sense of a brutal regime and people who will tolerate it no longer. It is a situation that must be changed. But no specifics are given in any of the modes. This is a clear case of the populist notions of the people being pitted against authorities. By populism, we mean a discourse that pits 'the people' against 'the elite'. The people are correct and knowing while the elite are despotic (more of this in Chapter 5).

(Continued)

73

The video does not address the original concerns of the protest (the environment and the government's privatization programme). There is no real articulation of the politics behind the movement. Though protesters want to be heard, what they are saying is absent. The video does not articulate the shortcomings of the government's neoliberal economic policies and their repercussions, such as public green spaces being sold off to private corporations for huge profits. There is no reference to the many government policies that have seen a rise in social and religious conservatism, a common complaint among those protesting. Though the video adds little to political discussions surrounding the issues the Gezi Park social movement raised, mainstream media ignored or backgrounded Gezi, so this video (and others) became a space where political issues became popularized and may have contributed in a limited capacity to public dialogue or even the scale of the protests.

Textual analysis

The video had received around 200 comments in Turkish at the time of writing. Though best avoided, translations are commonly used in CDA (van Leeuwen and Wodak, 1999; Wodak, 2001). To overcome any bias, comments were translated by three individual translators. Any discrepancies between translations were discussed and if we could not agree on a phrase or sentence, it was not used in the analysis.

In a previous publication, I found that comments that accompany music videos can be divided into four loose categories (Way, 2018a). We find that some support bands and their videos saying simply 'well done', or repeat words or lines from the song. In some cases, this makes up the vast majority of comments. Another category repeats slogans and key phrases associated with the song/ group's political outlook such as 'freedom' and 'the spirit of Gezi'. The third category sees posters simply abusing and insulting each other, a form of dialogue with interactions between posters. The last category includes more fully developed comments about the politics represented in the music videos. An analysis of these allows us to access the kinds of discourses that are used by viewers. Posters who write these fall into two groups: those who are against the perceived politics articulated in the video and those who support them. In the analysis that follows, we examine comments to reveal discourses articulated by posters both for and against the perceived politics of the video. We also focus on sequences of comments that take the form of a more developed interchange, to look at the way that these discourses interact.

In the analysis that follows we first analyse comments by posters who agree with The Ringo Jets' anti-government views and then comments that support the government (and not The Ringo Jets). We then analyse a sequence that takes the form of a more developed interchange, to look at the way these discourses interact.

Anti-government comments

What we find in these anti-government comments is not unlike the discourses found in the video itself. In the first place, we have a sense of the knowing people. For example, one comment reads:

I open my eyes, I don't jump into the games which are played on us. I read. I don't follow something blindly. I wish our people would lose the blinders and see what is going on.

Here pronouns are at work, constructing a positive representation of anti-government supporters. 'I' is in an emphasized position, at the beginning of each sentence activated, performing positive actions such as 'open my eyes', 'don't jump', 'read', 'don't follow' and 'wish'. None of these actions act upon someone else, limiting the representation of power. But this is not about power. This is about not being a victim of a game. The poster represents him/herself as clever through the metaphors of having open eyes and not jumping into games. The poster is intelligent, inferred because s/he reads and thinks instead of follows, s/he knows what is 'going on'. What is known is not stated but expressed metaphorically through the removal of 'blinders'. And what is already known once eyes are opened is not expressed in concrete terms but as a game being played on the people.

The pronouns 'us' and 'our' connote there is someone/something that is powerful. Though excluded, a strategy used to de-emphasize, we can assume it is the government represented negatively playing games on 'us'. Though represented negatively, there is no agent acting against the people, just a game pointing to something deliberate and malicious. To add to the discourse of negativity surrounding the elite and positivity about the people, grammatical strategies are used. Here, 'us' and 'our people' are namings for people living in Turkey. 'Us' appears at the end of a sentence in a prepositional phrase, de-emphasized and disempowered connoting victimhood and sympathy. Likewise, 'our people' are represented as the subject of the poster's 'hope' to see the truth as s/he does. Both these representations contribute to representing the elite as despotic and Turkish people as victims and protesters in the know.

Though anti-government posters represent themselves as intelligent, correct and knowledgeable, many comments also represent government supporters as being non-thinking. But this can also sometimes suggest that they may indeed be part of 'the people' and are victims. For example, a comment reads:

What happens if you win elections, you keep sinking. Win the election, it is nothing. What does it mean if crowded, useless herds win? It is good to see you struggle. Now fuck off.

(Continued)

Throughout these comments there is a lack of specificity as regard to who may characterize the different sides of the matter. This can be seen in the shifting sense of people and of 'us' and 'them' as discussed above and by Fairclough (2003). Above, government supporters are blinded and at other times part of 'crowded, useless herds'. In the comment above, 'you' are government supporters, distinct from 'I', 'we' and 'us' seen in the first comment. 'You' is represented three times, once in a secondary clause in a conditional phrase ('if you win') and twice negatively 'sinking' and struggling. Furthermore, government supporters are named negatively as unthinking metaphorically in 'crowded, useless herd'. We see yet another shift in defining government supporters as part of the self-interested elite in the following comment:

> You are the one negotiating with PKK, it is your prime minister who is dancing because he made Kurdistan, you have the shoeboxes, you are the thieves, you are the ones who slander people ... you are the ones who are continuing to cut trees which was illegal from the beginning although the court gave a stop order ... So are we – the ones that are objecting to these – the traitors? Fuck off you are the traitors.

This comment is in response to a pro-AKP comment. 'You' here refers to the AKP government and its supporters, a different grouping of the 'elite' than we have seen in previous comments. Here, 'you' are represented as powerful, active in a range of verb processes including 'negotiating', 'have shoeboxes', 'are thieves', 'slander people', 'continuing to cut trees' and 'are the traitors'. Some of these activations have agency, connoting power. But all of these vaguely point to corruption and controversial events involving AKP reported in the press. For example, 'you have the shoeboxes' references a corruption case involving millions of dollars found at the home of the manager of the *Halkbank*, run by the government. But in no comments are issues such as Kurdistan discussed, nor the processes of privatization of which Gezi was a part, nor the huge numbers of unemployed youth, as is characteristic of many contemporary societies across Europe. Important in this comment also is the sense of the 'we' who stand apart from 'you', active in 'objecting to these' injustices. Here, groupings have changed, though in each of these comments we see how there is a sense of an elite who are against the interests of the people, though how these are grouped shifts depending on who makes the comments and a shifting use of pronouns.

An important part of these anti-government comments is that nationalistic discourses are used to frame events. In the comment above, the government's negotiations with Kurdish leaders are represented as 'dancing because he made Kurdistan'. In nationalist circles, betraying the idea of a single Turkish entity by making

Kurdistan is part of a discourse that points to the Prime Minister being a traitor to the nation. This in itself is a complex issue, sometimes interwoven with more far-right and xenophobic views. But here it becomes thrown together as part of a list serving to de-legitimize. The idea of the 'traitor' is also recurrent as a naming strategy. Clearly, politicians serve their own ideologies, yet using the name traitor is part of a nationalist discourse, an act of claiming to represent the interests of a coherent and monolithic national citizenship and people, rather than constructing these as ideological differences that cut across society, ones that we need to discuss and understand. Consider how nationalist discourses can also be found in comments that show their support for Mustafa Kemal Atatürk:

> But your prime minister himself can't say I am Turk. He can't even call Atatürk 'Atatürk'.

In this case, patriotism and national identity are called into question. The pronoun 'your' in the last two comments clearly distinguishes between those who support Erdoğan and those who do not. We see this same strategy used by Americans who do not support Trump repeating phrases such as 'not my president' and 'your president'. In the above comment, Erdoğan is also represented in metaphorical verbal activations of 'can't say' and 'can't even call', connoting a lack of patriotism, of being a traitor. These attributed verbal activations are a way to recontextualize Erdoğan and AKP, prioritizing Islam as an identity marker over being a secular Turk. In this sense, the argument shifts away from the neoliberal drive to privatization that Gezi first symbolized to issues related to Atatürk, the founder of the modern secular Turkish Republic. Until very recently, it was unthinkable for any public figure to do anything but praise Atatürk. Comments do not make it clear whether or how such identity formulations align with those who are blinded or not. Elsewhere, posters make clear links between the elite and religion. Consider this comment:

> YouTube shows what the religious gang in the government does to its people, the shoeboxes, the way it benefits some individuals and itself.

It was, of course, not clear that such a religious/secular divide characterized those who protested and those who did not. Conservative Islamic groups such as the Radical Muslims and individual women who wore clothes associated with Islam were among protesters in Gezi. In this manoeuvre, religion is connected to the elite, a 'gang' who are self-interested and pitted against the knowing people. Choosing to name the government as a gang points not to a democratic body, but to a group who use violence and bullying to achieve their aims. Furthermore, the gang is

(Continued)

represented as active doing unnamed things 'to its people', while benefiting 'some individuals and itself'. Though no specifics are identified in terms of actions and circumstances, these actions all point to a religiously biased elite taking advantage of its position of power at the expense of 'the people'. This discourse about the prime minister's rule is common in popular expressions. This is important in the current Turkish political landscape where opposition political parties are based firmly in secular Kemalism and where the years of AKP have seen a shift to increasing state control of things like alcohol consumption and women's dress. But these things are not discussed or raised specifically.

In sum, these comments represent the government as an unpatriotic, bullying and self-serving religious gang who act against the interests of a common people. This elite is challenged on the grounds of national identity. There is a sense of people being blinded which prevents a more dramatic kind of event. Overall a range of complex issues are hinted at but never fully articulated. Given that Gezi began as a protest against privatization of public property and what this meant for Turkey, the anti-government comments are about something different. What is clear is that, in the first place, rather than analysing or commenting on the actual events of Gezi Park or on how they are represented in the music video, comments frame events around a set of personal interests defined in terms of the nation.

Pro-government comments

What we find in the pro-government comments are a similar lack of specific details about policies – the same homogenization and reduction. There is a similar kind of attempt to frame events in terms of wider interests using pronouns. Here, posters try to define just who 'the people' are and who the distant, self-serving elite are. As with the anti-government comments, these are not actually about Gezi, nor privatization, nor specific policies and which sections of the population benefit or not and in which ways. They are about legitimacy of national identity. In the following comment, see how 'the people' are no longer protesters and opponents to the government, as we see above, but government supporters and the government:

> You are 'çapulcu' [translation: street person] and … God know you didn't even leave your village you wannabe. Wannabe wannabe again wannabe. Ahh ahh you empty-headed çapulcu.

Çapulcu is the name protesters were given by Erdoğan. It is an insult and a nickname, connoting a lack of respect. But it was a strategic way to represent the millions of students, professionals, multi-religious and secular groups who were protesting for various reasons. They are collectivized as a 'you'. These people are from a village and 'empty-headed', connoting they do not understand things.

In other comments, çapulcu's lack of education is connoted in they 'haven't read a decent book in all their life and didn't improve themselves', comments that collectivize protesters while connoting negativity that is impossible to substantiate. The value of the protests and protesters' actions are further delegitimized by using the term 'wannabe' repeatedly, with a sense that there were people looking for their moment of fame.

As with the anti-government discourse, the idea of a self-serving elite is also important, though here it is represented as governments that preceded AKP. Pro-government comments often use a sense of past versus future. In some instances, the corruption is connected to a wider elite that exists internationally, although the links are never clearly specified. For example, a comment reads:

Did you start to pay taxes after Erdoğan became prime minister? You paid taxes before Erdoğan so where did this tax money go? Why are you always biased? But of course US and Israel was ruling the country before so you didn't raise your voice. We, including our prime minister's voice, were heard like ships ... Most importantly he paid the debt to IMF. Why the previous governments couldn't do that? Because they were busy eating and none of them cared about the country.

The elite here include 'previous governments' who are represented as corrupt and uncaring, metaphorically active 'busy eating' and not caring, connoting a despotic rule. But this elite also includes the USA and Israel 'ruling the country'. This is a popular largely anti-American discourse criticizing both former governments and AKP. Presented in this way it serves to gloss over the complexities of what in some ways has been a mutually beneficial web of relationships, although not without problems. But here it is used to connote that those against the government are unpatriotic, in favour of relations with the USA and Israel, here represented as 'ruling' Turkey.

Pronouns again play a key role in identifying those against the government in negative ways and distinct from those who support the government. While previous governments are referred to as 'they', 'you' are represented as not only supportive of them but not knowing in 'Why are you always biased' and 'you didn't raise your voice' against previous power relations. All the while, 'we' are aligned with the government. Many of the pro-government comments name the prime minister in ways that connote inclusiveness and respect. While in anti-government comments, he is named through abusive terms or as 'your prime minister', here he is named not only formally as Erdoğan and Prime Minister, but 'our prime minister'. The sentence 'We, including our prime minister's voice, were heard' makes

(Continued)

79

clear the Prime Minister is a part of the Turkish people, positively active opposing corruption and collusion with the USA and Israel. What exactly the people are doing is unclear, but a discourse of populism where the people are pitted against the elite is communicated.

Unsurprisingly, the pro-government comments represent AKP positively working for the people, but again never in specific terms. These comments usually are contrasted with negative ones of previous governments. For example, a comment reads:

This country will grow, develop and other countries will shrink. Look at today's Gezi Park, not yesterday's. It is better and good people will always win. As long as AK Party exists my country will be better.

Here, 'this country' is conditionally attributed with future growth and development. Gezi Park is 'better'. Though not directly attributed with these positive attributes, the last line of the comment does just that, by claiming AKP's existence ensures 'my country will be better'. Overall, it is in the co-text of 'my country', 'grow', 'develop', 'better', 'good people' and 'win', connoting more positivity.

The AKP government is also represented as leaders of the people, performing positive actions for the people and the country. Again, no details are given, just abstract positive attributes. These positive attributes are contrasted with other countries which 'will shrink' and yesterday's Gezi Park, yet another vague reference to the times before AKP's governance.

In sum, what we find is government actions and policies related to Gezi are absent. Instead, posters concern themselves with constructing the Turkish people as AKP and its supporters. AKP works for the good of the country while its supporters are clever. The elite pitted against them are former governments, protesters and even the USA and Israel.

What characterizes the discourses of both sides is that the events and the video are not commented upon in detail but rather there is an attempt to frame them by setting them into the interests of a shifting notion of a legitimate Turkish people at the mercy of self-interested elites. To accomplish this, popular history and reduced versions of events without connection are thrown together. The pressing socio-political issues in Turkish society, even issues like police brutality, or unemployment, are not discussed. What becomes clear is that this is populist politics where there is an easy and trustworthy mass public consensus and there are ignorant, self-interested elites.

Exchange of views

In this section, having looked at the political discourses used by pro- and anti-government YouTube posters, we look at the way these interact on the forum.

As stated earlier, many of the comments appear to have little relationship to previous posts, but air an opinion. Arguably, it is this tone of a lack of specific details and challenges to the collective other 'you' that leads to more comments of this type. As Coffey and Woolworth (2004) point out, such forums tend not to be characterized by attempts at deeper understanding of social relations. But on several occasions, there were some clear interactions. Here, we examine one of these involving three posters. These provide an excellent opportunity to understand how these discourses interact through a close examination of the representation of social actors.

The example starts after poster two claims the Prime Minister is great. Here is how the populist discourses held by each unfold when they meet:

Poster one: *Alright, you are used to being hoodwinked. They are stealing but show you that they are not. When you see reality, you will be shocked.*

Poster two: *Actually the ones that came before are the ones that robbed the country. You can't see the service that the government gives, I guess. Investments that are worth billions are made for the country. Go and look at how much money the third bridge which is being built now costs. Talking is not service. They didn't even drive a nail.*

Poster three: *Oh leave them alone, they love waiting in the sugar queues.*

Poster one: *Is there only Istanbul? The whole of Turkey. I don't live in Istanbul and I don't care about a third bridge. What has the government done as a service to this country? They used the earthquake money to make benefits available to their friends. They made 3 metres of road. It was ten times more than what it was worth. That money was my taxes. They didn't even deny all these accusations. There isn't a parallel state, is there any proof? What shall I do with this service if the people are not happy?*

Poster one is anti-government while posters two and three are pro-government. Poster one begins by constructing an elite, named as 'they', and active 'stealing'. Poster two and other government supporters are named 'You' and represented as victims 'being hoodwinked' by government theft and lies. This weak position reinforces the idea of a despotic elite victimizing the people, though specifics are excluded. Poster two replies by explaining that it was the former regime, impersonally named as 'the ones that came before' and 'they', both naming strategies used to dehumanize and distance social actors. 'They' act negatively, robbing the country, doing nothing: 'they didn't even drive a nail' and just 'talking'. Meanwhile, rather general evidence is given for what the present government is offering in 'investments

(Continued)

81

worth billions', 'service' and the building of a bridge, which in itself has come under much criticism from environmentalists and for being a poor use of money. Poster three throws in a snark comment drawing on the discourse of bad times in the past before AKP. Poster one continues to use 'they' to represent the government distinct from others. However, this time 'we' is replaced with the first person pronoun in 'I don't live in Istanbul and I don't care about a third bridge' and asks 'What shall I do with this service?' Though this lays out an argument for why he dislikes AKP, this poster personalizes his complaints and gives very few details of the actual problems with AKP. Poster one's comments also include vague references to AKP's clampdown on opposition after the banking scandal in 'there isn't a parallel state'. AKP's response to the banking scandal was to claim there was a parallel state within Turkey's judiciary, police and politics, headed by Fethullah Gülen, which is out to usurp AKP's power. This poster's flat denial of the parallel state is backed up with no counter claims or proof. This same lack of detail and context is seen in 'They didn't even deny all these accusations.' These serve the purpose of connoting a self-serving arrogant elite.

What is of note in this interaction is the significant role the representation of social actors play in posters articulating political discourses in comments. We find that hints and fragments of actual issues become fuzzy, fused with personalized perspectives of what it is to be a good Turkish national and framed in terms of established alignments and prejudices. What we might argue is that here we get a clearer sense of how many people do in fact manage the knowledge they come across about events and persons in civic society and in politics.

SUMMARY

This chapter started by examining what scholars say about the importance of our written comments in digital popular culture. They find that comments give us a chance to let off some steam by expressing our opinions on issues, events or people who inspire us to do so. Though comments are personal and at times confrontational, it is here we express our views and beliefs and are exposed to those of others. And this is political. Leaning on the seminal work of Fairclough (2003) and van Leeuwen (1996), we then considered how the representation of social actors in written comments is one good approach to analyse political discourses. These are vital tools needed in our analytical toolbox. With these tools, we have closely examined a sample of comments about a music video that was part of the Gezi Park protests in Turkey. Through using some of these tools, we have been able to unearth obvious and far less obvious political discourses. We have been able to see how the comments are not really about Gezi Park or even the music video. Instead, they are about personalized political views that define the nation, categorize people in opposing views as to what it is to be a patriot and who fits into this category and who does not. These tools are useful in a wide range of written or spoken texts – from news stories, to films, dramatic productions, posters, politicians' speeches. It is our job as critical discourse analysts to consider how people are represented and who benefits from such representations.

SUGGESTED READING

Anderson, B. (1991) *Imagined Communities: The reflections on the Origin and Spread of Nationalism*. London: Verso.

This seminal book examines the concept of the nation and nationalism. It is highly influential in scholarly thinking, making it a good place to start any research on the subject.

Chen, M. and Flowerdew, J. (2019) Discriminatory discursive strategies in online comments on YouTube videos on the Hong Kong Umbrella Movement by Mainland and Hong Kong Chinese, *Discourse & Society*, 30(6): 549–72.

This is a very interesting article on discursive strategies used in online comments. This is particularly useful for us as part of the study considers how online comments relate to various ideas of nationalism, as we do in this chapter.

Lange, P. (2018) Informal Learning on YouTube, *The International Encyclopedia of Media Literacy*. https://onlinelibrary.wiley.com/doi/pdf/10.1002/9781118978238.ieml0090

This is an interesting article because it demonstrates how comments on YouTube can be part of a positive, learning experience for users. This more positive assessment of comments is quite different from many other studies that demonstrate negative aspects of comments.

van Leeuwen, T. (1996) The representation of social actors, in Caldas-Coulthard C.R. and Coulthard M. (eds.), *Texts and Practices – Readings in Critical Discourse Analysis*. London: Routledge. pp. 32–70.

This seminal work categorises in great detail the many strategies used to lexically represent social actors. This chapter leans heavily on van Leeuwen's ideas expressed in this article.

5

ANALYSING MEMES

Authoritarianism in Visual Representations of Social Actors

CHAPTER OBJECTIVES

- Identify the importance of memes and their political potential.
- Understand Kress and van Leeuwen's (1996 and 2001) and Machin's (2007) analysis of the visual representations of social actors.
- Apply Kress and van Leeuwen's (1996 and 2001) and Machin's (2007) analysis of the visual representations of social actors to memes of US President Donald Trump.

KEY CONCEPTS

- Internet memes are pervasive and malleable remixes and iterations, viral texts that mutate and replicate. They are closely linked to the logic and rhythms of networks, social media and the ways a society expresses and thinks of itself (Denisova, 2019).
- Memes 'posit an argument, visually, in order to commence, extend, counter, or influence a discourse' (Wiggins, 2019).
- Kress and van Leeuwen (1996 and 2001) and Machin (2007) identify three broad categories of visual representations of social actors: positioning, kinds of participants and actions.

(Continued)

- Other composition choices that create meaning include the internal 'flow' of an image, what is salient and the chosen degree of modality.
- Authoritarianism 'prioritiz[es] collective security for the group at the expense of liberal autonomy for the individual' (Norris and Inglehart, 2019).
- 4Chan is made up of unarchived, subject-based boards with anonymous posting.
- The alt-right is 'a range of extreme far-right movements and positions broadly unified by their rejection of traditional, mainstream Christian conservativism and republicanism in favour of white nationalism and supremacism' (Merrin, 2019).

INTRODUCTION

Still imagery has a long history in how we communicate. As early as 40,000 years ago, people used cave painting in Europe as a means of communication (Clottes, 2019). Thousands of years later, but still before Gutenberg's movable type printing press, printers used woodcut illustrations in books. At this time, each page of a book had to be carved in relief into wood, inked and then stamped on to paper. The first of these illustrated typographic books (Figure 5.1) was published in Germany in 1461 (Boardley, 2015). Now, modern media, such as the printed press, depends on still imagery, where 'news images have always been instrumental in making meaning' (Allbeson and Allan, 2019: 70). Perhaps part of the reason for our love of the still image, and the photograph in particular, is the common belief that photographs are ostensibly ideologically neutral, that is, 'the camera never lies'. Though, indeed, we have become more cynical about media (think – 'Fake news', 'news bias', 'photoshop'), 'the sense of a technical, dispassionate point of view afforded by the camera continues to be central to journalistic authority' (Allbeson and Allan, 2019: 71). Our historical relations with still imagery is nothing compared in volume to the daily deluge of images we now experience, whether in online news, on Instagram or any of our digital popular culture. It is estimated we took over 1.2 trillion photographs in 2017, and we share more than 3 billion images across social media every day (Lavoie, 2018). Still imagery in memes is an essential part of our digital popular culture, and it is to this we turn our attention to in this chapter.

Figure 5.1 One of the first illustrated books *Ars Moriendi*, ca. 1487–1488.

Credit: Bamberg State Library, Bilder-Ars-moriendi. Photo: Gerald Raab. URN: urn:nbn:de:
bvb:22-dtl-0000001378

In this chapter, we consider how to analyse internet memes. Memes come in a variety of forms and deal with innumerable issues and subjects. One subject commonly represented in memes is politicians, especially US President Donald Trump. For this chapter, we examine a sample of such memes. Though our sample is restricted to memes that praise and criticize Trump, the aim is to illustrate how to analyse images in digital popular culture no matter what the content. By doing these analyses, we build our analytical toolkit in order to be able to analyse still imagery. For now, we set the stage for our analysis.

THE IMPORTANCE OF MEMES

Memes are a daily part of our digital lives, whether they be 'political', 'branded' or just a bit of fun. They appear on our social media feeds giving us a laugh, many times at the expense of politicians like Trump, his adversaries and Boris Johnson, as well as political events such as Brexit, all foregrounding a storm of allegations of Russian and alt-right interference in western politics (via 'meme farms').

We can trace the term 'meme' back to the biologist Richard Dawkins (1976) and his seminal book *The Selfish Gene*. Dawkins was not referring to memes on the internet, but memes as a way we pass on 'cultural information and ideas between individuals and generations' (Dawkins, 1976). He likened these to the passing on of genes between generations. Though indeed this Darwinian-inspired concept is novel, it is dismissed by scholars who examine internet memes (Denisova, 2019; Wiggins, 2019). Unlike genes, internet memes (hereafter memes) readily transform and alter due to purposeful human agency. The mutation of memes is desirable and often unavoidable. Besides, memes are more than imitations; they are remixes and iterations, viral texts that mutate and replicate. Denisova (2019: 2) notes 'memes are intrinsically linked to the logic and rhythms of networks and social media, as well as to the ways a society expresses and thinks of itself'. Though some definitions of memes include altered still imagery, GIFs (graphic interchange format, an animated image) and videos, in this chapter, we are concerned with the former. It is these image-based memes that are most pervasive and most malleable and of interest to us here (Wiggins, 2019: vii).

One distinction we need to make is the difference between viral media, emergent memes and memes. Shifman (2011: 190, emphasis original) claims viral media 'spreads to the masses via digital word-of-mouth mechanisms *without significant change*'. Memetic media involves imitation and remix (2011: 190). Some scholars add another category between viral media and memes: the emergent meme. Wiggins (2019) observes that when viral media are altered, remixed and/or parodied, they become 'emergent' memes. Memes are different in that they are 'imitations, remixes, and further iterations of the emergent meme' (Wiggins, 2019: 46).

Here, the path of the distracted boyfriend meme illustrates his point. Figure 5.2 is the original viral media, a photograph taken by Antonio Guillem. This image was first manipulated by a Facebook user adding text to make a comment about Phil Collins and his relations with popular music and progressive rock (see Figure 5.3). This is an emergent meme. Figure 5.4 is one of countless examples of where there is evidence of further manipulation, thus an internet meme.

Figure 5.2 'The Distracted boyfriend' viral image.

Photo credit: Antonio Guillem

Figure 5.3 'The Distracted boyfriend' emergent meme. Creator unknown

Figure 5.4 'The Distracted boyfriend' internet meme.

Credit: Adam Padilla (@adam.the.creator)

Memes are more than just a laugh, according to scholars. After all, 'memes are pop culture artefacts [and as such] they can provide insight into how "everyday" media texts intertwine with public discourses' (Milner, 2012: 9). Scholars have not always ascribed a political role to memes. Throughout the 1990s and 2000s memes went from a 'geek' culture in-joke to a mainstream gimmick (Denisova, 2019). With this popularity, they went 'from entertainment tools to the means of political and social deliberation' (2019: 10). They are a medium that, 'employ[s] popular culture for public commentary' (Milner, 2012: 2357). These political and social roles ascribed to memes are not like politicians' speeches. Instead, memes are 'a remixed, iterated message that can be rapidly diffused by members of participatory digital culture for the purpose of satire, parody, critique, or other discursive activity … Its function is to posit an argument, visually, in order to commence, extend, counter, or influence a discourse' (Wiggins, 2019: 11). It is through MCDS that we can best understand exactly how this is done.

ANALYTICAL TOOLS: THE VISUAL REPRESENTATION OF SOCIAL ACTORS

Memes we examine in this chapter are still images; some include written text. The still images, about Trump or any politician, not surprisingly, will include an image (possibly altered) of the said politicians. This being the case, it makes sense that one fruitful approach to examining memes is to consider the visual representation of social actors. In fact, a lot of previous research has demonstrated how examining the representation of social actors is central to revealing discourses (Billig, 1995; Wodak et al., 1999; Bishop and Jaworski, 2003; Wodak and Weiss, 2005). As is the case in all this book's analysis chapters, we also consider other aspects of representations that articulate discourses. In this case, compositional choices by producers. However, the focus is on the visual representation of social actors.

A number of scholars have considered how to analyse the visual representation of social actors. In this chapter, we build our analytical toolkit by using ideas from the seminal work of Kress and van Leeuwen (1996 and 2001) and Machin (2007). All three of these publications define three broad categories of visual representations of social actors: positioning, kinds of participants and actions. Let us take a closer look at these.

Positioning

How viewers are symbolically positioned in relation to participants in images through gaze, angle of interaction and distance is considered. A social actor may 'gaze' at us in a 'demand' image or not in an 'offer' image. These have repercussions in terms of

Figure 5.5 Demand image.

Photo credit: Houcine Ncib on Unsplash

representations of power and connoted engagement with viewers. In demand images (Figure 5.5), participants directly address viewers, creating symbolic interaction, suggesting power and demanding a response (Kress and van Leeuwen, 1996: 127–128). The demand being placed on viewers is determined by a number of factors. For example, if a social actor looks at us (symbolically) and smiles, this may 'invite[s] us in or allow[s] us to share in the joy of the moment', while a frown may suggest anger and danger or superiority towards us, while body posture may suggest welcome or aggression (Machin, 2007: 111).

Alternatively, participants in 'offer' images do not gaze at viewers, omitting contact and the power to address (Figure 5.6). These images are offered as information available for scrutiny (Kress and van Leeuwen, 1996: 124). In offer images, subjects do not engage symbolically with viewers. There is no symbolic relationship. This is ideological. Studies show how those with less power in society, like trade unionists in TV news, are positioned looking off camera, while politicians and news readers look at the camera (Hartley, 1982). In advertising, people tend to look off camera, treated more as exhibits (Machin, 2007: 112). A question worth asking is: who is granted connotations of power by looking straight at a camera and who is not?

Figure 5.6 Offer image.

Photo credit: Christopher Campbell on Unsplash

An image of a person can suggest power and engagement through other strategies such as both vertical and horizontal angles of interaction. Just as in real life, in images we can look up or look down on someone. These vertical angles of interactions speak volumes in terms of power, strength and status. Consider the vertical angles of interaction in Figures 5.6 and 5.7. I always ask my students in a classroom, why is it that I stand at the front of the class (sometimes on an elevated platform) while they sit. I am over six feet tall, so there really is no need for a platform! Part of the answer is they have to look up to me, connoting power relations within a classroom. If we share eye level with another, equality is suggested. If an image is shot looking up at someone, this not only accentuates height, but has metaphoric associations with strength, higher status, intimidation and/or superiority. Likewise, if a shot is taken from above someone, viewers look down at the person in the photograph. This suggests vulnerability, a lack of power.

Figure 5.7   Vertical angle of interaction.

Photo credit: Carol Magalhães on Unsplash

Horizontal angles also suggest levels of engagement with represented subjects. If we view a subject from the front, in a demand image, there is more engagement with the viewer than in an offer image. This is a continuum. Imagine starting in a demand image and moving the camera to the side of the subject. What happens is we have less engagement with our subject, losing eye contact and facial details. In my classes, I demonstrate this by looking at and talking directly to a student as we normally would. Then I turn away from them and look at other people in the room. When I ask what position feels like I am engaging most with them, the obvious answer is when we look at each other. The same can be said with images. Moving 'around the horizontal plane in this way reduces involvement and creates detachment' (Machin, 2007: 113). This works until an image is produced from the perspective of the viewer (like a first-person computer shooter game), connoting that we are aligned with them, as though we are standing with them, seeing the world from their perspective.

Another aspect of positioning is how symbolically close we are to the participant in the image. When we whisper to a lover, speak with a friend or converse with a stranger on the street, the distance between ourselves and the other changes. Physical proximity as such can also be connoted in still images in the form of shot types. The closer the image subject is framed, the more intimate they become. Close-up shots, such as in Figures 5.5, 5.6 and 5.7 are great at revealing who people are and how they are feeling. We can identify with them more as individuals. Just as in real-life situations, unwanted closeness connotes a threat to ourselves and possibly claustro-phobia. People in long shots, such as in Figure 5.8, become less individualized, lose a point of identification by becoming more generic and impersonal.

Figure 5.8 Long shot.

Photo credit: Yunming Wang on Unsplash

Kinds of participants

When we examine the kinds of participants in imagery, we consider if social actors are represented as individuals or groups, how they are categorized and who is included and excluded. All these choices carry with them connotations that draw upon specific discourses.

Participants may be represented individually or in groups. If represented individually, viewers are symbolically drawn closer to the individual represented. This is known as 'individualization' and comes in degrees, depending on a number of factors, such as shot type. In a close-up, individualization is accentuated where we can see details of the person and may understand how they feel due to clues such as a smile or where their eyes are looking. On the contrary, long shots detract from acknowledging individual traits (Machin, 2007: 118). Group shots reduce individualization even more and may connote 'collectivization'. This is when a group shot connotes homogenous 'types' or anonymous groups (Machin, 2007: 118–119). This is accentuated if everyone in the shot dresses similarly, performs the same action or strikes the same pose.

People can also be categorized culturally and/or biologically, these being either positive or negative depending on context. Cultural categorization can be achieved through dress, hairstyle, body adornments and the like. If we consider Figure 5.9 from promotional material for the film *Black Hawk Down* (2002), we can see how the subject is an American soldier. This categorization is achieved through his helmet, uniform and goggles. His surrounding of a high-tech helicopter also indicates sophistication and being an elite soldier. Biological categorization helps us easily identify certain social actors. In Figure 5.9, a big, strong, white man who is relatively clean cut with high cheek bones draws upon stereotypes of what it is to be a US elite soldier.

Figure 5.9 Visual categorization in *Black Hawk Down* promotional material. © Black Hawk Down. Ridley Scott. Sony Pictures Releasing, 2001. Film

Of course, these also work negatively. In many of my lectures, I display an image similar to Figure 5.10 and ask who these social actors are. Inevitably, students identify them as Taliban or Afghani terrorists. Reasons for this are cultural features such as their headdress, clothing, long beards, the AK47s, the bomb and being in a cave. Biological reasons that they give include long faces and big noses. This is not surprising considering these features typify representations of the Taliban in the news and in popular culture.

Figure 5.10   Visual categorization in a caricature of Taliban fighters.

Credit: Chappatte/Globe Cartoon

Obviously, who is included and who is not in visual representations has ideological repercussions. For example, the image from *Black Hawk Down* does not include victims of the American military intervention or a black soldier. Coverage of the Iraqi War included statements such as 'US soldiers begin attack on Falluja' yet 'visually, Falluja, the militia and the actual combat are not represented' (Machin, 2007: 121). This exclusion spared viewers unpleasant scenes of violence and death and helped legitimize US intervention. When we examine imagery, it is important we consider not only who is included, but also who is not and why.

Actions and agency

One aspect of visual representations that is key to discourses of power is who is represented as active, what actions are they represented doing and whether anyone is affected by these actions. In the next chapter, we go into great detail on this subject, but for now we need to consider this at a basic level and to identify in an image who is active and who is passive. To be represented as active is an empowering representation. This is especially true if the subject is acting upon someone else. This is known as having 'agency'. Being represented as active carries with it connotations of power, which generally is a positive thing. However, if someone is represented with agency, but doing something negative, this obviously carries with it very negative connotations.

Likewise, someone can be represented as passive, 'on the receiving end' of an action. This accentuates weakness and is generally a negative representation. Depending on the circumstances, however, this may instil sympathy in viewers. For example, as noted in the previous chapter, protest music tends to represent protesters as victims (Way, 2018a). Though indeed this accentuates weakness, this also creates a sense of sympathy and (hopefully) support for their cause.

Composition

Though the focus of this chapter is on the visual representation of social actors, we also need to consider a variety of composition choices when constructing images, such as the internal 'flow' of an image, what is salient and the chosen degree of modality of an image. We consider specific aspects of these in our analysis sections. Here, we consider them in broad terms.

How a meme or image, such as a print or digital advertisement, is organized carries with it meaning potentials. This includes where elements of the image are in terms of right and left, top, middle and bottom. These choices by producers contribute to an image's internal 'flow' (Kress and van Leeuwen, 1996). What is salient in an image and what is not is ideological and again a result of choices by producers. Salience is achieved through a number of visual devices such as potent cultural symbols, size, colour, tone, focus, lighting and foregrounding. Modality is also examined in some of this chapter's images and again this takes on ideological meanings. Modality is a literary concept associated with the amount of certainty a producer assigns to a statement. It 'refers to the way we communicate as *how true* or as *how real* a representation should be taken' (Machin, 2007: 46, emphasis added). For example, 'I go to the shop' has much higher modality than 'I will probably go to the shop'. In visuals, 'modality can be decreased or increased depending on how much the image departs from how we would have seen the image had we been there' (Machin, 2007: 46). Kress and van Leeuwen (1996) identify eight modality markers, including how the articulation of detail, background and depth contribute to how 'real' an image is perceived. All these visual strategies are part of our toolkit to help us analyse how images in memes articulate political discourses.

CASE STUDY ANALYSIS: MEMES ABOUT AUTHORITARIANISM OF DONALD TRUMP

Context: Authoritarianism

The focus of our chapter's analysis is on how Trump is praised and criticized in memes. Much of this is in terms of being authoritarian. As we will see, though most of this criticism in mainstream media is on Trump being too authoritarian, on 4Chan criticism is for not being authoritarian enough. To understand how this criticism is levelled at Trump, we consider what scholars say about authoritarianism.

According to *dictionary.com*, the adjective 'authoritarian' means 'favoring complete obedience or subjection to authority as opposed to individual freedom'. Though this definition is quite blunt, it encompasses what scholars identify as its main principles: the idea that authoritarianism 'prioritiz[es] collective security for the group at the expense of liberal autonomy for the individual' (Norris and Inglehart, 2019: 7). In fact, scholars identify three core components of authoritarian values which are: (1) the importance of 'security against risks of instability and disorder', (2) 'group conformity to preserve conventional traditions and guard our way of life' and (3) 'loyal obedience toward strong leaders who protect the group and its customs' (2019: 7). Do the phrases 'foreigners steal our jobs and attack our women', 'I alone can fix this' and 'are you with us?' sound familiar?

Authoritarianism is directly linked to the 'politics of fear', where there is a search for collective security of a dominant group, usually referred to as 'our people' against 'them', at the expense of personal freedoms. 'Our people' can be defined in terms of nationality and citizenship, or more locally as in-groups based on race, religion, ethnicity, location, generation, party, gender, or sex. Norris and Inglehart name such groupings as 'tribes', defined as 'social identity groups, often communities linked by economic, religious, or blood ties, with a common culture and dialect, typically having a recognized leader. Tribes involve loyalty, stickiness, boundaries, and shared cultural meanings and feelings of belonging' (2019: 7).

Some politicians in power at the time of writing this not only display authoritarian tendencies, but also populist ones. Populists 'pretend to speak for the

(Continued)

underdog ['the people'] whose political identity is constructed by opposing it to an elite' (De Cleen and Carpentier, 2010: 180). However, dependent on context, the way 'the people' and 'the elite' are defined is fluid. Think about Trump, a white, multi-millionaire property developer who represents himself as one of 'the people' while claiming 'I am draining the swamp', 'swamp' being his word for the political elite in Washington. His 2016 campaign 'continually articulat[ed] itself against the establishment, the elite, the mainstream, the political order, the neo-liberal economic order, the global order, the established way of doing things – against, that is, the entirety of the hitherto existing mainstream reality' (Happer et al., 2019: 4). The point is, populism, in whatever form, 'has a chameleon-like quality which can adapt flexibly to a variety of substantive ideological values and principles, such as socialist or conservative populism, authoritarian or progressive populism, and so on' (Norris and Inglehart, 2019: 3).

Scholars acknowledge populist discourses become a problem when combined with authoritarianism. In such circumstances, politicians tell us that in order to defend 'us' we need to restrict 'them'. This toxic combination results in policies that justify the restriction of immigrants, refugees, asylum seekers and foreigners. Authoritarian-populist politicians and parties have gained power in the USA, Austria, Italy, the Netherlands, Poland, Turkey and Switzerland. In other states they hold sway, such as 'UKIP's [and the Brexit Party's] role in catalysing Brexit' (Norris and Inglehart, 2019: i). Their discourse is reflected in more mainstream politics. Think of how Boris Johnson dealt with Brexit in 2019, itself seen as a reaction against the establishment (Happer et al., 2019:16). Johnson's governing style included attempting to prorogue parliament for six weeks leading up to a Brexit deadline of 31 October 2019, shouting 'traitors' at Members of British Parliament and using threatening language to address domestic and international leaders. These are all symptomatic of authoritarian-populism.

Context: Donald Trump

In this chapter, we focus on Trump, the person claiming the most headlines, academic responses and memes. Trump 'uses populist rhetoric to legitimize his style of governance, while promoting authoritarian values that threaten the liberal norms underpinning American democracy' (Norris and Inglehart, 2019: 3). He and his supporters have attacked 'the liberal press and their ideals of holding authority to account' (Happer et al., 2019: 15). All the while, he calls his opponents 'phoney' or 'dopey', labels media and journalists as 'corrupt' or 'fake news', while discourses of violence, racism and wider uncivility become the 'new' norms of social and political doing and acting (Krzyżanowski, 2020: 4). He has become the darling of the alt-right in the USA, admired and criticized for his style and actions. And it is this range of opinions in memes on 4Chan that we examine.

Context: 4Chan

4Chan is one of a number of websites that have become platforms to communicate far-right ideas (Happer et al., 2019: 13). 4Chan, set up by Christopher Poole in 2003, is made up of unarchived, subject-based boards with anonymous posting. It was 'part of the anything goes, libertarian culture of the internet, but its desire to shock and drift to the right would eventually make it and Reddit key sites for the alt-right' (Happer et al., 2019: 13). The alt-right, which 4Chan has embraced since 2011, is defined as 'a range of extreme far-right movements and positions broadly unified by their rejection of traditional, mainstream Christian conservativism and republicanism in favour of white nationalism and supremacism' (Merrin, 2019: 206).

4Chan is nasty. It is '[t]he modern online home of trolling and the spirit of chaos ... the must-see, cess-pit of the internet: as Obi-Wan Kenobi says (in a quote often applied to the site): "You will never find a more wretched hive of scum and villainy"' (Merrin, 2019: 204). Here, you will experience 'gratuitous pornography, misogyny, racism, most forms of "phobia", graphic insults, general grossness and maximum offensiveness' (2019: 204). If you have viewed a meme in the past few years, wretched or not, it is very likely to have come from 4Chan. Despite its notoriety, 'it has proven to be one of the most creative corners of the web, with its chaos birthing almost every major meme or aspect of internet culture over the last decade' (2019: 204).

4Chan is not only creative, but also political. It has run an attack campaign aimed at the Church of Scientology for attempting to censor content on the internet. It also aimed its rage at a woman game designer and then other feminist commentators in so-called 'Gamergate'. Here, they presented themselves as underdogs and victims, despite accusations of abuse by 'snowflakes, unicorns, cry bullies'. They pitted themselves against mainstream media and feminism, naming them as both 'impossibly strong' and 'laughably weak' (Lees, 2016). Not long after this campaign, 4Chan turned its attention to Trump. At first, his candidacy was seen as a joke, but then the site's content quickly evolved into support (Merrin, 2019). Its support for Trump is not surprising, considering 'his politics closely chimed with [4Chan's] the outsider-culture, anti-PC sentiment, racism and misogyny and the claims of post-truth "'shitposters'"' (2019: 208). Links between 4Chan and Trump are more than just shared political views. Trump and his staff retweeted alt-right videos and images created on 4Chan and 4Chan's memes were part of Trump's campaign to relentlessly tilt sentiment on social media in his favour. As one former campaign official said: 'He clearly won the war against Hillary Clinton day after day after day' (Schreckinger, 2017).

4Chan is important. Its /po/board 'is by far the most influential disseminator of memes in terms of the raw number of memes originating from it. In particular, it

(Continued)

is more influential in spreading racist and political memes' (De Cristofaro, 2018). It delivers an important youth demographic to the alt-right, playing a central role in attacks on mainstream media, mainstream politics, the culture of political correctness and left-wing identity politics. These attacks are evident on 4Chan and in Trump's 2016 election campaign. In fact, many memes that originate from 4Chan cross over into mainstream platforms such as Twitter to appeal to 'Normies'. These include the popular Trump train, You can't stump the Trump, the racist repurposing of Pepe the frog and The Deplorables memes. It was also instrumental in anti-Hillary Clinton campaigns such as Pizzagate and other conspiracy theories. These strategies Merrin calls 'mimetic warfare' because they are intentional and well organized. But 4Chan is also Trump's worst enemy. Even though mainstream media criticize Trump, this has little effect on his supporters, feeding into the narrative of Trump as an outsider. However, he is vulnerable to 'humour and satire: the same troll-culture that supports Trump and which he incarnates has become one of the most important weapons against him' (Merrin, 2019: 213).

Textual analysis

The images we analyse in this chapter are a few of the many that were in circulation on 4Chan in the spring of 2019, when this chapter was being researched. Daily, there are innumerable memes being made, manipulated and circulated in threads about Trump on 4Chan. This is not surprising, given its history of promoting not only Trump, but also the alt-right. Interestingly, as we see below, there is also a significant amount of criticism about Trump. This usually comes from those who position themselves even further to the right than Trump.

As noted by the scholars we have examined above and in Chapter 2, we know that the meanings we take from memes are very much dependent on a number of contexts. We need to know the event or subject the meme is commenting on for it to make sense. We also have to be aware of the intertextuality, that is the original media (remember the Gone with the Kim meme examined in Chapter 2). Furthermore, the political community one associates oneself with also contributes to the meanings a viewer takes from the meme. But what about the memes themselves? The actual texts? In this chapter, we examine how images in memes are used to articulate discourses about Trump. We identify strategies used in images that articulate these discourses. Specifically, we examine how visual strategies represent Trump as powerful and weak, which articulate discourses of Trump as invincible, a great leader, above the law, but also as weak and not nationalistic enough. Meme analysis is divided into dominant obvious themes seen throughout 4Chan: Trump as god-like, Trump as a powerful leader, Trump's relations with mainstream media and Trump as being weak. The aim of our analysis is to demonstrate the usefulness of our toolkit in examining the role images play in memes, whether about Trump or otherwise.

Images of god-like powers

One obvious strategy used to represent Trump as powerful is doing a visual mash-up with his head on a mythical character's body. God Emperor Trump is a series that appeared on 4Chan. These depict Trump as ruler of the world, wearing the armour of the immortal character Emperor of Mankind from the war game *Warhammer 40,000* and named as 'God Emperor' or 'Imperium of Man'. According to 'know your meme' website, these images first appeared on 4Chan on 16 June 2015. We now examine two of these images used in memes and found in threads during our time on 4Chan.

Figure 5.11 is typical of these God Emperor images. Trump stands tall. He wears the armour of Emperor of Mankind, culturally categorizing Trump as a super-being. Both the vertical and horizontal angle of interactions suggest strength. The camera looks up to Trump connoting great power (Machin, 2007). His body also faces the camera, though his face looks off to the side. This connotes that he is not here to engage with viewers in a demand image. He is posing to be admired. After all, viewers are mere mortals. Abousnnouga and Machin (2010: 144) examine war monuments and find that most of the subjects do not symbolically demand any-thing of their viewers, but look off to the horizon. This has the meaning potential 'of wanting the public to see the soldiers as part of a different world, one of the glory of God … metaphorically [looking] to the future and high ideals'. Here, Trump gazes in a similar manner, looking thoughtful, full of high ideals, powerful and into the future. Facial expressions are stern and forceful, making clear he is in power. His head is small compared to the massive body in the mash-up. However, both head and body are salient. Salience can be achieved through a number of strategies including size, focus and colour. His body is salient through its size – you cannot miss it! But the meme's message of Trump as powerful would be lost if his head

Figure 5.11   'God Emperor Trump' image in pro-Trump 4Chan thread. Creator unknown

(Continued)

was difficult to identify. Through light, focus and colour, his head is also salient. It is in focus and, importantly, the creator of the image has included what looks like a halo around Trump's head to guide our eyes towards him.

Compositional choices also contribute to Trump's mythical status. There is no distinguishable background, just modular shades of golden-red. Here, God Emperor Trump is decontextualized. There is low modality in this image; we do not know where Trump is or what he is doing. Where figures are represented without a background, 'it usually means that the image is symbolic rather than documentary', symbolic rather than descriptive (Machin, 2007: 51). This contributes to the notion that this image is less about real power and Trump's actions and more about vague notions or fantasies of Trump's power, however ill-defined these are (2007: 48).

The discourse of power, but not any real tangible power, is common in these series. In Figure 5.12, again this is not about 'real' political power, like the power to cancel Obamacare, build a wall, close the borders to Muslims or curtail criticisms in the press. This is symbolic power. Similarities between the two images include Trump's head mashed-up with the body of Emperor of Mankind. Both images see Trump's head small, yet salient through the use of colours and lighting and focus. Both images stress the symbolic representations of power over 'real' ones, representing Trump as a mythical character and using a low modal background.

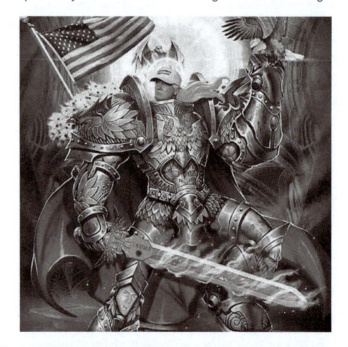

Figure 5.12 Symbolic power and nationalism in 'God Emperor Trump' images. Creator unknown

However, this image is different from the previous one. Now potent cultural symbols change the discourse to one that is one of nationalism and power. Salient are reminders of America. Perhaps most salient is the American flag, large and in focus. Also, an American bald eagle has submitted to Trump's power, it sitting on his left hand. It is not free to fly like the bird in the background of Trump's halo. But the America being promoted here is Trump's America. On the right knee of his armour, there is a demand image of Trump. He looks aggressive and powerful, yelling. A MAGA hat sits on top of Trump's and the bald eagle's heads. This cultural ornamentation is recognizable worldwide. MAGA, short for 'Make America Great Again', has become synonymous with a world view associated with Trump that includes controversial perspectives on race, immigration, the environment, politicians, authoritarianism and even knowledge (Makovicky et al., 2019). Part of this outlook includes being aggressive, symbolized by the flaming sword with 'Trump' written on the handle. This is not about America, but about a style of leadership that is unconventional, authoritarian and populist. Though imagery such as this connotes great power, it is not defined and suggests authoritarianism, a discourse some 4Chan users admire.

Trump as powerful president(ial candidate)

Trump's power is not just represented in god-like imagery. There are more descriptive representations of Trump's power, such as Trump represented positively as a powerful president and presidential candidate. Figure 5.13 is an example used in a thread in June 2019. The feed is made up of insults and bantering among users about the merits of Trump and his supporters. This image accompanied a post that claimed 'Losers lose their shit over how awesome this guy is.' What we can ask here is: why was this image chosen by one of his supporters? One answer could be the power this image connotes. This is a demand image with Trump looking straight at the camera, directly addressing viewers, creating symbolic interaction, suggesting power and demanding a response (Kress and van Leeuwen, 1996: 127–128). This empowers Trump. Furthermore, this is a close-up head shot, giving viewers a point of identification. Trump is looking confident with a slight smile on his face. A smile can take on a variety of meanings depending on context and, in some cases, 'there may be a kind of smile that invites us in or allows us to share the joy of a moment' (Machin, 2007: 111). Here, his smile indicates he wants us to share in his victory, emphasized by the 'we' instead of 'I' in the accompanying written text.

Though there is no action represented in the image, here Trump is represented strong through cultural categorization. His suit, white shirt and tie tell us this is a formal occasion and he is someone to be respected. The colours of the accompanying writing and surrounding boxes mirror those of the American flag suggesting a national event.

(Continued)

What has been 'won' is not indicated in the thread or image, but the clues suggest Trump's election in 2016. In any circumstance, this is an empowering image. But, like the images in the previous section, this is more symbolic than real. The image and context connote no real action and agency. Trump is not represented doing anything to anybody. The background, again, gives no clues as to any particular event or issue. Once again, this image is about power, though not defined and quantifiable.

Figure 5.13 Descriptive representations of Trump's power in 4Chan memes. Creator unknown

The slogan 'Can't stump the Trump' was started by Trump supporters during his campaign to become the Republican presidential candidate. It first appeared on 15 June 2015 on 4Chan, posted by a Trump supporter. The phrase was taken up by a number of conservative media outlets and Trump tweeted the phrase on 13 October 2015. The now famous meme (Figure 5.14) appears regularly on 4Chan and articulates discourses of Trump as a strong president(ial candidate), but once again in a symbolic rather than descriptive manner.

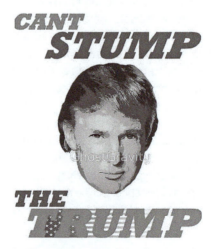

Figure 5.14 'Can't stump the Trump' meme on 4Chan. Creator unknown

As is the case with the previous image, Trump is salient, connoting his importance. Aside from written text, excluded are any details of where he is and what he is doing, suggesting it is all about Trump. Unlike any of the previous images, there is no background here further suggesting the image is more symbolic than descriptive (Machin, 2007: 34). And it is power that is symbolized. Trump's head has low modality. That is, the degree of realism is far less than in real life. Facial details, such as wrinkles, blemishes and faults are not present. There is a visual effect applied to the image that eliminates these realities and offers us a young, unreal version of Trump's head. Choosing a youthful version of Trump has more associations with strength than that of an old man. Power is also connoted in viewers' engagement with Trump. He stares at us in a demand image. Here his eyes are wide open as though he is afraid of nothing. His forehead slightly leans forward and his chin is tucked in, as though he is threatening viewers. Again, there is a slight sly smile, perhaps suggesting that, indeed, you cannot 'stump the Trump'. All this suggests Trump's power is beyond the realm of normal.

The composition of the meme also suggests power. Kress and van Leeuwen (1996: 193) claim that the position of elements in images create 'compositional structures' which have meaning potential. One structure is the 'triptych', where one element is centrally placed, acting as a mediator between other elements. Within this meme, Trump occupies the middle of the meme surrounded by colours of the nation, suggesting he is at the centre of America. This is emphasized with Trump's name integrated with the US flag, connoting a natural connection between the two (Machin, 2007: 154). In fact, by having Trump's name on top of the flag, overlapping occurs again indicating Trump's strength and importance in America (Eisner, 1985). Kress and van Leeuwen (1996: 193) also identify the top of compositions as the 'ideal', generalization or simplification of an image. The bottom is the 'real', factual and grounded in the everyday that adds weight and credibility to the ideal. Here, the ideal is 'can't stump' while 'the Trump' is the factual that adds weight to the ideal. This construction emphasizes Trump as unstoppable and clever in the context of power in America. What this is missing is any detail and specifics about exactly what is this power, who it affects and how.

IMAGES OF TRUMP'S RELATIONS WITH MAINSTREAM MEDIA

Trump's relations with mainstream media are combative at best, well documented and discussed in academia (see Happer et al., 2019). He makes no secret of his dislike for media that criticizes himself, a usual target for his angst in his political rallies and press conferences. This tendency to attack critical mainstream media is aligned with authoritarian notions of loyal obedience towards a strong leader. He also shares his views on Twitter, including a GIF in 2017 of him body slamming the CNN logo. This GIF resulted in a meme campaign instigated by 4Chan on 5 July 2017 named 'Operation Autism Storm' or the 'Great CNN Meme War'. The campaign urged users to engage in a meme war with CNN because the network threatened to reveal the identity of the producer of this controversial GIF. 4Chan and Reddit users began spreading anti-CNN images, videos and animated GIFs, including a 'best meme' in the 'Great CNN Meme War' contest and a compilation of said memes, clips and GIFs on YouTube. Much of this imagery is recycled and appears in feeds on 4Chan.

In this section we examine two images on threads during the spring of 2019, images that originate from the meme war. In both images, Trump is salient. His head, which is mashed onto other characters, is large, light in colour and is in the foreground of the images. Also, Trump is represented acting with agency in these – that is, doing something to someone. This is unlike the previous images we have examined and connotes great power (Fairclough, 1995b: 113).

As is the case with all memes, the manipulated images come from other primary media and knowledge of these contribute to the meanings of the imagery. The origins of Figure 5.15 is the game *Mortal Kombat*. It depicts a fatality sequence in which a character called Liu Kang (Trump here) turns into a dragon and eats the top half of his opponent. In the altered image, the Trump dragon dominates the image. He is much larger than the CNN character and in the centre of the image, a dominant position. His body is puffed out in a threatening position. Though the horizontal angle of interaction does not allow us to have any symbolic interaction with him, we are here to observe his strength. Trump's mouth is open, represented yelling and threatening as his eyes glare down at CNN, again emphasizing his power. CNN leans back, cowering under his threats. Here, representations of power are clear. Represented actions of yelling and threatening are a metaphor for Trump's actions and relations with mainstream media.

Figure 5.15   Meme of Trump as Liu Kang from the *Mortal Kombat* game. Creator unknown

In Figure 5.16, Trump again dominates the image. Here, his head is mashed onto the Hulk from *The Avengers* film (2012). In this image, Trump faces us, allowing viewers to witness his anger. The vertical angle of interaction emphasizes his strength. In the original film, the Hulk fights Loki, a villain. Here, Trump's head is mashed onto the superhero's body as he holds the villain by the feet in a sequence that sees the Hulk physically brutalize Loki. It is a one-sided fight due to the Hulk's enormous strength. Here, the superhero Trump physically brutalizes CNN. This show of strength and connotations of who is right and who is wrong would not be lost on viewers, again depicting Trump as very powerful and correct compared to CNN, a mainstream media outlet that dares to challenge his power. And again, we see how actions are not literal but metaphoric, while power is emphasized.

Figure 5.16 Trump as the Hulk from *The Avengers* film (2012). Creator unknown. Film still © Marvel's *The Avengers*. Joss Whedon. Walt Disney Studios Motion Pictures, 2012. Film

CRITICISMS OF TRUMP FROM THE FAR RIGHT

There is a lot of criticism of Trump in mainstream media and digital popular culture. Criticism is aimed at a large number of issues including his authoritarian tendencies, his (un)lawful actions, his style of governing and even his policies. Mostly, these come from a position that is less right wing than Trump. However, in our search of 4Chan in 2019, there was a lot of criticism of Trump from the right. He is depicted as not authoritarian enough and too tolerant of minorities such as the gay community, asylum seekers, Jewish people and Israel. In this section, we examine a meme to reveal some of the visual strategies used to connote negativity around Trump.

As noted above, viewers of 4Chan experience and express racism (Merrin, 2019: 204), evident in threads that defend and criticize Trump. One theme is an anti-Semitic discourse that includes the media being 'Jewish-controlled' and naming outlets 'Jewtube' and 'Faceberg', all part of a gambit of conspiracy theories whereby Jewish people are to blame. In the thread that accompanies Figure 5.17, we find some users attack Trump and some defend him. Trump is attacked as being weak, represented as following Israel in 'Trump is blind and Netanyahu is guiding him' and 'Make these shill memes that show him MIGA instead of MAGA.' We can only assume MIGA is an acronym that exchanges America for Israel in Trump's 'Make America Great Again' slogan. Elsewhere in the thread, the 'Jewish-controlled media' are attacked for being against Trump, who will 'destroy groping Joe [Biden] in 2020', while some users believe this thread is part of a Jewish-led conspiracy to turn voters against Trump.

Figure 5.17   An anti-Semitic far-right meme critical of Trump on 4Chan. Creator unknown

The meme is in the style of a before and after sequence. Scholars tell us an image can be organized from left to right where the left can represent the old while the right can represent the new, the possible (Halliday, 1985: 277). In this composition, the left is the past, something we already know, while the right is something new. In the left image, we see Trump the Crusader, culturally categorized. In popular fiction, the red on white cross we see on Trump's shield and chest plate is associated with not only the English flag, but also the Crusades and Saint George, England's 'patron saint'. Though not a symbol of America, this image resonates with Trump's policies towards Muslims, keeping in mind the eight Crusader wars were 'a series of religious wars between Christians and Muslims started primarily to secure control of holy sites considered sacred by both groups' (Crusades, 2019). The background, though low in modality, depicts a dry, desert-like landscape, a large sun and a building with a dome roof, all connoting the Middle East.

Interestingly, in this image on the left, Trump is salient, but not like we have seen with the memes that represent him positively. His head is mashed onto a knight, but his head is small and not in the foreground. The horse and American flag are far more salient, the flag being both large and a potent cultural symbol. Like the positive images examined above, Trump is looking to the horizon – a man with a vision. This image connotes positivity, though not as obvious as previous examples. It reminisces about a time when Trump had a vision as a candidate. His facial expression, though difficult to distinguish, is stern and serious, like a crusader, off to Make America Great Again.

The right-hand image has less certainty and positivity and lower modality than the left image. A 'realistic' photograph of Trump's head on the left is replaced with a caricature of Trump. It is biologically categorized based on racist stereotypes. He now has a large nose, squinting eyes and big eyebrows. Some of these qualities are used in Jewish hate literature. He looks untrustworthy connoted by his gaze which no longer looks to the horizon, but off to the side. He is now a flag bearer for Israel not America, indicated by the change in flag. What is connoted here is that he now works in the national interest of Israel. This is nothing short of treasonous behaviour for a president. He no longer is a warrior crusader fighting for America and its interests. Instead, he is a traitor, fighting for Israel and Jewish people. Though these criticisms are powerful, they are not specific. There is no articulation of an argument in the meme or in the thread of what Trump has done for or against America and/or Israel. Though these images may stir up nationalist feelings in 4Chan users, their lack of direct criticism is stark.

SUMMARY

In this chapter, we have considered how imagery in digital popular culture can articulate political discourses. We examined what scholars have told us about the power of memes. We summarized the seminal work of Kress and van Leeuwen (1996 and 2001) and Machin (2007) to add to our analytical toolbox, equipping us with tools on how to analyse the representation of social actors in images. We also considered some composition and visual organizational strategies that contribute to meanings

(Continued)

in imagery. With these in hand, we have analysed memes about Donald Trump's power. Whether pro- or anti-Trump, the power represented is not about any real tangible power or actions, but symbolic and/or metaphoric. We find many of these lean on discourses of nationalism, racism and authoritarianism, discourses close to many of its 4Chan audience members. Through these analyses, we have revealed how MCDS can disclose discourses, some obvious and others less obvious, in imagery. These tools are useful not just in the examination of memes, but in that of any imagery on- or offline. It is up to us to be critical and consider the deluge of images we come into contact with every day to consider carefully exactly what these are telling us and how this is being done.

SUGGESTED READING

Denisova, A. (2019) *Internet Memes and Society: Social, Cultural, and Political Contexts*. New York and London: Routledge.

This is an interesting study of the political role of memes. The first half of the book provides an in-depth theoretical context to the role of memes in politics. The second half of the book is (mostly) a case study of memes about Russia's annexation of Crimea.

Kress, G. and van Leeuwen, T. (1996) *Reading Images: The Grammar of Visual Design*. London: Routledge.

Here is another seminal book in the area of multimodal analysis. The authors provide a detailed examination on how to consider and analyse images from a discursive perspective.

Merrin, W. (2019) President Troll: Trump, 4Chan and memetic warfare, in C. Happer, A. Hoskins and W. Merrin (eds), *Trump's Media War*. London: Palgrave Macmillan. pp. 201–226.

This article is theoretically rich and argues that internet 'trolling' is an important political act. The case study of Donald Trump's presidential campaign is relevant and important for our understanding of how memes act politically.

Wiggins, B.E. (2019) *The Discursive Power of Memes in Digital Culture: Ideology, Semiotics, and Intertextuality*. New York and London: Routledge.

This book is an important examination of memes as discursive power. Case studies are relevant and provide solid evidence about the political importance and limits of memes.

6

ANALYSING ANIMATIONS AND MASH-UPS

Brexit in Lexical and Visual Representations of Social Action

---

CHAPTER OBJECTIVES

- Identify the importance of GIFs and mash-ups.
- Understand van Leeuwen's (1995 and 2001) and Kress and van Leeuwen's (1996 and 2001) work on the representation of social action.
- Apply an analysis of the representation of action to GIFs and mash-ups that represent aspects of Brexit.

KEY CONCEPTS

- Graphics interchange format videos (GIFs) are short animations comprising sets of images within a single file that appear as moving images.
- A mash-up involves producers sampling extracts of video, sound and music to create a new video.
- There are a number of ways to represent action, each with different connotations. For example, actions represented with transivity – that is, one actor doing something to another connotes power.

(Continued)

> - Van Leeuwen has categorized actions in terms of activation/de-activation, agentialization/de-agentialization, abstraction/concretization and single-determination/overdetermination, all contributing to discourses of power, legitimation and purpose.

INTRODUCTION

I remember as a kid enjoying re-runs of *The Jetsons* on Saturday mornings. This was an American animated situation comedy first aired in 1962 about a family who lived in the future. It was in colour, had a great theme song and everything seemed so futuristic: Rosie the robot did the housework, people drove aerocars and telephones included voice and moving images. As a little boy watching this on television, I did not imagine I would see some of this come true – that is, moving images on our telephones. My impression is not lost on others. As Tucker (2011: 285) points out, *The Jetsons* is 'distinguished in science-fiction lore by the fact that it is a rare attempt in this genre that actually succeeds in predicting the future'.

A big part of our daily interaction with digital popular culture is the moving image. It makes sense. Basic psychology tells us that we are biased towards motion: when something moves we notice it. This has its roots in the crucial fight or flight response. So, it only makes sense that we are attracted to movement on our phones. In fact, views of branded video content 'have increased 99% on YouTube and 258% on Facebook between 2016 and 2017'. On Twitter, a video tweet is six times more likely to be retweeted than a photo tweet. We watch around 100 million hours of video on Facebook every day ('Why video is exploding …', 2019) and YouTube's over 1 billion viewers spend a total of 1 billion hours a day watching videos ('YouTube by numbers', 2019).

As is obvious by the numbers outlined above, choices on what moving images to analyse are endless. In this chapter, we focus on animations and mash-ups that represent aspects of Britain's departure from the European Union (known as Brexit). The aim is to demonstrate the usefulness of approaching animations and mash-ups discursively. By doing this, we increase the breadth of our analytical toolkit so that we can apply these ideas to other media texts. Before our analysis, we need to consider context – in this case production and social/political contexts.

THE IMPORTANCE OF ANIMATIONS AND MASH-UPS

Animation is a method by which pictures are manipulated to appear as moving images. In traditional animation (including most animated films of the 20th century), images are drawn or painted by hand on transparent celluloid sheets which are photographed and exhibited on film. Today, most animations are made with computer-generated imagery. Animators' drawings are either scanned into or drawn directly into a computer system. Software is used to colour drawings and simulate movement and effects, creating a range of animation from very detailed three-dimensional to more basic two-dimensional offerings. In digital popular culture, animations are usually very short (under a minute) GIFs. A GIF, first developed in 1987, is a set of images within a single file that appears as a moving image, like a twirling icon or letters that get larger. Some animated GIFs loop endlessly while others present a sequence or two and then stop.

Mash-ups come from the word used in musicology meaning 'sample-based music where "new" songs are created entirely from "old" recordings' (Maloy, 2010: 2). Mash-up producers use 'found' extracts of voice and instrumentation taken from the internet as their raw materials. In audio-visual mash-ups, producers sample extracts of video, sound and music to produce a 'new' video. In this chapter, our analysis case studies are a sample of GIFs and a video mash-up. The aim of the analysis of both of these types is to illustrate how a variety of animated digital popular culture can be studied.

ANALYTICAL TOOLS: THE LEXICAL AND VISUAL REPRESENTATION OF SOCIAL ACTION

We can approach our MCDS analysis of GIFs and mash-ups by examining any number of things, such as the use of metaphors or how events are recontextualized. But, as we have stated before, one advantage of an MCDS is it can be tailored to individual projects, depending on research needs. We need to ask '[w]hat conceptual tools are relevant for this or that problem and for this and that context?' (Wodak and Weiss, 2005: 125). Video mash-ups almost inevitably involve social actors and their actions. This is partly due to the character of animation and video which allows opportunities to represent actions in ways other media, such as a still image, cannot. In this chapter, our analysis focuses on the representation of social actions in lexical choices and visuals.

How action is represented is important. It 'encode[s] different interpretations of, and different attitudes to, the social actions represented', a significant factor in articulating discourses (van Leeuwen, 1995: 81). Actions can be represented in a number of modes and contribute to discourses of power. In this chapter, we analyse social actions in lyrics and/or written lexica and images by closely following van Leeuwen's (1995) seminal work on the representation of social action. It is in this work that he classifies the representation of actions and reactions in ways that reveal discourses articulated in texts. Though this work looked specifically at written texts, this has since expanded to include visual representations (Kress and van Leeuwen, 1996 and 2001; van Leeuwen, 2005). These are useful for our current analysis.

Van Leeuwen (1995) claims there are three broad types of actions that may be distinguished from each other: mental processes, material actions and/or semiotic actions. Mental processes are most associated with reactions and a lack of power. They include thoughts, feelings and desires. Van Leeuwen (1995: 86) notes that 'As the power of social actors decreases, the amount of emotive reactions attributed to them increases'. Semiotic actions are speech acts that connote more power than mental processes because something is being done – that is, speech. In fact, speech acts can be transactive, a powerful representation involving two actors, as in 'she addressed him'. These can also be non-transactive as in 'she spoke'. Van Leeuwen found in his study that 'the actions of lower-status actors are more often represented as non-transactive' (1995: 90). Semiotic actions may include a quote and 'this is typically reserved for high status actors ... or used to enhance the credibility of an embedded representation' (1995: 91). This type of representation also is empowering, allowing an actor to represent the world in their way, giving voice to them as opposed to someone else.

The third type of action is material actions. This is an action involving someone doing something. These can be transactive (involving two participants) or non-transactive (involving only one participant). An action may be represented as transactive or not, connoting different types of power. For example, both 'police hit protesters' and 'police responded' can represent the same action(s), yet the second represents police differently than the first. Transactive representations, such as 'police hit protesters', are powerful in that they represent actions which 'have an effect on others, or the world ... [and] clearly the ability to "transact" requires a certain power, and the greater that power, the greater the range of "goals" that may be affected by an actor's actions' (van Leeuwen, 1995: 89–90). Non-transactive actions, such as 'police responded', represent an actor with less power.

There are a number of other ways actions can be represented which contribute to discourses of power, legitimation and purpose. Van Leeuwen has categorized these in terms of activation/de-activation, agentialization/de-agentialization, abstraction/concretization and single-determination/overdetermination. Though we do not use all of these categories in the analyses that follow, we outline them here for future reference.

Actions can be represented as active or de-activated, the latter 'represented statistically, as though they are entities or qualities, rather than dynamic processes' (van Leeuwen, 1995: 93). Two ways de-activation is achieved is through objectivation and descriptivization. Objectivated actions are realized by nominalizations or process nouns, such as 'migration', which can replace 'they migrate'. This has the effect of 'downrank[ing the action] in order to give priority to something else … [and/or] adds purposes and/or legitimations to the representation' (1995: 94). Descriptivations de-activate action, representing them 'as more or less permanent qualities of social actors' (1995: 94), like 'smiling', 'deaf' or 'specially trained'.

Actions can include an agent – that is, someone who is acting, such as 'the Headteacher has removed parents' role in policy-making'. Here, it is obvious that the 'headteacher' is acting. However, van Leeuwen also notes actions can be de-agentialized – that is, 'represented as brought about in other ways, impermeable to human agency' (1995: 96). There are three types of de-agentializations: eventuation, existentialization and naturalization. Eventuation represents an action as an event, as something that just happens – for example, 'Parents lose key role in policy-making' (1995: 96). Existentialization sees an action represented as something that simply exists, often beginning with 'there is', as in 'there is no role for parents in policy-making'. Naturalization sees actions represented as 'a natural process by means of abstract material processes such as "vary", "expand"," develop" etc., which link actions and reactions to specific interpretations of material processes' (1995: 97). An example may be 'Parental policy-making roles are contracting'.

Concretization involves representing an action with tangible details. Abstracted representations of actions are the opposite in that they 'abstract away from more specific "micro-actions" that make up actions' (1995: 99). Abstraction can come in the form of generalizations which abstract the qualities of actions and micro-actions that make up whole actions, pronounced in texts 'which are mainly concerned with legitimizing or de-legitimizing actions and reactions' (1995: 99). Representations of actions may be generalized, where a single term, such as pre-school 'milk time', represents a number of activities such as gathering on a rug, naming a colour and fetching milk. Representations which 'are mainly concerned with legitimizing or delegitimizing actions and reactions tend to move high up on the generalization scale, including only the names of episodes for whole social practices' (1995: 99). Distillations also abstract actions, but what is abstracted are qualities from the representation which 'not only highlight some aspect of an action at the expense of others, they also realize purposes and legitimations: purposes through the kinds of qualities highlighted' (1995: 99).

The last category of representation of actions is whether a representation is single-determined or overdetermined. Single-determination sees one representation accurately represent one action. Overdetermination is when one social action stands for more than one action. These come in two forms. First, symbolization such as the use of metaphors and allegories which 'highlight a quality of action rather than representing the action itself' (1995: 101). Second, 'inversion' occurs when an action is inaccurately represented to suggest a larger set of social actions that legitimize the status quo. The example van Leeuwen uses illustrates this well. In a children's book, which tries 'to reach children to comply with the rules of school and adopt the right behaviour' (1995: 85), a girl brings a lion to school. The lion 'engages in inverted actions such as "swishing his tail" threateningly during "registration time"' (1995: 102). It is this representation that reinforces the idea that the action of taking the register should be orderly, including leaving pets at home.

The categorization of social actions outlined above is a useful guide in analysing any text. These make up a vital part of our analytical toolkit. As always, we use the 'tools that fit the job'. Likewise, we also use other tools we are discussing in this book to enhance any analysis. What follows now are examples of how to put some of these tools into action. We perform a brief analysis of a sample of GIFs and then an in-depth analysis of a mash-up, all related to Brexit. This exercise illustrates how MCDS can be used to reveal political discourses articulated in animations and mash-ups.

CASE STUDY ANALYSIS: GIFS AND A MASH-UP RELATED TO BREXIT

Context: Brexit

Despite the fact that all good MCDS analysis requires contextual examinations, we do not dwell on describing Brexit. This topic is broad, complex and needs far more time and space than we can afford here. There are countless publications that consider a variety of aspects of Brexit, including those that examine it discursively (see Way, 2018b; Zappettini and Krzyżanowski, 2019). There have been a multitude of events that have happened since 23 June 2016 when 51.9 per cent of people who voted (or 17,410,742 out of a population of over 65 million) chose to leave the EU. At the time of writing, Boris Johnson has just 'Got Brexit Done', though there are likely many more years of negotiations before Britain will sever itself completely from Europe.

Brexit is an emotional topic for those who live in the UK and the EU. It raises emotions for those opposed to and for Brexit. This makes Brexit a hot topic in digital popular culture and a good one to examine.

CASE STUDY ANALYSIS ONE: GIFS FROM BUZZFEED

Context: Brexit

There are literally thousands of GIFs about Brexit. The vast majority of those collected for this research are against the idea of Britain leaving the European

Union. GIFs regularly appear on our Facebook and Twitter feeds and can be found in compiled lists. One of these, posted on 24 June 2016, is BuzzFeed's *13 GIFs That Perfectly Describe Brexit For Remain Supporters*. We briefly study these here to illustrate how analysing social action is revealing. A more detailed analysis follows in our examination of a mash-up below.

BuzzFeed was founded in 2006 in New York with a focus on tracking viral online content. It has now expanded into 'the world's leading independent digital media company ... reach[ing] hundreds of millions of people globally' ('About BuzzFeed', 2019). Its services include creating articles, lists, quizzes and videos (BuzzFeed Originals); producing original content for traditional and digital platforms (Buzz-Feed Studios); BuzzFeed Media Brands including Tasty, the world's largest social food network; and BuzzFeed News. Presently its executive chairman, Kenneth Lerer, is also co-founder and chairman of *The Huffington Post* (now *HuffPost*), known for its liberal political perspective. NBCUniversal, which owns NBC News, also has a $400 million investment in the operation. Since 2011, it has expanded into serious journalism, winning the 2018 National Magazine Award and being a finalist for the Pulitzer Prize, among other accolades.

Part of its entertainment services is the sharing of GIFs from other platforms. In the case of *13 GIFs That Perfectly Describe Brexit For Remain Supporters*, found at https://www.buzzfeed.com/lukebailey/13-gifs-that-perfectly-describe-brexit-for-remain-supporters, GIFs are sourced by Imgur. As an image and GIF hosting site, Imgur was ranked sixteenth among Alexa's top sites in the USA in 2016. Though originally developed to assist Reddit users, its content does not reflect any single political leaning. In the case of our sample, the GIFs are anonymous and most certainly communicate an anti-Brexit narrative.

Textual analysis

On initial inspection, what is evident in these GIFs is a discourse that Britain is engaged in self-harm. This is a dominant pro-Remain discourse and can be seen in a large number of news headlines and everyday conversations. For example, Sir Paddy Ashdown, former leader of the UK's Liberal Democratic Party, wrote an opinion piece for the pro-Remain *Independent* newspaper. Describing the march he perceived towards a no-deal 'hard Brexit' by the UK's government, he wrote: 'We are now embarked on a course that will bewilder future historians as the most remarkable example in modern history of a country committing an act of monumental self-harm while still in full possession of its faculties' (Ashdown, 2017). A similar discourse can be seen in these GIFs. But unlike the above article and politicians' speeches, the GIFs offer only a comical representation of self-harm with no room for examining facts to inform oneself about Brexit. On a closer examination of the representation of actions, other more sinister discourses emerge.

(Continued)

Through choices in editing and shot types, each GIF emphasizes an action and reaction that appears to be unstaged. The few seconds in each GIF captures a moment when a social actor acts upon an object and then there is a reaction. By editing out other parts of the sequence, these short visual representations focus our attention on these (re)actions. Long shots allow us to see the actions/reactions. These choices are at the expense of close-ups of actors' faces which would allow us to focus more on the actors and their feelings. They are shot on grainy CCTV cameras or consumer-quality camera devices, suggesting authentic (re)actions, as opposed to a staged event.

In each GIF, social actors engage in an activity that is meant to harm something, but their actions backfire and they harm themselves. For example, we see a man kick an A-frame sandwich board sign. He successfully puts his foot through the sign and the sign falls to the ground. Unfortunately for him, he cannot release his foot from the hole he has put in the sign and falls to the ground. In another, a school girl tries to kick a bird off the edge of a raised railway platform. She misses the bird, loses her balance and falls into the rail tracks while the bird flies away. In another, we witness a man with both of his fists tensely placed on the top of a plank of wood that is on the top of an open-topped steel barrel (Figure 6.1). He raises his left fist and punches through the board. Unfortunately, both halves of the wood lift from the sides of the barrel and hit the man on both sides of his face. In yet another, we witness a woman who walks towards a tall traffic cone set beside a parked car while she swings her keys (Figure 6.2). She kicks the cone. The cone first falls away from her then swings back and hits the woman hard in the stomach. All the other GIFs in this collection (and many other anti-Brexit GIFs) run a similar narrative. What can MCDS tell us about these?

Figure 6.1   Anti-Brexit GIF: man hits wood.

GIF credit: u/mattsgotredhair on Reddit

Figure 6.2 Anti-Brexit GIF: woman kicks cone.

GIF credit: AFVOfficial on Imgur

If we break down the visual representation of each actor's actions, discourses become evident. In all cases, the actor performs a material process with agency, like 'man kicks sign', 'girl attacks bird', 'man punches wood' and 'woman kicks cone'. In all these, the actor is represented as powerful, subjecting an entity (goal) to the actor's action. All these actions may be considered negative, such as attacking a bird, vandalizing a street sign or kicking a traffic cone. Others are less negative, such as punching a piece of wood, though again 'showing off' can be seen as negative, especially if it backfires.

What follows next are 'reactions' to these actions. For the most part, the goals of the initial actions are inanimate objects (with the exception of the bird). These objects obviously have no human agency; however, these reactions have transivity, connoting power, such as 'cone hits woman', 'wood hits man', 'sign trips up man', 'bird causes girl to fall'. What all these reactions have in common is, first, they are the result of an actor's negative actions. Second, the reactions are transitive, causing harm to the actor – harm the actor was not expecting.

What do these tell us about Brexit? To fully answer this, we need to identify who the actors in the GIF represent. The title of this list, *13 GIFs That Perfectly Describe Brexit For Remain Supporters*, makes clear there is a group of 'Remain supporters' who are distinct from Leave voters (not represented in the title). It is presupposed that Remain voters do not understand Brexit and need the GIFs to have Brexit 'perfectly describe[d]'. The GIFs illustrate how a 'bad' action results in a 'bad' reaction. This initial 'bad' action becomes a metaphor for voting to leave the EU which culminates in a harmful reaction to those voters. This allows Remain voters to laugh at Brexit supporters in the GIFs.

(Continued)

Like the 51.9 per cent of voters who chose Leave in the referendum, the actors in the GIFs are represented with agency. Like the self-harm discourse, their actions harm themselves. Also similar to the Brexit self-harm discourse is the idea that what happens next is unpredictable. The discourse in the GIFs, however, is different than the public discourse in two ways. First, in the GIFs, Brexiteers suffer the consequences of their 'bad' actions, allowing Remainer audiences to laugh at them. However, the public discourse (and the reality) is how one voted and feels about Brexit is not a factor in how it will affect voters. Second, unlike the public discourse, where there are arguments, comments and discussions about how much harm Brexit will cause and if indeed there will be harm, in the GIFs harm is as certain as the initial act of voting to leave.

These findings agree with some findings of previous research, but also show slight differences. Similar to Denisova (2019) and Wiggins (2019), our analysis reveals that GIFs provide little room for debate on issues. In the political arena, though most agree Brexit will harm the UK's economy, there is a wide range of opinions on how much harm, with some Brexiteers claiming it will benefit the UK's economy (Mason, 2019). With our GIFs, there is no room for debate. The negative consequences of initial actions are as clear as the initial actions. Our analysis of social actions has also found differences between our findings and those of Denisova (2019) and Wiggins (2019). These previous studies have found that memes articulate dominant public discourses. What the analysis of social actions reveals is GIFs articulate discourses similar to dominant Remain discourses, but not the same. We find an oversimplification of facts which results in slightly different discourses to dominant ones. It is Brexiteers who get injured in the GIFs, not the whole of society. This is a dangerous discourse because these comical offerings do not reflect a discourse about the harm Brexit will do to all UK residents. It is all who live in the UK, Brexiteers and Remainers, who will suffer equally when Brexit finally does materialize.

CASE STUDY ANALYSIS TWO: 'JACOB REES-MOGG'S MESSAGE FOR THE COMMON PEOPLE' BY JOE.CO.UK

This is a visual and audio mash-up, where visuals and sounds from multiple sources are edited together to appear as a unified text. Here, some video elements from Pulp's 'Common People' are edited with images of UK Conservative MP Jacob Rees-Mogg. The audio mash-up is a simplified instrumental version of

Pulp's song edited with speech excerpts from Mogg's voice taken from speeches, media interviews and public speaking engagements. It has received over 1 million views at the time of writing. Before we start our textual analysis, we need to examine who Jacob Rees-Mogg is, who made this mash-up and what the source video is.

Context: Jacob Rees-Mogg

Since 2010, Jacob Rees-Mogg has been a high-profile Conservative Party British Parliamentarian for North East Somerset, serving as Leader of the House of Commons and Lord President of the Council since 2019. He was born into privilege, being the son of William Rees-Mogg, a former editor of *The Times* newspaper. He was educated at Eton College and the University of Oxford. He has amassed a substantial fortune working in the City and co-founding Somerset Capital Management, an investment management firm, making him one of the highest-earning politicians in the country (Wilford, 2017; Bennett, 2018). He is a divisive figure, due to his conservative public persona. He is nicknamed 'the Honourable Member for the 18th century' due to 'his Latin quips and penchant for three-piece suits'. On the one hand, this has led to him being idolized by right-wing, pro-Brexit voters who claim he can 'lead the Conservative fightback' (Wilford, 2017). On the other hand, he is reviled by the left for his support for zero-hours contracts and his opposition to raising benefit payments in line with inflation (Wilford, 2017).

Since January 2018, Mogg has been a regular feature in mainstream news due to his Chairmanship of the European Research Group (ERG). This group was first formed in July 1993 in response to growing concern about Britain's continued integration into the European community through the Maastricht Treaty. Today, the ERG is a vocal alliance of pro-Brexit Tory MPs whose focus is on withdrawing from the EU. Its membership is not public knowledge, though it is estimated that between 21 and 60 Tory MPs (including cabinet members) are part of the group. In the lead-up to the Brexit referendum, ERG members acted in an official capacity for the Vote Leave campaign. After the referendum, it was influential in shaping Theresa May's Brexit negotiations. Mogg is the media face and voice of this group.

Context: JOE.co.uk

JOE.co.uk is a part of *Maximum Media*, a digital publishing company based in Dublin, Ireland, that boasts being home to four of Ireland's most popular digital lifestyle brands, attracting 8 million users each month (Maximum Media, 2019). In March 2015, JOE.co.uk was launched and now attracts 4 million unique users. Its business model uses branded content, which relies on profits from editorial content that is paid for by advertisers (Webb, 2015).

(Continued)

Its content has been described as 'lad-lite', that is 'for men, not lads' (Southern, 2016). Unlike the now failed 'lad' publications of the 1990s such as *Loaded* and *FHM*, which have been accused of being sexist, Maximum Media founder Niall McGarry claims, 'We never spoke about women in an objectionable way; we never dallied in "lad" culture or advocated the use of drugs or getting boozed up all the time ...We targeted men interested in fashion, news, comedy and sport, who want to better themselves' (in Southern, 2016). JOE.co.uk offers short, snappy and irreverent pieces alongside longer-form content on issues like men's health and mental illness, with around 50 per cent of its content in video form.

Though there is nowhere in their publicity that claims to be of any political affiliation, a cursory view of their content reveals they are against Brexit. Furthermore, they have released a large number of video mash-ups which are critical of Conservative politicians, such as 'Theresa May's Brexit deal suffers the largest Commons defeat in history' with close to 5 million views. At the same time, JOE.co.uk also has plenty of mash-ups that positively represent the UK Labour leader (at the time) Jeremy Corbyn, such as 'No one spits bars like Jeremy Corbzy' (Figure 6.3). Uploaded in June 2017 during the UK's general election campaign, this mash-up has Corbyn's face superimposed on to Grime artist Stormzy's face in his 'Shut Up' video, while he raps a list of Labour policies. According to D'Urso (2018), mash-ups like these matter because they are aimed at young people who are traditionally hard to reach. This becomes even more relevant when we consider the 'Corbzy' mash-up has been viewed over 453,000 times (more than any video posted by a political party) while it 'clearly distils many of Labour's key policies into a 38 second long video, and was aimed at a young audience unlikely to watch a conventional political broadcast' (D'Urso, 2018).

Figure 6.3 UK Labour Party-supporting mash-up: 'No one spits bars like Jeremy Corbzy'.
Credit: JOE.co.uk

Context: 'Common People' by Pulp

'Common People' by Pulp was released in May 1995 and reached number two in the UK a month later. Pulp's frontman Jarvis Cocker wrote the song as a 'memoir about a fellow art student from his time at Central St Martins College of Art and Design: a rich girl who wanted to slum it with the "common people"' (The making of..., 2014). The song, was a critical examination of class in the UK. The song 'railed against class tourism, the naive desire of bohemian sons and daughters of fortune to blend into the underclass as some sort of cultural experience' (Keppler, 2018). It is political because 'Cocker revealed a bleak assessment of working-class life, wasting away at jobs and pool halls, "with no meaning or control", their desolation unfathomable from the outside' (Keppler, 2018). The three-chord sequence played throughout the song was composed by Cocker, while the video is dominated by Cocker dancing in a way he describes as 'just a little dance I made up on the spot ... stupid things you do' (Cocker, in The making of ..., 2014). Choosing to represent Mogg singing 'Common People' is ironic. He is a parliamentarian from a privileged background who is praised and reviled for supporting policies which do not benefit those most in need in society. The word 'common' has not only connotations of lower class, or 'the people', but also being 'common', unsophisticated and, according to Cocker, 'a real insult' (The making of ..., 2014).

Textual analysis

This mash-up is an audio and visual mix of a number of elements. The written and spoken/sung lexica are cut and paste words and sentences from Mogg edited together. This is mixed with a simplified musical version of Pulp's song. The visuals include scenes of Mogg talking in various public engagements, such as in a radio studio and a public speaking event. Other scenes have Mogg's head superimposed onto Pulp's original video. As this description indicates, there are the modes of written and spoken lexica, visuals and musical sounds. In this chapter, we concentrate on how lexical choices and visuals represent social action. We look at musical sounds in the next chapter.

Lexical analysis

The lexica to the mash-up are:

She came from Greece

She had a thirst for knowledge

(Continued)

I explained 'I went to Eton college',

That's when she …

… laughed at me.

I told her that my dad was loaded

And how I'll profit if the pound imploded

And then she cried.

Because her visa had expired.

And I said …

I want to leave the Common Market

I want to leave the Customs Union, too

Want to leave the Common Market

Want to keep out …

Foreign people like you.

But I didn't understand

Why she refused to shake my hand

We let the people have their say

Then we convinced them not to stay

Sold them falsehoods on a bus

Deflect all the blame from us

Still, May will never get it right

A no-deal Brexit is in sight

Causing Irish talks to stall

If the backstop fails we can build a wall (laughs)

I want to leave the Common Market

I want to leave the Customs Union, too

Want to leave the Common Market

Wanna watch it all slide out of view

And leave the whole economy screwed

'Cos I've got nothing else to do-o-o-.

Alright!

Lexical choices throughout the mash-up create two distinct groups of actors: Mogg and elites who support Brexit; and 'the people' who are victims of Brexit. Personal pronouns play a role in defining both groups. According to Laclau (2005) and De Cleen and Carpentier (2010), 'the people' is not a prefixed natural category, but a signifier that acquires meaning through a diversity of discourses. Its meaning changes and is fought for by different groups (Laclau, 2005: 74). For example, in their study De Cleen and Carpentier (2010) identify how 'the people' are constructed differently by Belgian extreme right-wing political groups and those opposed to them. This discursive construction is in conjunction with 'the formation of an internal antagonistic frontier separating the "people" from power' (Laclau, 2005: 224). In our mash-up, 'the people' are personified by a woman from Greece represented as 'she' and 'her' ('you' is used once), while the wider 'people' are represented as 'the people' and the pronouns 'their' and 'them'. This group is distinct from Mogg, who is represented as narrating the mash-up, so uses pronouns 'I', 'me' and 'my', while including himself as a Brexit-supporting elite, indicative in the pronouns 'we' and 'us'. Named as such, an 'us' group of Brexit-supporting elites are distinct from third-person 'she' and 'they' used to represent 'the people'.

There is only one other personal naming throughout the mash-up. This is ex-prime minister Theresa May, who is named as 'May'. This naming omits any honorifics, limiting representations of authority and power (see van Leeuwen, 1996, and Chapter 4). This negative discourse about May is reinforced with the line 'May will never get it right', where she is activated in low modality and vaguely in 'will never get it right'. This is likely referring to the many actions May performed when in charge of Brexit. This is a clear example of an overdetermination where a represented action ('never get it right') is substituted for a multitude of actions. Represented as such, no details of May's (mis)handling of Brexit are made clear, but negativity is articulated.

Mogg is emphasized and represented negatively, though not represented as powerfully as he could be. He is named 'I' eleven times, far more than any other actor. In most lines he is active and, at the beginning of each line, a prominent sentence position used for emphasis (van Dijk, 1991). In fact, 'I' is active in 'explained', 'told', 'went', 'profit', 'said' and 'want'. Most of these do not represent Mogg with transivity, suggesting a lack of power, though they all connote negativity. For example, the line 'And how I'll profit if the pound imploded' is a conditional

(Continued)

125

sentence suggesting uncertainty. Unlike 'the people' who it is presupposed will suffer because Brexit will 'leave the whole economy screwed', Mogg is represented immune to this, actually profiting from Brexit. This line recontextualizes Mogg's Somerset Capital Management company setting up a second investment fund in Ireland, after it warned its clients about the financial dangers of a hard Brexit (Quinn, 2018). Not surprisingly, this information has been used by political opponents who note the discrepancy between his company's statements about the dangers of Brexit, his company's interests in Ireland and his actions as an MP when he 'repeatedly dismissed the concerns of those worried about the financial risks of Brexit' (Quinn, 2018). Though indeed, it is likely someone with the financial clout of Mogg is likely not to suffer from the negative effects of Brexit, it is unlikely he will actually benefit from a decline in Britain's economy.

Elsewhere, the lines 'Then she cried because her visa had expired' also represents Mogg negatively while not empowering him. This is an example of an 'eventuation de-agentialization' where an action is represented as an event, as something that just happens (van Leeuwen, 1995: 96). Mogg could be represented far more powerfully with a line such as 'I refused to renew your passport'. Representations like these emphasize Mogg and negative actions without empowering him, a strategy seen throughout this mash-up.

Mogg and the elite are also represented as privileged, used to delegitimize. Being an economic elite is evident in: 'I explained "I went to Eton College"'. Here, as is the case in most lines, Mogg is active ('I explained' and 'I went'), connoting a degree of power, though neither are material processes with agency. His elite status is suggested by being educated at Eton, school to UK's most privileged since King Henry VI. Elsewhere, his economic status is represented as 'I told her that my dad was loaded'. Here, Mogg is represented in a semiotic process with agency by 'I told her', connoting a degree of power. But he is also delegitimized. We learn that Mogg is privileged not from his own hard work, but due to his father's wealth. Indeed, Mogg's father was a Baron and Lord, editor of *The Times* and filled a number of other high-profile positions. All the same, Mogg is an active businessman and the strategy used here is to discredit Mogg as one who enjoys undeserved privilege, a discourse used against other elites, such as Donald Trump.

There are also more direct ways of representing Mogg working against the people's interests. In the first chorus, Mogg sings '[I] Want to keep out Foreign people like you'. Though 'want' is a mental process, 'keep out … you' is a material process with transivity, a representation of power. However, again, these representations connote negativity. The 'you' he is addressing is the female student with an expired visa. Taking (back) control of immigration was one of the discourses of the Leave campaign and one of many reasons why people voted to leave. Some of this discourse was fuelled by racism (Shaw, 2019). Here, Mogg is represented working against a section of 'the people' actively wanting 'to keep out Foreign people', suggesting Mogg's motives for Brexit may also be racist.

But, Mogg is also represented working against all 'the people'. He sings that he wants to leave the Common Market and the Customs Union and '[I] Wanna watch it all slide out of view, And leave the whole economy screwed'. Again, though this is a mental process, suggesting limited power, presuppositions suggest something different. Presuppositions are 'a taken-for-granted, implicit claim embedded within the explicit meaning of a text or utterance' (Richardson, 2007: 63). These are powerful ideological tools (Fairclough, 1995a: 14; Richardson, 2007: 64), defined as '[t]he unsaid, the already said, the presupposed, is of particular importance in ideological analysis, in that ideologies are generally embedded within the implicit meaning of a text rather than being explicit' (Fairclough 1995b: 108). These implicit 'taken for granted' claims enforce ideologies without questioning them (Richardson, 2007: 187). Here, three things are presupposed: Brexit will ruin the economy, Mogg 'wants' to ruin the economy and he is in a position to affect the economy. Though there is almost unanimity concerning Brexit and its negative impact on the economy, there is considerable debate about what will be the effect. To represent it as 'screwed' is simplistic. The presupposition that Mogg is powerful enough to impact the economy again should be questioned. Although he is influential in the Conservative government, he is only one of a large number of voices, many of whom do not want a hard Brexit. And, finally, the presupposition that Mogg indeed wants to ruin the economy ought to be questioned. Though he wants a hard Brexit, which will be bad for the economy, it is unlikely he, as a businessman, wants to ruin the economy. It is in his interest for the UK to have a strong economy. However, these lines represent Mogg as callous, emphasized by the following line "Cos I've got nothing else to do-o-o". This is an addition, a reaction which 'represent[s] the private feelings of participants' (van Leeuwen and Wodak, 1999: 98), an action difficult to substantiate. All the same, this addition draws upon a discourse that Mogg is callous in his attitude towards 'the people'.

As mentioned previously, the pronouns 'I' and 'we' are used to construct a group of pro-Brexit elites. Like 'I', 'we' is active, but unlike 'I', 'we' have agency in most lines, connoting power, acting upon 'them', 'the people'. In lines 'We let the people have their say', and 'Then we convinced them not to stay', the elites are represented in a position to *allow* the people to have a referendum and then in an empowered position to 'convince'. Though empowerment for the most part, is a positive attribute, actions are negative, made clear with lines such as '[We] Sold them falsehoods on a bus, Deflect all the blame from us'. As part of the Vote Leave campaign, 'We send the EU £350 million a week, let's fund our NHS instead' was painted on the side of a bus. This claim has since been proven false, both in terms of how much we pay into the European Union and how post-Brexit politicians will fund the NHS.

However, in this mash-up, referring to this political campaign stunt as 'falsehoods' and deflecting blame draws upon a discourse of deceitful elites.

'We' is also used to further represent pro-Brexit elites negatively in 'If the back-stop fails we can build a wall (laughs)'. Here, the Irish border is linked to Trump's wall on the Mexican border. Both plans have caused controversy. The Irish back-stop is 'a position of last resort, to maintain an open border on the island of Ireland in the event that the UK leaves the EU without securing an all-encompassing deal' (Campbell, 2018). This was a sticking point in Brexit negotiations. At the same time, Trump tried to secure funding for a wall across the US–Mexican border to control immigration. The laugh by Mogg following the line again draws on a discourse of Mogg being uncaring and part of a 'we' with Trump, known as a right-wing populist, through the conditional representation of building a wall. Though some Brexiteers do indeed share some views with right-wing populists, there are many Brexiteers with very different views. Grouped and acting as such, a very negative discourse of Mogg and Brexiteers is articulated.

In contrast to the elites, representations of the people's actions see them represented as victims. In almost all circumstances, 'the people' are either passivated by the elite (see above), or acting and reacting to elite actions. Emotive reactions are associated with powerlessness (van Leeuwen, 1995: 86) and here 'the people' are represented as such. This creates sympathy for a powerless people opposed to a powerful and callous elite. The Greek student 'laughed' and 'cried', both semi-otic processes reacting to Mogg's actions of being educated at Eton and having an expired visa. Powerlessness is further connoted by crying, a semiotic process associated more with women than men (Caldas-Coulthard, 1994: 306). She also reacts emotively to Mogg's actions associated with keeping out foreign people by 'I didn't understand why she refused to shake my hand'. Though indeed this is a material process, it is an emotional reaction to Mogg. These reactions create sympathy towards the student and 'the people' in general. Only once are 'the people' acting and not reacting in 'She had a thirst for knowledge', though again this is a mental process. This represents the student positively, and is a far cry from some Brexit arguments which represent foreigners as out to steal UK jobs and burden the welfare state. This positive representation of the people draws upon a discourse of the people being not only victims of negative actions by the elite, but also a people who are good and correct.

Visuals

Representations of actions in the mash-up's lexica connote a (somewhat) powerful and callous pro-Brexit elite who work against the interests of 'the people' who are victims and correct. Visuals articulate similar discourses, though in very different ways. When analysing the representation of social actors, van Leeuwen (2005) tells us that one strategy to consider is who is included and who is excluded. One obvious feature is Mogg is in all visuals, connoting his importance. Though all-inclusive, he is represented negatively. Figure 6.4 sees Mogg's face edited onto Pulp frontman Jarvis Cocker. Kress and van Leeuwen (1996) and Machin (2007) note that salience can be expressed visually through devices such as potent cultural symbols, size, colour, tone, focus and fore-grounding. Mogg is salient here, as is the case throughout the mash-up. Though this is a long shot, Mogg's face is in focus and lit more brightly than the rest of the scene. Furthermore, he is 'centre stage'. However, he looks ridiculous. He is active, in a material process of 'dancing' and a semiotic process of 'singing'. These actions could be part of a positive representation, but here they are not. Cocker describes the dance Mogg is doing as the 'stupid things you do' (The making of ..., 2014). In this part of the dance, Mogg dances energetically, kick-ing like a chorus-line dancer in a Los Vegas show. Furthermore, this scene ridicules Mogg's conservative public persona through not only his actions, but also his clothing. He wears Cocker's bright-coloured jacket, black shirt open at the collar and a tan-coloured tie. This is very different than his normal conservative apparel seen in all his 'in situation' shots. In all of these, he wears a dark jacket, white shirt and dark tie.

Figure 6.4   Rees-Mogg delegitimized as ridiculous in mash-up.

Credit: JOE.co.uk

Figure 6.5 accentuates his difference to 'the people'. Here, he is in formal attire including a bow tie, something only worn on very formal occasions. Mogg is active in a semiotic process with agency, 'speaking to an audience'. This act, along with

(Continued)

his clothing, suggests his elite status as one who addresses audiences. But his audience is different to himself. This is noticeable by the representation of the spectator to the left of Mogg. He is more salient than the others through lighting, focus and being close to the centre of the image. He wears 'normal' clothes, including a dark T-shirt, as he frowns at Mogg. Though this is an emotive reaction, connoting weakness (as has been seen in the words), it also undermines Mogg, showing disapproval towards him.

Figure 6.5 'Othering' of Rees-Mogg through dress and audience reaction.

Credit: JOE.co.uk

Mogg's actions also connote a lack of engagement with viewers and the people. These draw on a discourse that the elite are not to be trusted and not one of 'the people'. Figures 6.6 and 6.7 exemplify this. In both images, Mogg is active in a semiotic process of speaking, connoting a degree of importance. However, he does not engage with the viewer, his gaze looking off camera. These are 'offer images', where images are offered for our scrutiny, connoting a lack of power, symbolic interaction and empathy with the viewer (Kress and van Leeuwen, 1996: 124). In fact, in the whole video, there is no instance where Mogg's gaze directly addresses viewers. Eyes are always off to one side. In western culture, this also signifies a lack of trust, where we are suspicious of people who do not look us in the eye when speaking.

A lack of power is further connoted through choices in camera positions. Most shots are close-ups which grant viewers a point of identification. However, many of these are taken from a high angle (notable in Figures 6.6 and 6.7), belittling his power, metaphorically not being one to look up to (Kress and van Leeuwen, 2001). These images accompany words that tell us he does not care, further drawing upon discourses of an uncaring, deceitful elite.

Figure 6.6   Rees-Mogg's lack of engagement with viewers through gaze.

Credit: JOE.co.uk

Figure 6.7   Lack of trust in Rees-Mogg through camera angles and gaze.

Credit: JOE.co.uk

The people are for the most part excluded from this mash-up. The rare few times we see them, they are visual metaphors or metonyms for 'the people'. The audience member examined above in Figure 6.5 is a metonym for the disapproving 'people'. In the dance scenes of the original Pulp video, dancers represent 'common people'. In Mogg's mash-up, dancers react to Mogg, copying his dance moves (Figure 6.8). Furthermore, they dance with a lack of energy and conviction, robotically and mindlessly doing as they are told. Here, 'the people' are victims of the elite; powerless by metaphorically being manipulated and reacting to the elite's (Mogg) actions.

(Continued)

Figure 6.8   'The people' as victims of Rees-Mogg and the elite.

Credit: JOE.co.uk

Musical sounds

Musical sounds play a significant role in articulating discourses of an elite that is out of touch with the people. However, this chapter's focus is on the visual and lexical representations of action. A comprehensive look at sounds comes in Chapter 7 and this mash-up is used as an example of how musical sounds articulate discourses in digital popular culture.

SUMMARY

In this chapter we briefly studied animations and then performed a detailed analysis of a mash-up. These are significant parts of our daily consumption of digital popular culture. We dipped into our toolkit and decided that one very useful tool for analysing these is considering the lexical and visual representation of social action. Our analysis of GIFs reveals discourses similar to the popular dominant ones drawn upon, though simplification of facts result in discourses that are not quite the same. We found that GIFs represent Brexiteers as self-harming, which allows Remainers to laugh at them. This is a discourse somewhat different than the public discourse that the UK is harming itself. Though indeed, these make us laugh because we are 'taking the micky' out of the perceived stupidity of Brexiteers, the GIFs ignore the fact that it is not just Brexiteers who are paying for Brexit. Indeed, the economic, cultural and social burden of Brexit will be shared across the whole of the UK and Europe regardless of one's stance on Brexit. In this sense, analysing the representation of social actions reveals that the GIFs are misleading and not something which contributes to dialogue, but misinforms.

Likewise, the analysis of social actions in our mash-up also uncovers discourses that are based on the simplification of facts. Here, it reveals that Brexit has been reduced to a polemic of 'us' the people struggling against 'them' Brexiteer elites. Discourses lean on a type of populism, where the elite are represented as callous and working against the interests of the people. Though this is a discourse we experience daily in other media, there is no room in these mash-ups for thought. They are indictments of guilt before trial. So, although this mash-up is good fun and brings to light actors involved in Brexit, issues are distorted and people's views are simplified. This results in hardening of positions, not engaged discussions. Our analysis also reveals how very complex issues are simplified, relying on stereotypes of elites, groups of voters and a unified people. These representations are far from reality. These do little to inform debate about the merits and dangers of Brexit. What they do is polarize positions into simple binary opposites, leaving little room for informed debate. It is through this detailed analysis that we can reveal such ideological work.

Examining the representation of social actions is only one of many 'tools' we can use to analyse GIFs and mash-ups. Even the above analyses were not restricted to just this 'tool'. We also considered the representation of social actors, the role of presuppositions and the use of camera shots, to name but a few. However, we have expanded out toolkit to give us more ways into a text. In the next chapter we delve deeper into the role of metaphors, representations of place and musical sounds in promotional music videos.

SUGGESTED READINGS

Laclau, E. (2005) *On Populist Reason*. London: Verso.

This seminal work is a cornerstone of thinking on populism, making it essential for understanding the intricacies of populism. It is highly recommended for anyone who wants to learn more about this subject.

van Leeuwen, T. (1995) Representing social action. *Discourse and Society*, 6(1): 81–106.

This article, like most writings from Theo van Leeuwen, offers a set of well-thought-out analytical tools. It is a great way to become acquainted with analysing the representation of social action. Though this article considers lexica only, the ideas from this article run through this chapter's multimodal analysis. Van Leeuwen's later work on multimodal communication also does this.

Way, L. (2018b) Turkish newspapers and how they use Brexit for domestic political gain, in Ridge-Newman, A. (ed.) *EU Referendum and the Media: National And International Perspectives*. London and New York: Palgrave Macmillan. pp. 281–294.

This chapter is an example of how to consider the representation of Brexit in news discursively. It is one chapter in a collection that offers a wide international survey of how the media dealt with Brexit. Most of this is not from a discursive perspective, but it adds a lot of understanding about Brexit and the media globally.

Zappettini, F. and Krzyżanowski, M. (2019) 'Brexit' in media and political discourses: from national populist imaginary to cross-national social and political crisis. *Critical Discourse Studies*, 16(4): 381–388.

This article is a very good example of how we can use critical discourse analysis to reveal discourses about Brexit in the media from two distinguished critical discourse analysis scholars.

7

ANALYSING MUSIC VIDEOS
Protest Against Politicians in Musical Sounds, the Representation of Place and Metaphors

---

CHAPTER OBJECTIVES

- Identify the importance of music videos.
- Understand how metaphors play a key role in music.
- Understand the importance of the representation of place in music videos.
- Understand how 'domains of music' produce meanings and play a role in articulating discourses.
- Apply an analysis of the sounds used in a musical mash-up.
- Apply an analysis of metaphors, the representation of place and sounds to a 'political' music video.

KEY CONCEPTS

- Digital popular culture has deeply affected not only *what* music we experience but also *how* we experience it.
- Both 'official' promotional videos and fan-made ones entertain, inform and help form identities and social relations.
- Metaphors are a representational strategy in which power operates.

(Continued)

- Representations of place in music affect our understanding of places, rein-forcing myths and providing listeners with a sense of identity, ethnicity, social activism and politics.
- Scholars (Cooke, 1959; Tagg, 1984 and 1990; van Leeuwen, 1999; Machin, 2010) have produced a semiotics of sounds that is context dependent.
- Van Leeuwen (1999) categorizes these into domains of sound (perspective, inter-acting sounds, timing, melody, voice, modality), each with meaning potential.

INTRODUCTION

I remember when MTV was launched back in August 1981. I was not wit-ness to the airing of 'Video Killed the Radio Star' by The Buggles, the first video aired by MTV, but whenever I found a venue that played MTV, I would be there. I remember feeling the world of pop music had just opened up a whole new realm of pleasures and I was able to experience music like never before. The slick visuals were completely different than those on television programmes like *Top of the Pops*, album covers or still photographs in music magazines such as *NME*. This was a chance to see my heroes differently. I have had a similar experience with YouTube. Unlike during the time of MTV, when most of the videos the VJ selected were not anything I wanted to see or hear, YouTube gives me the same access to music videos – but now I get to choose.

In this chapter, we are going to delve into one of digital media's most used areas – music. Specifically, we are going to consider how to analyse popular music artefacts on YouTube. To do this, we need to consider the importance of music video. We then add to our analytical toolkit by consid-ering not only how to analyse sounds, but also the important roles played by metaphors and the representation of place, essential components of music video. We perform two analyses in this chapter. First, we consider the roles of musical sounds in the 'Rees-Mogg's message for the common people' ('Mogg's message') mash-up examined in Chapter 6. We then analyse the roles of musical sounds, alongside the visual and lexical representation of place and metaphors in Eminem's 'The Storm'. It is through these examples that we can observe how musicology-informed MCDS can reveal discourses in music in digital popular culture.

THE IMPORTANCE OF ONLINE MUSIC VIDEO

Digital popular culture has deeply affected not only what music we experience but also how we experience it. Where once we would go buy a CD, now we are more likely to view a video on YouTube; music video has 'segue[d] seamlessly into emergent digital modes of production and, more recently, distribution' (Arnold et al., 2017: 2). Music video platforms (YouTube, Spotify, MySpace) not only offer commercial official promotional videos, but also an 'influx of "homemade" music videos' (2017: 9). Sometimes, fan-made videos become 'official' ones, such as Kate Tempest's 'Europe is Lost' and Saian's 'Feleğin Çemberine 40 Kurşun'. Furthermore, 'Since video editing technology first became ubiquitous across web-enabled electronic devices, YouTube's user generated content has arguably been as important as Vevo: the multinational collaboration between Sony Music Entertainment and Universal Music Group which is responsible for a large amount of 'official' music video on YouTube' (2017: 12). Yes, downloads, streaming and video platforms such as YouTube offer new spaces for commercial consolidation and creative freedom, but music video can be source material or disguarded as 'of more significance [are] online videos made by vloggers and YouTubers' (Manghani, 2017: 37). These new media artefacts which source videos include parody, as we examine in Chapter 8. These internet videos, along with their originals 'provide a means for a younger generation to communicate and experiment with the forming of identities and social connections – a process which still typically concerns itself with the "pleasures" of fashion and the body within a limited political purview' (2017: 40).This discussion thus far suggests our 'listening' behaviour has also changed. Though always multimodal in nature, digitally distributed pop has 'created a state where some listeners now listen to music by looking at it. Adding this layer has allowed artists to add new nuance, new depth, new ways to convey their messages' (Arnold et al., 2017: 5).

Music video consumption is important. Not only does it allow artists and fans to communicate in different ways than simply listening to a song, it also allows fans to make their own statements. This can be in the form of making their own video to an artist's music, making their own video to their own song, bypassing the industry, or watching, liking and/or commenting on videos (see Chapter 4). This is not without its limits, as we also discussed in Chapter 4. Although fan-sourced videos do offer political possibilities, Manghani (2017: 39) states that 'It is notable, for example, that YouTubers are generally almost all middle-class, upwardly mobile young people (though this is equally true of most pop musicians over the years).'

ANALYTICAL TOOLS: METAPHOR, THE REPRESENTATION OF PLACE AND MUSICAL SOUNDS

In this chapter we consider how to examine political discourses in two musical artefacts. Our lyrical and visual analysis will use the tools we have considered thus far in the book, as well as the role of metaphors and the representation of place. Our musical analysis will examine the six domains of sound. Let's take a closer look at our new analytical tools.

Metaphor

According to Dictionary.com, a metaphor is 'a figure of speech in which a term or phrase is applied to something to which it is not literally applicable in order to suggest a resemblance'. But the choice of what figure of speech to use carries with it connotations which lean on particular discourses at the expense of others. We, as analysts, must consider what metaphors are used to represent something/ somebody and what discourses they articulate. This can be thought of in terms of how producers map a 'source' domain on the semantic field of the 'target' domain (Lakoff and Johnson, 1980). The role of metaphors is highlighted in this chapter because popular music tends to rely on metaphor, possibly more so than other communicative modes (Way, 2015). Though aesthetically pleasing, metaphors are a powerful representative strategy. It 'is not only a matter of language usage or poetic license, but a functional mechanism which affects the way we think, act and experience reality' (Lakoff and Johnson, 1980 in Flowerdew and Leong, 2007: 275). They are a powerful tool used to represent aspects of the world in certain ways (Lakoff and Johnson, 1980). They can have specifically political roles, strengthening, reproducing or subverting relations of power. Mottier (2008: 184) notes how 'metaphors classify and order reality, social and political classifications and ordering … [they are] the vehicle through which power operates'. It is for these reasons that we examine them in detail.

Representation of place

Representations of place are also revealing. These are powerful, affecting our understanding of places, reinforcing myths and providing listeners with a sense of identity (Forman, 2002). Naming bands after local places such as Ladysmith Black Mambaso and Cypress Hill are 'evocative of place, and often history and rurality' (Connell and Gibson, 2003: 43). Place can also be represented in lyrics and visuals. Of course, genre deeply determines how places are represented.

For example, rapper xxxtentacion singing about country streams and flowing prairie grass sounds as strange to us as Garth Brooks singing about life in New York slums. In song, analysis of settings is 'highly revealing about the world being communicated' (Machin, 2010: 92) and 'can be used to understand broader social relations and trends, including identity, ethnicity, attachment to place, cultural economies, social activism, and politics' (Johansson and Bell, 2009: 2). Representations of place also suggest authenticity. Urban dwelling is an important part of authenticating bands within rock genres and movement is associated with 'freedom and adventure' (Connell and Gibson, 2003: 37). Certain aspects of urban landscapes, such as 'the hood', are essential in authenticating rap. In contrast, rural settings are part of authenticating folk and country, with rural spaces echoing mobility (2003: 82). References to the outdoors draw upon folk and country aesthetics and authenticity, favouring rural areas which produce an 'invented geography ... of a bygone natural environment' (2003: 39). So, this is part of our analysis.

Musical sounds

As discussed in Chapter 2, musical sounds communicate to us affectively, meanings deeply influenced by context. A critical approach to studying meanings in music must recognize the importance of context and 'knowingly position the interpreter [of music] in relation to [context]' (Cook, 1990: 123). Scholars from a number of fields have studied the semiotics of sounds in order to consider their meaning potentials. Critical musicologists such as Walser (1995) have examined popular music songs including Public Enemy's 'Fight the Power' considering in detail the role of musical sounds. Some cognitive linguistics have also considered the semiotics of music. For example, Zbikowski (2015: 148) believes 'specific sequences of patterned sound' are key to understanding music's meanings, along with social and cultural context. In trying to ascribe meanings to music we need to understand that music is not a language in the same sense as written text. As Philip Brett tells us, music is 'only by imperfect analogy called a language, "the" language of feeling' (in Cook, 1990: 122). It is in this theoretical context that we consider the semiotics of sound.

Scholars that we lean on in this chapter are Deryck Cooke (1959), Philip Tagg (1984 and 1990), Theo van Leeuwen (1999) and David Machin (2010). Each of these scholars have built on the work of their predecessors. Much of this has formed the bedrock of almost all examinations of music and meaning from a MCDS approach (see Way, 2018a, for a summary). This work is informed not just by each other's work but also by musicology. As such, our approach builds on this previous work, giving us a 'hindsight' advantage of employing what works best in revealing discourses articulated in music.

139

What follows now is the work of these scholars summarized for convenience, following the six domains of sound outlined in van Leeuwen's (1999) *Speech, Music, Sound*. These are perspective, time, interacting sounds, melody, voice quality and timbre, and modality. For the most part, I apply these ideas to recorded sound, as this is what we experience in online music videos.

Perspective

Perspective refers to both a metaphoric social distance and a hierarchy created by the 'closeness' of sounds. Social distance in music is similar to the idea of how an image is framed – a close-up suggesting a small social distance as opposed to a long shot (see Chapter 5). How voice and instruments are recorded, usually related to microphone position, connotes not just physical distance, but also social distance. So, intimacy can be connoted through a whispered voice and address us as though we share a personal relationship. For example, famous crooners like Frank Sinatra and Nat King Cole sang sentimental songs with the help of a closely miked voice to connote an 'intimate, personal relationship with fans that worked best for domestic listeners' (Frith, 1988: 19). We can compare this to the rasping voices of hard rock, loud and high, shouting and screaming to be heard over the noise of the city (Tagg, 1990: 112). So, informality and intimacy is connoted through the closely miked, relaxed, casual voice while distance and (at times) formality is conveyed through the louder, higher and tenser voice.

Perspective is also realized by the relative loudness of simultaneous sounds. Sounds can be recorded so they sound close, middling or far away or as 'figure', 'ground' and 'field' (Schafer, 1977: 157). Deciding what sound become the figure or the field connotes a hierarchy where some sounds are treated 'as more import-ant than others' (1977: 157). Most pop music and advertisements individualize a singer, shown importance in a hierarchy of sound by being 'on top' of the musical accompaniment (Tagg, 1990: 111). It is sounds that are the 'figure' that listeners 'must attend to and/or react to and/or act upon, while background sounds are "heard but not listened to", disattended, treated as something listeners do not need to react to or act upon' (van Leeuwen, 1999: 16).

Time

Time can be natural, such as the cycles of days, or artificial, manufactured by humans, such as the movement of hands on a clock. Since the Middle Ages, west-ern music has become divided and measured, 'overwhelmingly dominated by the principle of a regular, unvarying, machine-like beat, to which all voices and instruments had to submit' (Harman et al., 1962: 122; van Leeuwen, 1999: 38).

Music complying by the 'rules' of clock time or the metronome connote just that: compliance. For example, dance music (such as disco) 'represents a high degree of affective acceptance of and identification with clock time, digitally exact rhythm and hence with the system in which this time sense dominates' (Tagg, 1984: 32). Subverting metronome timing by notes in the melody anticipating and delaying the beat is common in Afro-American-inspired music such as blues and rock. It is an attempt to 'gain some control over time through musical expression' by 'subvert[ing] the implacable exactitude of natural science, computers and clock time' (Tagg, 1990: 112).

Tempo of a song is another important aspect of timing. Most pop songs' tempos are in the same range as our heart beats. So, like the speed of our hearts, a faster tempo in music may connote excitement or fear while a slower tempo relaxation or fatigue. Tempo is 'an important parameter in determining the human/biological aspect of an affective relationship to time' (Tagg, 1984: 22). Timing in music outside our normal heart beat range is 'non-human' and may signify supernatural events (van Leeuwen, 1999: 53).

Interacting sounds

Sounds can 'interact' sequentiality and simultaneity, both having meaning potential related to relations of power. Turn-taking is called 'antiphony' and suggests difference or opposition between two (or more) groups of voices. These are usually not equal groups, commonly in the form of call and response where the caller is represented as a leader with power. Scholars note that most times in popular music, this is gendered where 'the leader is a male singer and the chorus a group of female "back up" vocalists, which enacts (from the point of view of the musicians) and represents (from the point of view of the audience) a relationship of male dominance' (van Leeuwen, 1999: 73). Connotations of power are further articulated if there is a single male lead. Monologues can 'express dominance', though also 'extreme isolation and loneliness' depending on context (1999: 72).

For the most part, musical sounds in western music interact simultaneously. How these interact again suggests power. Sounds can 'interlock', meaning no sound is dominant while each does different things, such as when a band warms up. The effect may be one of 'integrated, contrapuntal unity, or extreme heterogeneity and diffuseness' (Lomax, 1968: 156). 'Social unison' involves all voices and/or instruments singing or playing the same notes at the same time. This carries connotations of 'solidarity, consensus, a positive sense of joint experience and belonging to a group' but also 'conformity, strict disciplining and a lack of individuality' (van Leeuwen, 1999: 79). 'Social heterogeneity' sees several voices and/or instruments combine and intertwine, with each sound possessing musical interest and value. This connotes that 'there is no sense of individuality as something in opposition to or irreconcilable with society … people say their own thing, yet fit together in a harmonious (or occasionally disharmonious) sounding whole' (1999: 80). Finally, 'Social domination' involves one dominant voice with other sounds as accompaniment, support and back-up. This is common in most popular music where sounds are hierarchized and dominance such as leader–group interaction is suggested.

Melody

We examine six aspects of melody that contribute to meaning-making. Melodic continuity relates to the key of a song. In western music, a melody usually finishes on the key note of the 'tonic'. This makes the melody sound finished, having a unifying function. Melodies that do not finish on the tonic suggest unfinished business. Melodic patterns consider the upward or lower direction of the melody. Cooke (1959: 133) tells us that ascending melodies express 'outgoing', 'active' emotions, descending melodies suggest 'incoming', 'passive' emotions, and arched melodies combine the two. This aspect of melody is closely related to pitch movement. Ascending melodic movements are more 'active', more 'outgoing' and 'dynamic' than descending melodies (1959: 102). This is also a consideration in our efforts as we sing: ascending movement requiring more effort, descending decreasing effort. Van Leeuwen (1999: 103) suggests 'Rising pitch can energize, rally listeners together for the sake of some joint activity or cause. Falling pitch can relax and soothe listeners, make them turn inward and focus on their thoughts and feelings.' Depending on context, a descending pitch movement can also suggest a lack of energy and negativity.

Pitch range is another aspect of melody with meaning potential. Melodies can move in large or small intervals. A wide pitch range takes more energy to produce and connotes the venting of strong feelings such as excitement, shock, grief or joy. A narrow pitch range suggests the constraining of strong feelings due to any number of reasons such as the desire to conceal emotions, modesty, tiredness, or being scared. Pitch level again relates to the amount of effort needed to vocalize. To sing at a higher pitch level generally takes more effort than a lower one. Male rock singers raise pitch by about one octave above normal speech to express 'despair, celebration or anger, the dominant character of vocal delivery in rock is one of effort and urgency' (Tagg, 1990: 112). High-pitched voices tend to be loud, assertive and 'public', as in the case of the male rock singer, but they are usually produced by small people, animals and machines; lower pitched sounds are usually produced by large people, animals, music instruments and machines. These 'are often seen as threatening and dangerous' (van Leeuwen, 1999: 108). Articulation of the melodic phrase considers how notes are 'attacked' by producers. They can be smoothly put together or in short separate stabs, each connoting levels of energy. It takes more energy to perform a series of separate attacks than one long connected motion, so a disjunctive sound production can come to stand for 'a lively and energetic approach, or a bold and forceful attack' while connectivity suggests a smoother, more relaxed or sensual approach (1999: 110).

The final aspect of melody we consider is the notes played and sung by music producers. This aspect of our musical analysis is one of the very few areas for which we need a working knowledge of music. Saying that, you can find most of the notes you need for analysis online. Cooke (1959) believes different notes and patterns of notes in a melody are commonly used in western music and communicate certain ideas and moods to its audience. To do this part of the analysis, you have to know the key of the song and the notes that make up the scale associated with the key. You have to know the eight notes that produce the octave associated with the key. In this analysis, note one and note eight are one octave apart. Each one of these notes (one to eight) has a meaning potential, according to Cooke. Machin (2010: 218) summarizes these meaning potentials well and I replicate them here:

1 – anchoring, stable

2 – something in between, the promise of something else

3 – stable and happy

Minor 3 – stable but sad or painful

4 – building, creating space

5 – stable, like the 1st note

6 – generally happy like the 3rd

7 – slightly thoughtful and longing

Minor 7 – pain, sadness.

Voice quality and timbre

Think about how your voice 'sounds different' than your mother's or your father's voices. This is what we call our voice quality and timbre. Voice qualities include rough versus smooth, tense versus lax, breathiness, soft and loud, high and low, and vibrato versus plain. And all these qualities carry meaning potentials.

A rough voice has the characteristics of friction, hoarseness, harshness, rasp while smooth is clean-sounding, well oiled. Rough voices are mostly heard in male voices or low-register instruments and are linked to male assertiveness (Lomax, 1968: 192). These are valued by some music genres (blues, jazz, gospel, rock) and not in others (western classical music and some pop). We can easily manipulate some aspects of our voice. For example, when we tense the muscles in our throat, our voice becomes higher, sharper and more tense. This is not only usually associated with us being tense, but it also represents tension and may connote aggression, repression, excitement, fright, anguish, scorn and sarcasm, 'whenever things are not casual, laid back and informal'; the opposite is suggested by a wide open relaxed throat sound (Fonagy and Magdics, 1972: 286; van Leeuwen, 1999: 131). Another strategy used with our voice is the amount of breathiness. Think about when you are very close to someone, you are likely to hear them breathe while they talk. In recorded music, breathiness in voice and instruments is associated with softness and intimacy. Recordings of Marilyn Monroe come to mind.

Some aspects of our voice overlap with more general observations already discussed. For example, the softness and loudness of our voices are associated with distance and social distance. High and low pitch range have also been discussed, though here we can consider gender. Men use a higher pitch range to assert themselves and dominate, while speaking in a low range can be used to make themselves vocally small, unless enhanced with booming bass which can be overbearing. Women may use low pitch to be assertive, though loudness decreases – creating the 'dangerous woman' stereotype. They may also speak in a high pitch that can be seen as 'belittling themselves' or loud which evokes the 'shrill'.

'Vibrato' is the trembling/wavering sound we hear in people's voices. This is associated with emotions such as love and fear. On the contrary, a voice which is flawless in these terms may suggest an uncompromising, unwavering solidness. Nasality is a vocal sound associated with tension which explains why 'pinched and nasal tones pervade many of the sounds of pain, deprivation and sorrow' (Lomax, 1968: 193). There are usually negative value judgements associated with nasal sounds while less nasal sounds may connote inhibition and repression, stress, control or restraint.

Modality

Modality is the act of assigning a degree of truth to a representation. In written language we can write 'I am walking to the shop' or 'Perhaps I may walk to the shop'. The first representation has far more certainty than the second one. So, 'speakers or writers assign modality to their assertions to express *as how true* they would like these representations to be taken' (van Leeuwen, 1999: 156, emphasis original). This can also be expressed musically by manipulating pitch range, duration variation, dynamic range, perspective depth, degrees of fluctuation, degrees of friction, absorption rate and degree of directionality. These aspects of sound may be recorded to sound 'natural' to increase their certainty, believability or manipulated to sound unnatural. Depending on context, these may be used to emphasize emotions or de-emphasize humanity.

CASE STUDY ANALYSIS: A MUSICAL MASH-UP AND A MUSICAL CYPHER AGAINST GOVERNMENT POLICIES

It is how metaphors are used, places are represented and sounds are manipulated by music producers that helps determine meanings in online music offerings. As is the case with all social semiotics, these factors alone do not dictate what fans understand, but they identify experiential meaning potential. Intertextual, social, political, consumption and production contexts all play roles in defining these potentials. It is now time to apply some of these concepts to two case studies. In the first case study, we return to the music mash-up we analysed in the previous chapter. We confine our analysis to the musical sounds, seeing as we have already examined how the visuals and lyrics represent social action. In the second analysis, we look at all three foci of this chapter in a music video. In both, it is obvious that these aspects of music play key roles in articulating political discourses.

CASE STUDY ANALYSIS ONE: 'REES-MOGG'S MESSAGE FOR THE COMMON PEOPLE' MUSICAL MASH-UP

In the last chapter, we analysed how the representation of social action in visuals and lexical choices in 'Mogg's message' articulates discourses of populism where the elite are represented as out of touch, cold and calculating and 'the people' as their victims. We now return to this mash-up and consider the role musical sounds take.

(Continued)

The music in the mash-up is a simplified version of Pulp's 'Common People', though both are based on a three-chord progression (C, G7 and F) in the key of C. Musical choices by this mash-up's producers connote a lack of emotion. With lyrics and visuals, this quality can be ascribed to Mogg. Together lyrics, visuals and musical sounds articulate a discourse that the elite, personified in Mogg, are 'inhuman' and callous while they victimize 'us the people'. For this analysis, we apply as many of the musical domains identified above that are relevant to our analysis.

Remember, perspective is concerned with the relative closeness of sounds. In the mash-up, Mogg's voice is upfront in the mix. This suggests that what he is saying is important. Seeing that most of this articulates a discourse of an unfeeling elite (see last chapter), this is emphasized in the mix. Behind his vocals, instrumentation is simplistic, unlike in the original song by Pulp. In the original, there is a large list of instruments, both electronic and acoustic that 'filled a 48-track tape and created a multi-layered sound' (Classic tracks: Pulp, 2013). In 'Mogg's message', many of the tonal characteristics such as keyboard sounds remain. However, what is missing are the flourishes, instrumentation and nuances noticeable in the original. Historically, protest songs, from 'zipper' songs by the Weavers in the 1950s to songs that accompanied the American civil rights movement, have been simplistic. This is key to remembering, playing and reusing music for a variety of causes (Eyerman and Jamison, 1998: 102). In 'Mogg's message', the same simplicity is heard. Other than ease of remembering, playing and reusing (the mash-up itself a reusing of Pulp's song), simplicity serves other purposes. The simplistic instrumentation in 'Mogg's message' helps us focus more on Mogg's voice, his voice not having to compete for our attention with other sounds. Its simplicity also connotes a type of certainty, or modality about 'Mogg's message' – a simplistic certainty that elites are callous, out of touch and against the 'people's' interests.

The manipulation of time contributes to the idea that Mogg is uncool, 'unhuman' and inauthentic, being part of the system. In the original Pulp song, tempo fluctuates between 90 and 160 beats per minute. Producer Chris Thomas claimed this fluctuating 'is absolutely intrinsic to the [song's] excitement'. In 'Mogg's message', timing remains perfectly consistent at around 72 beats per minute. This choice has two connotations. First, like our heart beats, a slower tempo in a song suggests less excitement than a faster one. Compared to the original song, this slower tempo presents Mogg as a bit of a bore. Second, the consistent tempo suggests an 'unnatural' mechanical obedience to 'the system' (Tagg, 1984), emphasizing the idea that Mogg is unhuman, robotic and uncaring, which is reinforced in the lyrics and visuals.

A number of melodic choices further connote negativity surrounding Mogg and the elite. The song's melody relies on the first, fourth and fifth notes. These choices of notes suggest Mogg is boring. The first and fifth (C and G7) anchor the melody and connote stability, but also the pedestrian, the everyday, boring, stuffy (Cooke, 1959). The fourth (F) is associated with building or moving forward. In the context of the mash-up, relying on these notes suggests Mogg is not only boring and uncool. They also suggest there are changes afoot. Images and lyrics point to negative changes associated with the actions of the elite and Brexit.

Pitch movement in singing phrases can be characterized as descending. This makes sense. In the original song, Cocker represents the hardships of working-class life negatively, not as something students should glamourize (see Chapter 6). This same melodic pitch movement is present in 'Mogg's message'. Near the end of every two or three lines, the singing melody descends. This is most obvious in the choruses. In the final chorus, Mogg sings 'I want to leave the Common Market, I want to leave the customs union too, Wanna watch it all slide out of view, Leave the whole economy screwed, 'Cos I've got nothing else to do'. During this section, we see the most variation in notes sung throughout the mash-up. Figure 7.1 is a visual representation of the notes sung, where the number one and eight are the key note of C. As this image illustrates, though pitch range is fairly static (more on this below), the general pitch movement is descending, the chorus starting on the F, rising to the G, before slowly descending down to the C. This downward pitch movement connotes a lack of energy and negativity towards Mogg (Cooke, 1959), further articulated in lyrics and visuals.

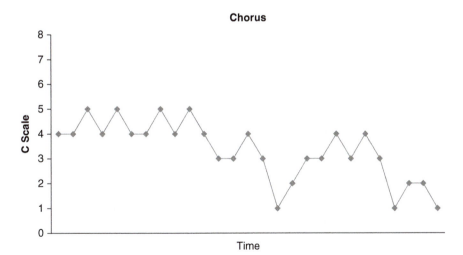

Chorus

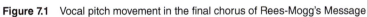

Figure 7.1 Vocal pitch movement in the final chorus of Rees-Mogg's Message

(Continued)

Despite a downward pitch direction in vocals, the song's instrumental and vocal melodies may be characterized as fairly static. As mentioned above, the song is based around a three-note progression of C, F and G7. Figure 7.2 is a visual representation of a typical vocal line in the chorus. This is fairly static for the most part with most of the line sung on one note (F) and then moving up one note on the scale twice to the G. A melody like this connotes 'very little outward giving of emotion or positive energy' (Machin, 2010). Again, the original is good to use as a comparison. For the first minute and 40 seconds, Cocker sings the same few notes, like 'Mogg's message'. Here, constrained emotional 'coolness' is connoted. In the case of 'Mogg's message', there is also a coolness in emotions, though without Cocker's positive connotations. Both Cocker and Mogg sing in a low pitch, suggesting 'feeling down' and also gravity (Cooke, 1959; Machin, 2010). However, in the second half of the original, Cocker raises his voice a whole octave as the tempo increases. Together these connote excitement, agitation and possibly anger. On the contrary, Mogg sings the whole mash-up without change in pitch, suggesting a lack of emotion despite lyrics that many viewers would find emotionally charged, further connoting callousness.

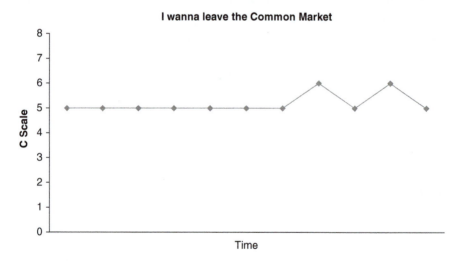

Figure 7.2   Static vocal melody throughout most of Rees-Mogg's Message

Vocal style further alienates listeners from Mogg and the elite. Again, a comparison with the original helps emphasize this point. In the original, Cocker's voice at times during the first minute and 40 seconds is very breathy, sometimes a whisper, connoting intimacy (van Leeuwen, 1999). Later, when pitch is raised, his throat tenses suggesting agitation and excitement. Between lines, we can hear his breathing, suggesting he is close to us, even when he is excited. In 'Mogg's message', throat muscles sound tense throughout. Many of the bass tones disappear, making him sound higher, sharper and 'more tense'. Breathiness is omitted. These choices do not connote a warm and compassionate politician, but one who is cold and calculating.

Choices made in the mash-up's production contribute to a modality that suggests Mogg is unhuman. This is seen in the simplification of instrumentation (discussed above) and in the manipulation of time in Mogg's vocal montage. As observed above, in Pulp's 'Common People', vocal tempo is variable, at times excited and at other times giving us time to contemplate lyrics. In 'Mogg's message', the vocal montage includes unnatural pauses and rhythms. It is a very rough montage, a lot like a mechanical recording we hear in airports announcing flight numbers and arrivals. This unnaturalness of his voice is further enhanced by the use of auto-tune. It is obvious that auto-tune has been used extensively on his voice so that he sounds like he is actually singing the words in tune to the instrumentation. However, this is done in a way that makes him sound robotic, reducing how real or authentic he sounds. Auto-tune can be done in much more subtle ways, evidenced in many of the pop songs we enjoy. But here, it has been left rough, to enhance an unnatural sound. The unnaturalness of his voice is also noticeable in the speed of his speech. Here, it is consistently very fast. This is unnatural if you think about the way we normally speak and the original song, both characterized by pauses and changes in speed. These are used for emphasis, to express excitement and to give listeners time for contemplation. By representing Mogg without these qualities, he is again represented as unnatural. The exception to this is the pause that follows the line 'Want to keep out Foreign people like you'. Here, a pause is added for emphasis. It makes this racist line stand out, emphasizing a discourse that Mogg and Brexiteers are racists.

As we can see, musical choices communicate a lot to us listeners. The above analysis illustrates how musical sounds, in relation with other intra-textual modes (lyrics and visuals) and extra-textual factors, articulate political discourses. This analysis is informed by these contextual factors outlined in the previous chapter. What follows now is an analysis that considers all three foci of our chapter: metaphors, representation of place and the role of musical sounds.

CASE STUDY ANALYSIS TWO: EMINEM'S 'THE STORM'

Context: Eminem

Marshall Bruce Mathers III, or Eminem, has been a global success since his debut album *Infinity* in 1996. He has won numerous awards including Grammies and Academy Awards, as well as racking up American and worldwide best-selling albums. He has also never been shy of articulating his political views in and out-side his music. In 2002's 'the Eminem Show' music video, his character rips up the American constitution. Lyrics in 2004's 'Encore' attack George W. Bush's Iraq war. In a 2012 interview, he confirmed he had voted for President Obama, while in 2015, in a freestyle rap, he critiqued both Donald Trump and Hillary Clinton as presidential candidates. In 2016, he used a freestyle rap to express his concerns about the dangers of Trump as president and the following year led a 'Fuck Trump' chant at the Reading Festival (UK).

But in this chapter we consider his video recorded freestyle rap 'The Storm' which he revealed on Twitter and was played at the Black Entertainment Tele-vision Awards on 10 October 2017. It has been considered 'one of his most upfront freestyles ever, blasting the "racist" Donald Trump in a series of brash, take-no-prisoners lines' (Milton, 2017). It directly addresses Trump 'on topics including the NFL protest, America's recent spate of hurricanes, Trump's lavish trips to "his golf resorts and his mansions" and more' (Connick, 2017). These topics and more are represented in the lyrics of his rap, Marshall claiming the rap is a protest over 'injustices' he ascribes to Trump. Referring to his rap, he claims 'We have a president who does not care about everybody in our country; he is not the president for all of us, he is the president for some of us. He knows what he's doing' (Songfacts, 2017). This rap is his chance to 'speak out' over the president. What we do here is consider how Eminem uses representations of place, metaphors and musical sounds to not only express his political views but also authenticate himself as the voice of Black America. Before we examine these in detail, we define what we mean by authenticity.

Context: Authenticity

Though authenticity in music generates considerable debate (Moore, 2002), recent studies have found it useful to view it as the quality of 'sincerity' or 'play-ing from the heart' that listeners ascribe to performers (2002: 210). How this is assigned is socially, historically and genre-dependent – by music producers and fans alike. Notions of authenticity have their roots in the Romantic tradition where artistic creativity was seen as coming from the soul, as opposed to something that emerged from society (Machin, 2010). These beliefs contribute to the dichotomy of authentic verses 'establishment'. Authenticity is dependent on 'the inauthentic other', such as authentic rock versus inauthentic pop (Auslander, 1999: 71).

Different semiotic resources are used based on genre and subgenre to connote authenticity. So, a tightly choreographed dance routine may signify authenticity in a soul-influenced pop group but would be disastrous for a rock group. Rock's authenticity is determined by live performance and being anti-establishment (Frith, 1981; Auslander, 1999: 70). But even within the genre of rock, there are 'many forms of rock authenticity', varying between its many subgenres and across time, constantly reinventing what is authentic and new and what is not (Grossberg, 1992: 202). Likewise, in American hip hop, the genre associated with our case study, authenticity is articulated through lyrics which reveal personal truths, representing a geographical background linked to lived experiences in predominantly black urban neighbourhoods (Fraley, 2009: 43).

Fans are also active in decisions about authenticity (Moore, 2002; Hibbett, 2005; Machin, 2010). Authenticity and inauthenticity are decided on by fans based on how they 'judge people's sincerity generally' (Frith, 1996: 71). We, as fans, determine the legitimacy of political intervention by a musician (Street, 2013: 50). And this legitimacy is 'not simply there in the music; they are there because the way we think about music puts them there' (Cook, 1998: 14). These judgements are based on not only musical sounds, 'but also [on] prior musical and extramusical knowledge and belief' (Auslander, 1999: 76). This is important in our study of Eminem, who has been represented over time as legitimate, living in Detroit and making political statements throughout his career.

But authenticity is not just about musicians. Music commodities also express ideas of authenticity about fans and others multimodally. Moore (2002) identifies three levels in which authenticity can be articulated and experienced. There is first-person authenticity which 'arises when an originator (composer, performer) succeeds in conveying the impression that his/her utterance is one of integrity, that it represents an attempt to communicate in an unmediated form with an audience' (2002: 214). Second-person authenticity 'occurs when a performance succeeds in conveying the impression to a listener that that listener's experience of life is being validated, that the music is "telling it like it is" for them' (2002: 220). This authenticates listeners by articulating a place of belonging which distinguishes the music from other cultural forms, performers represented as powerful and correct and 'telling it like it is'. Third-person authenticity, according to Moore (2002: 218) 'arises when a performer succeeds in conveying the impression of accurately representing the ideas of another, embedded within a tradition of performance'. For

(Continued)

151

example, Eric Clapton, a white Englishman, is renowned for authentically playing country blues music associated with the black community in the Mississippi Delta in America. Our analysis focuses on first-person authenticity – that is, Eminem – authenticating himself as the voice of Black America.

Textual analysis

Representations of place

We could write pages and pages of analysis about this video. This has been done many times in the popular music press, evident through a quick scan of the internet. But in this section, we concentrate on the role of the representation of place in articulating discourses of authenticity.

Place is mostly represented in the visuals. The opening image tells us this is 'DETROIT MI', a black majority city synonymous with urban decay, crime and poverty and the home of Eminem. This is relevant. He chose to record the rap four days before its airing in a car park in Detroit and tell his fans this in the opening image. The song's 'authentic' voice would have been very different if Eminem had chosen to record this rap in tall prairie grass with the first image telling us this is 'Montana' or the like, instead of this urban setting (Connell and Gibson, 2003). Representations of place communicate a variety of social issues including 'identity, ethnicity, attachment to place, cultural economies, social activism, and politics' (Johansson and Bell, 2009: 2). Here, Eminem chooses a Detroit car park to identify himself in terms of race (a well-known white rapper showing support for the black community), and sympathy towards black rights, politics and activism, topics articulated in his lyrics.

Other aspects of the representation of place in this video further articulate the idea that Eminem is the urban voice of Black America. In almost every shot, Eminem raps to the camera, gesticulating and leaping in a performance space in the foreground. Surrounding his performance space are four cars. These are dated, large American Buicks and Cadillacs. Cars like these do not connote affluence and privilege the way Porsches, Mercedes or Jaguars may. These are cars associated with hard times and driven by criminals, pimps and gangsters in films, television shows and American rap videos. Here, cars link Eminem to 'the streets'.

The rap is filmed in a darkish car park, the darkness further suggesting being from the dangerous 'mean' streets. Unlike a brightly lit scene that may suggest truth, hope and clarity, darkness has the universal meaning potential of evil, danger, a lack of clarity and untruths (Machin, 2007: 70). The cars' headlights are on, seemingly lighting the dark car park. Though close-ups of Eminem suggest lighting is actually from off-screen sources to Eminem's right, headlights from the background connote a 'budget', authentic, impromptu urban lighting. These choices in the representation of place do not suggest this is a carefully constructed and choreographed piece of entertainment, but something quite authentic. It is here where Eminem speaks to us, offering us his political ideas.

Role of metaphor

Popular music tends to rely on metaphor, possibly more so than other communicative modes (Way, 2015). In Eminem's rap these are mostly in the lyrics, though also evident in visual choices. Throughout the whole rap, the visuals see Eminem active and empowered, rapping and moving aggressively in front of nine young black men. They wear clothes associated with rap such as hoodies and baseball caps, though nothing flashy like the gold chain Eminem wears around his neck. They stand legs apart, sit or lean on the bonnet of the aforementioned cars. All look in the direction of the camera and Eminem. For almost the whole rap, they are shot as a group in a long shot behind Eminem, de-emphasizing their individuality. A few times, we get a very short closer look at members of the group, but again these are almost always group shots and all of them are offer images, omitting power and symbolic engagement with viewers. Furthermore, they are not active. They do not move and, importantly, they do not add any sounds to the rap. This is a silent, disempowered representation. As such, these visual choices are a visual metaphor for the state of the black community in America and Eminem being empowered as a spokesperson for this community.

There are a large number of metaphors in the lyrics. These are used to articulate two discourses: Eminem is strong and dangerous and Trump is delegitimized. The first line in the rap is an example of how a metaphor represents Eminem as strong and dangerous. The line reads: 'It's the calm before the storm right here'. Here, Eminem represents his rap as a 'storm' and beforehand as 'the calm'. The storm Eminem refers to is his political anger.

Later in the video, Eminem raps: 'The fact we're not afraid of Trump, Fuck walkin' on egg shells, I came to stomp'. Here, Eminem uses the eggshell metaphor to distinguish his robust 'stomping' criticisms of Trump from those who do not 'tell it like it is'. To stomp demonstrates Eminem's power and a lack of concern for consequences as opposed to the careful measured navigation connoted in eggshells.

Though stomping suggests a lack of concern and power, some metaphors see Eminem as clever, seen in lines like: ''Cause like him [Trump] in politics, I'm usin' all of his tricks'. So, here the metaphor 'usin' all of his tricks', works in two ways to delegitimize Trump but also connote intelligence in Eminem. The line presupposes that Trump is indeed 'using tricks'. Politicians are supposed to be honest and their

(Continued)

dealings transparent. To claim one is 'using tricks' carries with it connotations of bending the rules, manipulation and possibly wrong doings. Additionally, these lines state that Eminem 'is usin' all of his tricks'. Though using tricks carries with it negative connotations, it also suggests you can manipulate and bend rules. Unlike a politician, for a rapper from Detroit, with symbols of urbanization and 'the street' in abundance, this adds street credibility to Eminem. He is not only strong and does not care, he is also a clever operator who is against Trump.

There are a large number of other metaphors that more directly delegitimize Trump. Eminem claims that the administration 'we got in office now's a kamikaze, that'll probably cause a nuclear holocaust'. Though indeed many commentators have expressed concerns for Trump's foreign policies and his unconventional manner, representing him as a suicidal war pilot suits Eminem's political agenda. The rapper also demasculinizes Trump in a number of lines such as:

Trump, when it comes to givin' a shit, you're stingy as I am

Except when it comes to havin' the balls to go against me, you hide 'em

'Cause you don't got the fuckin' nuts like an empty asylum

Racism's the only thing he's fantastic for

'Cause that's how he gets his fuckin' rocks off and he's orange.

Here, demasculinizing metaphors of 'having the balls … you hide 'em', 'don't got the fuckin' nuts' and 'gets his rocks off' are used against Trump. In the first two lines Trump is represented as being uncaring except for being confronted by Eminem. Here, not only is Trump represented as uncaring and weak, Eminem is also represented as strong. In the last three lines, again demasculinized metaphors are used to strengthen an argument that Trump is racist, it being the only issue that he finds exciting. Using sexualized metaphors indeed may invoke anger and delegitimize, but none of these lines provide any information, evidence or proof to claims of being uncaring and racist. They paint a very negative picture of Trump at the expense of sexualizing topics that could benefit from serious contemplation. Together, the metaphors we have examined and others in the rap articulate discourses of power and delegitimation, further articulating discourses of Eminem as a legitimate voice of Black America.

Musical sounds

This is an acapella rap, so the role of voice is the focus of our analysis, with some other aspects of sound being far less important. Though Eminem's voice is in the foreground, there is also atmospheric 'noise' in the background. This was not recorded in a studio where this can be tightly controlled and even eliminated, but outside in a car park. Most of this noise is edited out, but some has remained. Alongside the noise is a 'natural' echo to the sounds from Eminem. This is especially noticeable between lines. Both background noise and echo remind fans of the authentic urban space where this is recorded which connotes a street-wise authenticity associated with Eminem.

Eminem's voice is recorded at a close proximity. Although close, he does not whisper to us like a lover, but more like an angry friend venting his anger. This perspective allows us to feel his anger up close, us being a part of an anti-Trump group led by Eminem. There are no interacting sounds. Eminem is singled out as the sole source of sound, other than the background noise. This is all about him. Though monologues can be about isolation and loneliness, this video is about something else with lyrics representing 'us' as anti-Trump Americans ('we' used eight times) and visuals showing Eminem surrounded by nine men who agree with him. It is about Eminem expressing dominance as a powerful voice of Black anti-Trump America. This is made clear by choosing to have no musical accompaniment or other voices.

Lyrics and visuals make clear Eminem is angry. This is further connoted in his style of rapping: tense, rough and almost yelling (at times), not relaxed and smooth. His tense throat results in his voice becoming higher, sharper and tenser, connoting 'aggression' and 'scorn' (Fonagy and Magdics, 1972: 286; van Leeuwen, 1999: 131). This is used, for example, in the 'kamikaze' lines above, emphasizing Eminem's scorn and aggression towards Trump. These choices in vocal delivery represent Eminem's outflowing of emotions, his sincere and authentic anger.

His authentic, angry passion is further suggested by timing in his rapping. There is no adherence to clock time. He is rapping in natural time, slow at some points and faster at others following his emotions. At times, in a fit of anger, he raps very fast. At other times, between lines he stops, it all being too much. Here we hear him breathing in what gives us the impression of unmediated circumstances. But these choices in timings reflect the way we talk when we are emotionally engaged. We naturally leave pauses when we want people to contemplate our ideas or need a break. We talk faster when we get angry or excited and stop when we are filled with emotions. Like us, Eminem's breathing is agitated as he gets excited, noticeable between lines, again adding to a 'real' feel. What is represented here are real emotions expressed in authentic ways. This is very different to the reality of a well-rehearsed recorded piece of entertainment for a glitzy awards ceremony.

Some strategies are used to not only articulate authenticity, but also to emphasize anti-Trump discourses articulated in other modes. Eminem uses vibrato or a wavering of his voice, to do this in many of his lines. This wavering is not like

(Continued)

one we may hear in a classically trained vocalist, but a breaking of his voice. This suggests intense emotions. Although this can be heard throughout the rap, it is especially noticeable in the word 'bastards' in the line 'He says, "You're spittin' in the face of vets who fought for us, you bastards!"'. Here the emotions attached to Trump and patriotism are emphasized, this line being part of a discourse that sees Trump as being unpatriotic and using patriotism for his own ends. Anti-Trump discourses are also leaned upon in the use of nasal sounds. Eminem mimics Trump supporters in the lines 'He's gonna get rid of all immigrants!' and 'He's gonna build that thing up taller than this!' He raps these with more nasality than the rest of the song, with an accent we may associate with the South of the USA. These lines link Trump, his supporters and (an oversimplification of) his policies in an overly nasal way to connote negativity.

Choices in musical sounds are used to articulate discourses seen in other modes: Eminem is authentic and Trump is bad. Sounds also articulate negative ideas about Trump supporters. Together with an examination of metaphors and the representation of place, our analysis reveals that this video is more than just an authentic rant about US President Donald Trump. It is a well-rehearsed, well-presented piece of entertainment that criticizes Trump as well as authenticating Eminem.

SUMMARY

This chapter has examined the role of musical sounds in online musical offerings from mash-ups to music videos. Our detailed description of the semiotics of sound, based on the work of a number of scholars from semiotics and musicology, demonstrates how we can understand the roles musical sounds play in articulating discourses. Our examination also highlights the importance of not ascribing rigid meanings to sounds, but considering their potential meanings in light of other modes of communication (such as visuals and lyrics) as well as social, political, historical and consumption contexts. Armed with these insights, we are able to reveal the roles musical sounds play in a musical mash-up. We found musical sounds emphasized discourses articulated in other modes. We then also analysed a music video by not only considering the role of musical sounds, but also metaphors and the representation of places. This has proved to be revealing in terms of showing how anti-Trump ideas are articulated, but also authenticity.

With these new tools added to our analytical toolkit, we are now in a position to analyse a much wider range of artefacts in digital popular culture. After all, sounds are an integral part of much of what we engage with online. With these tools, we should be in a position to think more broadly in terms of not only how we can analyse online digital popular culture, but also what we may wish to consider as a potential sample for consideration.

SUGGESTED READING

Cooke, D. (1959) *The Language of Music*. Oxford: Clarendon Paperbacks.

This short seminal book examines the semiotics of classical music. It is clear and easy to read, though an understanding of music is a great advantage. It is the cornerstone of a lot of work on the semiotics of music and influences much of what we consider in this chapter.

Machin, D. (2010) *Analyzing Popular Music*. London: SAGE.

This book examines how to analyse popular music from a multimodal perspective. Though politics is not its focus, it describes in great detail how to uncover ideological discourses in popular music artefacts including posters, album covers, musical sounds, lyrics and more.

Tagg, P. (1990) Music in mass media studies: reading sounds for example, in
  K. Roe and U. Carlsson (eds), *Popular Music Research*. Sweden: Nordicom.

This chapter examines music through the lens of semiotics. It is part of a wide range of publications by Tagg, many of which are highly influential in the field. Like most of this work, its appeal lies in its accessibility, aimed at scholars and students who do not study music.

van Leeuwen, T. (1999) *Speech, Music, Sound*. London: Macmillan Press.

This book is a treasure trove of information on a wide range of views on the semiotics of sound. It summarizes what others say and offers many new (at the time) insights. What makes it especially important is it categorizes aspects of sounds in a systematic way, allowing us to use many of these ideas when we analyse sounds in multimodal media.

Way, L. (2018a) *Popular Music and Multimodal Critical Discourse Studies: Ideology, Control and Resistance in Turkey since 2002*. London: Bloomsbury.

This book summarizes not only what semioticians say about musical sounds, but what cultural studies scholars tell us about relations between popular music and politics. It uses this information to offer a musicology-inspired approach to multi-modal critical discourse studies. This approach is applied to a number of Turkish popular music case studies.

8

ANALYSING PARODIES

Environmental Protest in the Recontextualization of Social Practices

---

CHAPTER OBJECTIVES

- Consider the roles and importance of online comedy.
- Outline how comedy can be political.
- Describe the concept of recontextualizations.
- Consider texts as recontextualizations of social practice.
- Analyse a parody of a news reporter's 'off-camera' rant as a recontextualization of social practice.

KEY CONCEPTS

- Parody is a humorous or satirical imitation while satire uses irony, sarcasm, ridicule, and more, in exposing, denouncing, or deriding vice, folly (dictionary.com).
- Scholars of comedy believe satire results in a 'reduction of argument scrutiny' (Young, 2008).
- Eight elements (activities, participants, performance indicators, times, places, tools and materials, dress and grooming, eligibility conditions) make up a social practice.
- Recontextualizations involve transforming social practice into a representation that 'selectively appropriates, relocates, refocuses and relates other discourses to constitute its own order' (Bernstein, 1996).

INTRODUCTION

A large and fun part of our digital popular cultural experiences involve humour in the forms of memes, jokes, mash-ups, parodies and much more. Though humour amuses and makes us laugh, it also functions socially by conveying social norms and transmitting factual information (Attardo, 1994). By its very nature, humour is 'sociopolitically contextualized but may have varying degrees of critical reflexivity' (Calhoun, 2019: 28). Politically critical comedy is one popular form of digital humour and of interest to us in this chapter. Its popularity cannot be understated. For example, Vine was a popular short-video platform on Twitter between 2013 and 2017, boasting 25 channels of which its most popular two channels were comedy ones. King Bach played by comedian Andrew Bachelor was the most-followed person on all Vine channels with over 25 million followers. Bach's humour was political, delivering 'anti-hegemonic racial humor center[ing] around issues affecting Black Americans' (2019: 27).

This type of comedy is not easy to perform. Comedians of anti-hegemonic 'political humor must represent dominant discourses and beliefs in order to position them as objects of critique, and comedians who use this form of humor must do so in a way that clearly conveys that they do not subscribe to the ideologies they present' (2019: 29). Satire and parody are two closely interconnected tools used within this wider umbrella of political humour. Dictionary.com defines parody as 'a humorous or satirical imitation of a serious piece of literature or writing', satire as 'the use of irony, sarcasm, ridicule, or the like, in exposing, denouncing, or deriding vice, folly'. Comedians can use imitation to criticize, as a 'playfully critical distortion of the familiar' (Feinberg, 1967: 19). Abrams (1999) claims satire uses laughter as a 'weapon to diminish or derogate a subject and evoke toward it attitudes of amusement, disdain, ridicule, or indignation' (in LaMarre et al., 2014: 402). Prickly relations between the powerful and those who use satire to criticize them are nothing new. Plato proposed laws against satirists (Feinberg, 1967) and in 1600s England it was forbidden to publish satire (1967: 401). Even today, state-sponsored censorship and hostility towards satire continues. For example, Iran threatened to start an international Holocaust cartoon competition in response to worldwide protests of countries whose newspapers published political cartoons of the Islamic prophet Muhammad. The public's interest in satire is also long running due to it leaning on universal values, problems and issues that transcend any one society (Feinberg, 1967). Today is no exception. Who does not enjoy watching excerpts on YouTube of *Saturday Night Live*'s Alec Baldwin imitating Trump or Randy Rainbow parodying a news reporter who interviews politicians? One of my favourites is when Rainbow parodies first a news reporter and then Justin Beiber. To the tune of Bieber's 'Despacito', he criticizes Trump by singing 'Desperate Cheeto' while wearing a blond Bieberesque wig (Figure 8.1). Here is an example of a satirical parody that is 'anti-hegemonic', representing and challenging hegemonic discourses by poking fun at people and institutions with power and their biases and faults (Gilbert, 2004; Santa Ana, 2009).

Figure 8.1   Randy Rainbow's parody 'Desperate Cheeto' criticizes Trump.

Credit: Randy Rainbow

In this chapter, we take a close look at satirical parodies. We consider what draws us to anti-hegemonic ones and what role(s) they play in articulating politics. We examine these critically using a new (for us!) set of analytical tools in order to expand our capacity to analyse texts. As is always the case, we intend to demonstrate how our MCDS approach can reveal the politics articulated in digital popular culture.

THE IMPORTANCE OF SATIRICAL PARODIES

What role(s) can satire and parody play in politics? As mentioned above, comedy can inform us. Studies have shown how late-night US satirical parody shows are used by audiences to learn about politics, politicians and current affairs. Though not a substitute for more conventional sources of information, studies demonstrate how young people use these shows as a complement to more traditional forms of news, particularly online news, television news and talk radio (Young and Tisinger, 2006). Some research has also demonstrated that this programming can influence attitudes, political knowledge and political participation (Baumgartner and Morris, 2006; Hoffman and Thomson, 2009; LaMarre et al., 2009; Young and Tisinger, 2006). Other research has found even wider influences in society. These programmes have been credited with 'grabbing an audience's attention, bringing ideas to the top of people's minds, increasing source likeability, and inducing a positive affective state' (Polk et al., 2009: 203).

Scholars make a distinction between US satirical late-night comedy shows, such as *The Daily Show* and *The Colbert Report*, and punchline-oriented joke shows such as those hosted by Leno and Letterman (Holbert, 2005). The former focus on issues, policies, political rhetoric and the institutions of power (Baym, 2005), while the latter on punchline jokes and caricatures of public figures. Scholars claim 'this difference in content may make policy and issue stances more salient to viewers of satire' (Hoffman and Young, 2011: 167). These programmes are also credited with breaking down 'divisions between news and entertainment, public affairs and popular culture, affective consumption, and democratic discourse' with more than half of their stories addressing policy issues (Brewer et al., 2013; Brewer and Marquardt, 2007; Hollander, 2005).

Satire is complex for us as fans to process and this affects the political roles it can play. When faced with satire, we are forced to understand both the humour and the intertextual links between the satirical and the original. This 'is often complex and requires deeper thought [than punchline-oriented jokes]' (Polk et al., 2009: 206). This has positive and negative consequences in terms of potential political role(s). On the one hand, Hoffman and Young (2011: 164) 'found a significant and positive indirect effect for both satire or parody and traditional TV news on [political] participation'. Programmes interpret other media texts by satirizing them and by doing so they inform us, provoking reflection and re-evaluation of issues, texts and genres (Brewer et al., 2013: 327; Gray et al., 2009: 18). On the other hand, this is demanding on audiences. Fans must make sense of ideas and texts relative to other texts, rather than in isolation from one another (Gray et al., 2009: 18). This taxing mental processing creates a possible 'reduction of argument scrutiny'. There are a number of theories as to why this happens. One of these claims this is due to us wanting to understand the joke, thereby depleting our cognitive resources and 'reducing the listener's ability to scrutinize message arguments' (Young, 2008: 124). Another position claims the positive affect we experience from jokes disrupts our 'motivation to scrutinize the premise of the message' (2008: 124). In other words, we let facts slip us by in order to enjoy the joke. All the same, although some information in jokes may be discounted and subject to less message scrutiny, the content appears to increase in persuasion over time (Nabi et al., 2007). Whether by depletion or motivation, both positions point to the idea that 'when arguments are delivered in a humorous way, recipients are less likely to scrutinize the claims presented – particularly in a challenging or critical way' (Young, 2008: 134). This sees a decrease in 'audience counter argumentation and facilitates attitude change simply by reducing the audience's cognitive resistance' (Polk et al., 2009: 203).

The object of this chapter's analysis is Jonathan Pie's seven-minute 'The Extinction Rebellion Returns' video available on YouTube and Facebook. Like its American television counterparts, in this and other videos, Pie uses parody and satire aimed at television news, issues and politicians. We can credit Pie with many of the attributes of *The Daily Show* which uses the television news format and 'highlights inconsistencies in political rhetoric and satirizes the norms governing the typical news media through ironic inversions of the day's news' (Young and Tisinger, 2006: 117–118). Like *The Daily Show*, Pie employs irony to reveal the gap 'between what is and ought to be' and highlights 'differences between vice and virtue, between good and bad, between what man is, and what he ought to be' (Bergson, 1956: 127; Griffin, 1994: 36).

There is no shortage of comedy in digital popular culture, as outlined in our introduction. Comedy online can utilize the affordances offered by digital technologies. Some comedians have 'taken advantage of platforms' various features', using its multimodal capabilities 'such as text, image, and/or audio – to create a wide variety of online communicative styles' (Calhoun, 2019: 31). Some have adapted to new digital genres and forms, evident by King Bach's success and the technical resourcefulness of Randy Rainbow. But what about the political role(s) characteristic of digital comedy?

Of course the political role(s) of parody and satire outlined in the above section also apply to digital parody. However, are there any roles unique to digital parody? Denisova (2019: 36) considers how comedy works in digital memes, leaning on Bakhtin's (1984) concept of carnivalesque resistance. In short, Bakhtin (1984) claims the medieval carnival used to ridicule those in power and, unlike in most other aspects of life, this was tolerated by those in power. It was tolerated because it was confined in terms of time and place and it 'allow[ed] the population to let off steam and then return to the status quo' (2019: 37). Though there are obvious similarities, digital carnival is different. Digital carnival is not constrained by time like its medieval counterpart, though it is constrained by the boundaries of hyperspace. Like its medieval counterpart, dissent is tolerated, even in restrictive regimes, as long as it remains online.

However, Denisova notes that there are different levels of tolerance between the two types of carnival: 'What makes digital carnival different from the original medieval carnival is that it operates under the *implicit* permission of the elites. The medieval carnival was clearly sanctioned by the governors, while digital carnival seems to happen in the free space of open-access social networks' (2019: 37, emphasis original). Saying that, there are cases where those responsible for sharing memes that mock those in power have been prosecuted. In 2014, Turkish doctor Bilgin Çiftçi was put on trial for sharing a meme that compared Turkish President Erdoğan to the character Gollum from *Lord of the Rings* (Figure 8.2). He was indicted for violating Article 301 of the Turkish constitution that punishes those who 'denigrate state officials'.

163

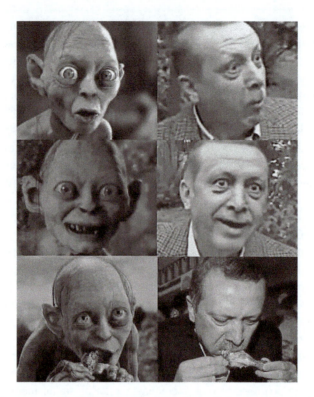

Figure 8.2 Meme comparing Turkish President Erdoğan to Gollum from the *Lord of the Rings film*. Creator unknown, first use, source: Know Your Meme

Like parody on television, digital parody is intertextual and context-sensitive – parody makers need to draw clear links to the political and social environment to make criticism sound and timely (Denisova, 2017). So, satirical recontextualizations have a role to play in politics as long as audiences can make the links between the parody, the original texts and the issues. For digital parody to play a role (other than letting off steam), it needs to successfully be a part of actions both digital and outside the digital realm (Denisova, 2019: 37).

ANALYTICAL TOOLS: RECONTEXTUALIZATION OF SOCIAL PRACTICE

In this chapter, we expand our analytical toolkit while utilizing analytical strategies we have used before. The analytical focus of this chapter is considering satirical parodies as recontextualizations of social practice. Again, we try to pick the right tools for the job. We can approach satirical parodies as texts that represent an issue, people and set of social practices in a certain way. From this perspective, satirical parodies are the recontextualization of social practice. To clarify, we consider the concepts of social practice and recontextualizations. Van Leeuwen (1993a and 1993b) claims social practices always include the following:

1. Activities – the core of a social practice is a set of activities, sometimes in a set order and usually fixed by habit, convention or prescription. To illustrate this and the following ideas, we use the examples given in van Leeuwen (1993a and 1993b). The social practice of going to a lecture may include activities such as going to the correct room, finding a seat, taking out a pen and notebook and the like.
2. Participants – those involved in practices take on certain roles such as instigator, agent, affected or beneficiary. In a lecture, participants include a lecturer and students, taking turns in the roles outlined above.
3. Performance indicators – these represent how the activities are performed as a whole or specific parts of it. A lecture may be judged on a number of criteria such as pace, how well it was understood and the like.
4. Times – these may include overall timing of a social practice, or segments of the practice. A lecture starts and finishes at precise times whereas when the lecturer gives examples and when s/he sums up ideas are more flexible.
5. Places – social practices are usually related to specific places. Our lectures usually take place in a specific lecture room or hall.
6. Tools and materials – social practices require certain tools and materials. Our lectures usually require students bringing a tablet or a pen and paper while a lecturer may use a projector, digital imagery and/or power point presentations.
7. Dress and grooming – social practices come with expectations on how we dress. As a lecturer, it would be frowned upon for me to turn up in a pair of speedos and swimming goggles.
8. Eligibility conditions – to be engaged in social activities, eligibility conditions apply. In a lecture hall, students expect the lecturer to have relevant qualifications (like a PhD) and students to have completed secondary school.

A representation of some kind of social practice may be considered as a recontextualization. What does this mean? Some of what we communicate may represent some social practice or another such as taking part in a lecture, going to the shops or having a chat with your mother. These discursive acts are constructed representations of events (van Leeuwen and Wodak, 1999: 93). What we do is turn a social practice into a representation of a social practice, an activity that takes

165

place outside the context of the represented practice. One way to consider these representations is to consider them as 'recontextualizations'. Back in the 1990s, education sociologist and linguist Basil Bernstein (1990 and 1996) examined how pedagogic discourses were recontextualized by various social actors, such as education boards, head teachers and teachers. Here, he found an actor who recontextualizes pedagogical discourses 'selectively appropriates, relocates, refocuses and relates other discourses to constitute its own order' (Bernstein, 1996: 47). These transformative recontextualizations are not neutral. Bernstein (1996: 49) notes how recontextualizations modify not only 'the *what* of pedagogic discourse, what discourse is to become subject and content of pedagogic practice, but also recontextualizes the *how*; that is the *theory of instruction*'. These changes become detached or 'abstracted' from their original 'social base, position and power relations' (1996: 53, emphasis original).

Bernstein (1990) identifies some guiding principles on how texts are transformed in recontextualizations. These same principles can apply to any social practice as it is transformed. The process of recontextualization inevitably ensures that the text is different from the original in the following ways: '1. The text has changed its position in relation to other texts, practices, and positions. 2. The text itself has been modified by selection, simplification, condensation, and elaboration. 3. The text has been repositioned and refocused' (1990: 53).

How social practices are recontextualized is determined by a number of factors, such as a producer's intended audience and what discourses they want articulated. To illustrate what I mean, we consider a meme we saw back in Chapter 3 which appeared on my Facebook feed a while back (Figure 8.3). This meme was sent to me by a friend who dislikes the UK Conservative Party. The two people in the image are David Cameron who was the UK's prime minster

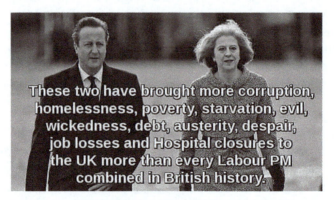

Figure 8.3   Recontextualization of social practices: 'These two' meme. Creator unknown

from 2010–16 and Theresa May who was the subsequent prime minister from 2016–19. Both premierships included policies one does not associate with conservatism, such as introducing legislation on gay marriage, as well as ones which do, such as an austerity programme aimed at bringing down the nation's budget deficit by cutting funding to public services. Despite a vast array of policies, announcements, actions and societal repercussions related to these, Cameron and May's social practice(s) of governing the country are recontextualized into a list of nouns in a sentence.

Some of the recontextualized repercussions of their policies can be substantiated through looking at government reports and statistics, such as the numbers of homeless, levels of poverty, jobless rates and the number of hospitals closed. Some of the other recontextualizations are far less clear, such as 'debt' – whose debt are they referring to? Government? Individuals? Households? Municipalities? And other recontextualizations such as 'starvation', 'evil', 'wickedness' and 'despair' are difficult to verify, though contribute to a very negative representation of Cameron and May. Their terms in government involved thousands of social practices. Much of these are excluded or represented in vague ways in order to vilify these two politicians. Though some of us may believe at least some of these accusations, we need to consider such recontextualizations more carefully.

As seen above, Cameron and May's premierships are transformed into a very negative recontextualization. In our case, this is an anti-Tory meme. Our job as analysts is to consider critically how a text represents a social practice. That is, we need to consider the decisions that are made that represent social practices in certain ways, how a social practice is transformed in this process.

There are four types of transformations we need to consider when analysing a text. These are deletions, rearrangements, substitutions and additions. As analysts, we need to appreciate that not every aspect of a social practice can be fully represented. Some things are deleted, while others are included. Whole aspects of an action or event may be deleted or more specific deletions can be made. For example, 'two people were shot' deletes who is performing the shooting. This is a sentence with passive agency and in CDA we find this significant in articulating discourses. In the meme above, details of some representations are deleted, such as whose debt is increasing, as well as whole aspects of their premiership such as legislation on gay marriage. These may be socially and/or politically important.

Rearrangement involves recontextualizing elements within a social practice in an order different from the order in which they actually occurred. Why is this important? Think of when we read a news story: most people read the first few paragraphs of a story and then move on. News producers know this, so stack the most important information at the start. Rearranging can happen in most texts, and 'in various ways which relate to the interests, goals and values of the context into which the practice is recontextualized' (van Leeuwen and Wodak, 1999: 97). In the above meme, the actions and repercussions of Cameron's and May's times in office are not obviously in chronological order, but rearranged as a list to articulate a discourse of negativity.

Communication, such as memes or online satirical videos, involve substituting social practices for signs. The mode of representation used offers a range of possible ways of representing an activity, in the case of the above meme, a sentence and a photograph. Part of substitution involves how people are named, for example 'these two' and 'every Labour PM' and how activities are represented. These may involve a range of strategies (see Chapter 6) such as abstractions and generalizations where a loss of detail occurs with (de)legitimation of a group of people. In the above meme, 'these two' could easily have been 'our last two prime ministers', the latter connoting importance and respect by identifying their roles in the UK. Their activities and results of these are represented in vague terms delegitimizing the politicians, suiting the aims of an anti-Conservative producer.

Finally, elements including reactions, purposes and legitimations can be added to representations of social practices. These obviously can be ideological. Reactions are representations of the private feelings of participants, such as their worries, fear, hopes, desires, joys and griefs. So, in our meme above, 'despair' in the UK is represented. Adding this feeling to this recontextualization adds more negativity and delegitimation towards the two politicians. The purpose of social practices or parts of social practices can be represented in different ways depending on the recontextualization. In the above meme, though the purpose of Cameron's and May's governance is not made explicit, some of the attributes such as corruption and evil indicate that the purpose of their premierships were most definitely not for the benefit of 'the UK' and possibly for their own benefit. Legitimations represent 'why' social practices are as they are. In the meme above, this recontextualization serves to delegitimize Cameron and May and legitimize support for Labour.

In this chapter we analyse how Jonathan Pie recontextualizes the social practices of a number of actors involved in some way or another with the 2019 Extinction Rebellion protests in London. He recontextualizes these through his 'off-air' parody of a news reporter's satirical comments while covering the protests. There are a number of actors and their social practices recontextualized in this satirical parody. In the analysis that follows, we examine those of Extinction Rebellion, British Prime Minister Boris Johnson, US President Donald Trump and Jonathan Pie himself.

CASE STUDY ANALYSIS: JONATHAN PIE'S 'EXTINCTION REBELLION RETURNS'

As with all our case studies, we need to consider text and context. The video can be found at https://www.facebook.com/JonathanPieReporter/videos/142504575766 1077/. To contextualize our textual analysis, what follows is a brief examination of the character Jonathan Pie, then the environmental positions of Extinction Rebellion, Boris Johnson, Donald Trump and Greta Thunberg. After our contextualizations, we consider how Jonathan Pie recontextualizes the social practices (including the environmental ideas they communicate) of these actors to articulate discourses that legitimize Pie and those he agrees with and delegitimizes populist right-wing politicians.

Context: Jonathan Pie

Jonathan Pie is a fictitious British news reporter, created and played by British actor and comedian Tom Walker. Pie first appeared online on 21 September 2015 and since then has appeared regularly in a series of video clips distributed on YouTube and Facebook. In these short videos, he appears as an off-camera television reporter who rants about political events (usually in the UK and USA). These rants go against the reporters' convention of neutrality by revealing his personal opinions to the camera before or after filming a regular news segment. This chapter's analysis looks at one of these rants. Aside from these, he appears online in BBC's *Jonathan Pie: Back to the Studio* and on television, appearing occasionally on an Australian satirical news programme, on BBC Three's *Jonathan Pie's American Pie* mockumentary and on RT UK (for three months in 2016).

Pie is a self-declared 'proper old-school socialist', a persona closely aligned to Walker's Labour-supporting views. His rants target not only the political right, such as the UK's Conservative Party, Trump and Scott Morrison (Australia's right-wing Prime Minister at the time of writing). He also targets 'his left-wing fan base' (Comedy interview, 2018). Ironically, his most viewed video targeted the latter in 'his liberal-blasting tirade in the wake of Donald Trump's presidential victory [that] has attracted more than 150 million online views alone' (Comedy interview, 2018). In the video that we analyse below, he not only attacks Johnson and Trump, but also London's Labour mayor Sadiq Khan, the left-leaning newspaper the *Guardian* and those on the left and right who complain about the protests.

(Continued)

Context: Extinction Rebellion and Greta Thunberg

Extinction Rebellion came to the media's attention when, on 31 October 2018, 1500 of its members assembled on the UK's Parliament Square in London to announce a Declaration of Rebellion against the UK Government. The next few weeks saw 6000 protesters peacefully block five major bridges in London, plant trees in Parliament Square and super-glue themselves to the gates of Buckingham Palace while reading a letter to the Queen. Extinction Rebellion's actions are 'non-violent civil disobedience in an attempt to halt mass extinction and minimize the risk of social collapse' (About us, 2020). They promote mass 'above the ground' civil disobedience – in full public view. This means economic disruption to shake the current political system and civil disruption to raise awareness. They do not use petitions or write to MPs but use civil disobedience 'as a tool' to promote government action.

Since these initial actions in 2018, there have been others such as two represented in Pie's satirical parody: one in April 2019 and the other beginning 6 October 2019. The latter was organized 'to demand governments tell the truth on the Climate and Ecological Emergency – and act' (About us, 2020). In this protest, thousands of protesters disrupted capital cities around the world. In London, Extinction Rebellion blocked Trafalgar Square, Westminster Bridge, Lambeth Bridge, Millbank, Victoria, The Mall, Whitehall, Victoria Embankment, Horseguards Parade, Victoria Street and Smithfield Market. Extinction demands were, 'that governments and other institutions must tell the truth and declare a Climate and Ecological Emergency, must act now to halt biodiversity loss and reduce greenhouse gas emissions to net zero by 2025 and must create and be led by the decisions of Citizens' Assemblies on climate and ecological justice' (This Monday, 2019).

Greta Thunberg is another face of environmental activism. She came to prominence around 20 August 2018 when she did not attend school for three weeks to demand the Swedish government reduce carbon emissions in accordance with the Paris Agreement. She protested by sitting outside the parliament every day during school hours with a sign that read 'School strike for climate'. Since then, through social media, she has built up a global following, striking on Fridays outside the Swedish parliament, attending protests and giving speeches. She has joined various student protests around Europe, and has spoken at various forums and parliaments including the British, European and French. She has addressed the 2018 United Nations Climate Change Conference; the January 2019 World Economic Forum, when she declared: 'Our house is on fire'; the US House Select Committee, to give testimony in August 2019; and the UN Climate Action Summit in New York City in September 2019. That same day, she (with a group of other children) made an official complaint against Argentina, Brazil, France, Germany and Turkey for not meeting their emission reduction Paris Agreement pledges.

In her speech at the summit, she told world leaders: 'This is all wrong. I shouldn't be up here. I should be back in school on the other side of the ocean. Yet you all come to us young people for hope? How dare you! You have stolen my dreams and my childhood with your empty words.' Some of these addresses and Trump's reactions to these are recontextualized by Pie.

Context: Politicians

Boris Johnson, the UK's populist Conservative Prime Minister, made news with his public reactions to Extinction Rebellion's protests. In the same week London's mayor Sadiq Khan was telling the protesters their methods were incorrect, Johnson dismissed the protesters as 'uncooperative crusties' who should stop blocking the streets of the capital with their 'heaving hemp-smelling bivouacs' (in Rawlinson, 2019). He also referred to them as 'importunate nose-ringed climate change protesters … [saying] the best thing would be for them to stop blocking the traffic.' Referring to the UK's iconic Conservative politician Margaret Thatcher, Johnson claims 'she took it [climate change] seriously long before Greta Thunberg' and protesters should 'learn about a true feminist, green and revolutionary who changed the world for the better.'

Trump's position on climate change, like his positions on many issues, is unclear and constantly in flux. Despite this fluidity, his approach to the environment is one that may be characterized as an obstacle for businesses to make a profit. During his 2016 election campaign, he famously claimed that climate change was a Chinese government hoax, a plot to sabotage American manufacturing. Once elected as president, he has given support for the coal industry, dropped out of the Paris Climate Agreement and made cuts to environmental groups and organizations, such as the Environmental Protection Agency, while promoting fossil-fuel consumption in policies such as the America First Energy Plan. Not surprisingly, Pie has a dig at both these politicians.

Textual analysis

Our contextualization has had to cover a lot of ground. One of the reasons for this is that Jonathan Pie covers a lot of ground in terms of events, social actors and social practices. Not all of these are analysed here. Our analysis focuses on the social practices associated with the social actors described in our contextualization section. This is more than enough to reveal the dominant discourses articulated in Pie's rant. Also, we will not go into any great depth on the visuals in this parody. This is because the focus of this chapter is on how social practices are

(Continued)

recontextualized in Pie's dialogue, articulating discourses of legitimacy for himself and activists and delegitimacy for politicians.

Throughout the video, Pie recontextualizes the social practices of Extinction Rebellion, politicians, the media and the public at large in regard to the global climate crisis. These social practices are not listed and discussed in any chronological order, but rearranged in ways that delegitimize some and legitimize others. Many times this is done by rearranging practices, events and issues as binary opposites. Will Wright (1975) observed how Western films adhere to a basic structure that shapes concerns and a lack of comprehension about social changes into simple binary opposites, where individuals or groups represent each side. This is a discursive strategy that can represent wider issues and anxieties present in society at particular times. Here we see binary opposites between right-wing politicians and environmentalists. We will see this recontextualization strategy on several occasions in this analysis. But one clear and dramatic example is the end of the video when Pie dramatically rips off his microphone and says the following:

It's up to you Tim [the unseen co-worker who speaks to Pie through his headphones], you have a choice, are you going to be one of the contrary little twats like Boris or are you going to be a decent human being and do what you can? 'Cause I've made my choice. OK. Are we done? Are we done? OK. Where's the fuckin' super-glue, because I'm off. I'm off to save the fuckin' planet.

Here, Pie sets up binary opposites of 'contrary little twats like Boris' opposed to 'decent human being' who 'do what you can'. The social practices of people who do not support protesters, such as Johnson, are presupposed to not be those of 'a decent human being'. If we remember from Chapter 7, presuppositions are 'a taken-for-granted, implicit claim embedded within the explicit meaning of a text or utterance' (Richardson, 2007: 63). Substituting these names (the informal naming of 'Boris' and the very negative 'contrary little twats like Boris') for the many social practices of those who do not support the protesters is an extreme simplification of the many positions and social practices one may engage in as a non-protester. This again substitutes those who do not protest with 'contrary little twats like Boris', connoting negativity. Opposed to this are those who 'do what [they] can'. This substitution for social practices can mean recycling, donating money to causes, sending letters to the government, patronizing companies and institutions who support climate change and avoiding those who do not. However, here, through actions and dialogue, Pie defines this as protesting. He tells us 'Where's the fuckin' super-glue, because I'm off. I'm off to save the fuckin' planet'. Here, Pie represents himself as an authentic environmentalist, like Extinction Rebellion.

He recontextualizes gluing oneself to somewhere (he does not make this clear), as 'off to save the planet'. Again, though indeed these protests are an important tool in raising awareness of the global climate crisis, recontextualizing them as 'saving the planet' adds legitimacy to this practice and Pie himself.

Visuals in this part of the video help further to legitimate Pie. Throughout the whole video, Pie faces the camera in a close chest shot (Figure 8.4). He is salient throughout and always looking directly at the camera in a demand image. This is empowering and creates symbolic interaction between Pie and his fans. He connotes authenticity in his hand movements and facial expressions all communicating heartfelt sincerity. He waves his hands in anger at times, points to us, sneers, laughs, yells at times, all to connote true emotions. Even his hair, which at the beginning of the video looked neat and 'in place', loses its form. In the last scene, when he storms off camera, sincere anger is brought to the fore (Figure 8.5). For the first time in the video, he moves away from his front of camera position. He is still salient, though now he moves off to the side so that the protests behind share in salience. This is where Pie is going. His actions of ripping out his earpiece and microphone, shooting a V-sign at Tim and storming towards the protests further legitimize Pie, not as a cool-headed objective journalist reporting a protest, but as a 'decent human being' doing what 'he can' by joining Extinction Rebellion in their protest. These visuals work with his dialogue to emphasize the legitimacy of both Extinction Rebellion and Pie.

Figure 8.4 Symbolic interaction connoting a sincere Jonathan Pie.

Credit: Jonathan Pie/Tom Walker

(Continued)

Figure 8.5 Actions connoting sincere anger and a legitimate Jonathan Pie.

Credit: Jonathan Pie/Tom Walker

Legitimizing Extinction Rebellion and environmentalists involves a number of transformative strategies, deletions playing a critical role. All the while, politicians' social practices are recontextualized in a way that acts as a binary opposite to these. Consider:

> *the fact that Thatcher was talking about climate change 30 years ago and the planet is still boiling itself to death kind of proves the point that all these crusties are making … if any politician comes out and says we know there's a problem but this isn't the way to tackle it the question is what would you suggest? A strongly worded email? You actually start doing something and these people might stop gluing themselves to shit … yes, saying you are aware of the crisis and then doing nothing about it makes you a pretty vile human being and a fuckin' useless politician.*

In 1988, British Prime Minister Margaret Thatcher warned of the dangers of global warming. Between that time and Pie's video, 31 years passed and a lot of social practices have contributed to global warming. These include the social practices of politicians of all walks, industrialization, an ever-increasing global population and a lack of will on the part of many in society (politicians, business, the wider population) to make the sacrifices and changes needed to reduce climate change. In Pie's recontextualization, all these practices have been deleted. In their place are politicians who 'are aware of the crisis and then doing nothing about it … like Boris Johnson'. Here, the social practices of politicians are recontextualized as 'doing nothing about it'. Though, indeed, many believe politicians should do more, deleted from here are the many actions the UK government is involved in, such as signing the 2015 Paris Climate Accord and initiating environmental impact studies on all major projects such as the High Speed Rail Link to the North of England. The point is, governmental actions have been deleted and substituted for 'doing nothing about it', articulating a discourse that delegitimates Johnson.

Opposed to politicians (again) is Extinction Rebellion. Their actions are legitimized by creating a false choice in 'what would you suggest? A strongly worded email? You actually start doing something and these people might stop gluing themselves to shit'. Here, the addition of 'A strongly worded email' creates a false choice between gluing oneself to a street, gate (like Extinction Rebellion) in an act of protest or sending an email. Deleted are all the other possible actions one can take to express opposition to government policies. As such, their actions seem legitimate. Furthermore, Pie adds purpose to these actions by linking them to politicians starting 'doing something'. Though it is likely that the purpose of Extinction Rebellion is indeed to get politicians to act on climate change, here purpose is added to simplify dynamics between politicians' actions and protests, further legitimizing protesters' actions.

Elsewhere, Extinction Rebellion's actions are directly legitimized through recontextualizations. Consider:

Last time Extinction Rebellion got the government to declare a climate emergency OK this time they're asking what it intends on doing about it ... it's a pretty reasonable question ... This sort of thing works.

In this sentence two demonstrations a year apart are represented together. In the first part of this sentence, the government's response to Extinction Rebellion's ten-day demonstration beginning on 15 April 2019 is recontextualized as 'Last time Extinction Rebellion got the government to declare a climate emergency'. These protests may have been one of many reasons why the UK's House of Commons declared a climate emergency on 1 May 2019. However, here we see deletions and additions that recontextualize a number of social practices that suggest the protests were a success. Deleted from Pie's account are all the political (and other) factors that contributed to the House of Commons making this declaration, such as similar declarations made by Scotland (28 April 2019) and the Welsh National Assembly (29 April 2019). Besides, making declarations are a vote winner. They do 'not legally compel the government to act' due to there being 'no single definition of what that means' (UK Parliament declares, 2019), yet appeal to many concerned voters. These deletions legitimize Extinction Rebellion's social practices of protesting.

(Continued)

175

Additions also play a role. Added into this recontextualization is a presupposed direct link between protesting and the UK government's declaration of a climate emergency. However, the government did not declare an emergency. The Environment Secretary (at the time) Michael Gove did not back Labour's demands to declare one. What happened was MPs approved a motion to declare an environment and climate emergency that 'demonstrates the will of the Commons on the issue but does not legally compel the government to act' (UK Parliament declares, 2019). So, indeed, it was a victory for environmentalists, but it was not a government declaration as it is recontextualized by Pie. It was a political victory for Labour Leader Jeremy Corbyn who proposed the declaration and other politicians who backed him. As such, Pie's recontextualization of a political victory by some MPs connotes legitimation of Extinction Rebellion.

The second part of this extract shows further additions that legitimize Extinction Rebellion in 'they're [Extinction Rebellion] asking what it intends on doing about it … it's a pretty reasonable question … This sort of thing works'. Here, one of Extinction Rebellion's demands (declaring an emergency) is represented as 'asking', connoting a 'softer' more reasonable stance and perhaps less militancy than a 'demand', the term used by Extinction Rebellion. There are also two additions of 'it's a pretty reasonable question' and 'this sort of thing works'. The first addition recontextualizes the demand in a positive manner, it being 'pretty reasonable'. The second addition again legitimates their actions as ones that produce the desired results in 'this sort of thing works'. If we consider the three demands Extinction Rebellion had, actually none of them were achieved. Their demands were, first, that the government declare an emergency. This was not met (see above). Extinction Rebellion's second demand was that 'The UK must enact legally binding policies to reduce carbon emissions to net zero by 2025' (Extinction Rebellion are, 2019). Presently, the UK is aiming for zero carbon emissions by 2050. Its third demand was 'A citizens' assembly must be formed to oversee the changes needed to achieve this goal' (Extinction Rebellion are, 2019). Again this demand has not been met. However, Pie recontextualizes these demands and their results as 'this sort of thing works', legitimizing Extinction Rebellion and its social practices.

Many parts of Pie's video recontextualize Johnson in a way that delegitimates him by his position opposite to authentic legitimate environmentalists. Here, deletions and additions play a key role. Consider:

Why not point out the hypocrisy of Boris Johnson who won't be photographed with a disposable coffee cup because it's not a good look and who declares that the climate change is a real thing and then ridicules those people who are willing to give up their civil liberties to push for change.

In this excerpt, Johnson is delegitimized by recontextualizing his practices as hypo-critical. He is worried about his image and ridicules protesters while declaring climate change is real. Deleted from this recontextualization are all the social prac-tices the government is engaged with that reduce climate change (as discussed above). Furthermore, we find binary opposites where Johnson is not a legitimate environmentalist while those in Extinction Rebellion are. Extinction Rebellion are legitimized as 'people who are willing to give up their civil liberties to push for change'. This is an addition of protesters' thoughts used here to connote authentic, 'true' environmentalism opposed to inauthentic hypocritical politicians.

Though many segments of the video serve to legitimize Pie and Extinction Rebellion, a dominant discourse throughout is delegitimizing politicians, espe-cially Johnson. This is evident even in the first sentence of his off-camera rant which reads:

> *Just in case you needed any more evidence that Boris Johnson is an utter prick he gives his assessment of a global movement to tackle catastrophic climate change [mocking posh accent] gurble gurble they're all a bunch of crusties gurble gurble … taking another leaf out of the Donald Trump's guide to leadership book.*

In this opening gambit, Johnson is substituted by the names 'Boris Johnson' and 'an utter prick'. There are countless other words Pie uses to substitute for Johnson such as 'pretty vile human being' and a 'fuckin' useless politician' throughout this video. Obviously, these namings are very negative, even the first depriving Johnson of his honorifics of prime minister. Pie recontextualizes Johnson's public statement he made at a book launch where he said:

> *I am afraid that the security people didn't want me to come along tonight because they said the road was full of uncooperative crusties and protest-ers of all kinds littering the road. And they said there was some risk that I would be egged.*

In Johnson's statement, he does not directly call protesters 'a bunch of crusties', as Pie says. Johnson recontextualizes a statement by 'the security people' who he rep-resents in indirect speech as saying this. In Johnson's statement, he links 'crusties' with traffic in 'littering the street' and a risk of being egged. However, Pie recontex-tualizes Johnson's statement as 'his assessment of a global movement to tackle catastrophic climate change'. Here, substitutions and deletions are made to represent Johnson as far less environmentally friendly than he may be. Furthermore, he

(Continued)

delegitimizes Johnson further by mocking his accent as those of the elite, connoting he is out of touch with the people. Finally, Pie includes the addition of 'taking another leaf out of the Donald Trump's guide to leadership book' to delegitimize Johnson further. This addition suggests Johnson made this statement because he follows a similar political agenda to Trump. Though indeed both are right-wing populist leaders, such an addition is impossible to substantiate, though it connotes a direct link between the two leaders. Given Trump's very negative public views on the environment, this statement delegitimizes Johnson even further.

Trump is also delegitimized by Pie's satirical parody. In the video, Pie recontextualizes Trump's conduct at a number of public engagements and rearranges them in a way that connotes Trump acts like a child. Consider:

When you [Trump] deny science and sit there with your arms crossed getting angry at an autistic teenager 'How dare Greta tell me I ruined her childhood' You sound like a small little man ... you sound like a contrary wanna be edgy prick ... you sound like a nasty human being.

Here, substitutions and rearrangements are used to recontextualize a number of public engagements involving Trump and Thunberg, including a chance meeting and public statements in New York's UN building in September 2019 and the World Economic Forum 2020 in Davos, Switzerland. In New York, both Trump and Thunberg spoke at different meetings on the same day. Thunberg addressed a UN summit on climate change while Trump organized a meeting on religious freedom. During Thunberg's address, she made the claim that 'You have stolen my dreams and my childhood with your empty words'. Trump did not attend Thunberg's summit, but they crossed paths in a corridor. They did not speak to each other; Thunberg glared at Trump while he apparently did not notice her. Thunberg's stare made the news. Later, Trump quote-tweeted a video of Thunberg's speech and captioned it: 'She seems like a very happy young girl looking forward to a bright and wonderful future. So nice to see!' In response, Thunberg changed her Twitter bio to 'A very happy young girl looking forward to a bright and wonderful future'. At the World Economic Forum a few months later, they both spoke, but again they did not meet.

In Pie's recontextualization of these (non)meetings, statements associated with them and tweets, social practices are rearranged to connote Trump acts like a child. This is a dominant anti-Trump discourse. For example, mainstream media and memes regularly include images of Trump crossing his arms and looking angry, such as Figure 8.6 taken during the 2018 G7 meeting in Canada. In Pie's rant, events are rearranged in an order that suggests Trump responds to Thunberg's criticisms by crossing his arms in '[you] sit there with your arms crossed getting angry at an autistic teenager "How dare Greta tell me I ruined her childhood"'. Here, Trump is represented responding to Thunberg, a representation that connotes a powerful Thunberg (van Leeuwen, 1995). Trump is delegitimized, responding in his 'spoilt brat' manner by crossing his arms and getting angry. This negative discourse is further articulated with the addition of Trump being named three times in this section as 'a small little man', 'a contrary wanna be edgy prick' and 'a nasty human being'. In the meantime, sympathy towards Thunberg is connoted in naming her as 'an autistic teenager'.

Figure 8.6 'Childlike Trump' image from G7's 2018 meeting, Canada.

Photo credit: Jesco Denzel/German Federal Government via AP Images

SUMMARY

In this chapter we analysed (mostly) the monologue of Pie's 'Extinction Rebellion returns' video. We learned how satirical parodies such as this are an extremely important part of our digital popular culture. They entertain and can play political role(s). We dipped into our toolkit and decided that one very useful tool for analysing these is to consider them as the recontextualization of social practices. Our analysis reveals that though many of us may agree with Jonathan Pie's assessment of politicians and environmentalists, these recontextualizations lean on a simplification of positions and the creation of binary opposites between politicians and environmentalists. The danger is that these simplify complex social practices, reducing them to simplistic opposites and ignoring more subtle differences typical of social practices.

(Continued)

Examining how social practices can be recontextualized is only one of many 'tools' we can use to analyse parodies. As you may have noticed, a lot of our other tools were also used in our analysis. Likewise, we can analyse a whole range of texts as recontextualizations of social practice. The hope is, after all these chapters of analysis, we now have a large toolkit to consider texts critically. In the next chapter we tie this all together in order for us to be critical analysts of digital popular culture.

SUGGESTED READING

Bernstein, B. (1996) Pedagogy, symbolic control and identity. *British Journal of Sociology of Education*, 18(1): 119–124.

This article and Bernstein's (1990) book go into great depth explaining the concept of recontextualization. Though these works examine the recontextualization of pedagogical discourses, the concept of recontextualization is useful for us as we analyse how other discourses are used in different contexts.

Calhoun, K. (2019) Vine racial comedy as anti-hegemonic humor: linguistic performance and generic innovation. *Journal of Linguistic Anthropology*, 29(1): 27–49.

This article has a good literature review on relations between comedy and humour. It then uses the case study of King Bach on Vine to explore how humour on social media can be political.

Esralew, S. and Young, D. (2012) The influence of parodies on mental models: exploring the Tina Fey–Sarah Palin phenomenon. *Communication Quarterly*, 60(3): 338–352.

This is one of a number of articles involving Dannagal Young in which she examines late-night American parody and satirical television shows. Though not from a discursive perspective, these studies help inform our study on the roles and limits of satires and parodies.

Polk, J., Young, D. and Holbert, R.L. (2009) Humor complexity and political influence: an elaboration likelihood approach to the effects of humor type in The Daily Show with Jon Stewart. *Atlantic Journal of Communication*, 17(4): 202–219.

This is another article that examines the role of humour in American television shows. It is particularly interesting for us as it looks specifically at the role of satire and parody in influencing voters' behaviour.

van Leeuwen, T. and Wodak, R. (1999) Legitimizing immigration: a discourse historical approach. *Discourse Studies*, 1(1): 83–118.

This article uses the case study of Austrian imimigration documentation to analyse how social practices are recontextualized. The discussion on recontextualizing social practice is clear and systematic. The article is also a good example of the discourse-historical approach to critical discourse studies.

9

SUMMARY OF OUR APPROACH AND FINDINGS

CHAPTER OBJECTIVES

- Summarize our approach to the analysis of digital popular culture.
- Consider how our approach reveals what politics are articulated in digital popular culture and how these are articulated.
- Identify the importance of critically analysing digital popular culture.

KEY CONCEPTS

- MCDS is a well-suited approach to analysing digital popular culture.
- MCDS exposes the use and abuse of communication to articulate discourses of inequality and power to the detriment of others.
- In each chapter, we have added analytical tools to our toolkit.

Digital popular culture is an important part of our lives. It is here we are entertained and informed in a personalized stream of jokes, memes, comments, animations, music videos, parodies, mash-ups and the like. These are laden with opinions and values that inform our own perspectives, sometimes confronting these and at other times conforming to and substantiating ours. That makes digital popular culture political.

Though there is a large range of approaches on how to examine digital popular culture and politics, we have looked at these relations from a multimodal critical discourse approach. The advantages to using this approach are threefold. First, it can be adapted to take into account the range of modes of communication employed by digital popular culture, such as still imagery and written texts of memes or lyrics, moving images and musical sounds of mash-ups and music videos. Second, this approach considers texts in context, an essential factor in determining the meaning potential of texts. An essential part of understanding the meanings in much of digital popular culture, we have to be able to 'finish the sentence'. This requires knowledge about the social and political context (Denisova, 2019). It also requires us to connect our digital experience to other media, or understand digital popular culture intertextually (Wiggins, 2019). For example, a meme needs to refer to the 'subject' as well as to other texts for it to have political potential. With MCDS's emphasis on texts in context, this approach is well suited to digital popular culture. Third, through a detailed analysis of texts in context, we reveal not only what discourses are articulated but also how this is done. MCDS uses 'the power of description so useful for drawing out buried ideologies in linguistic-based CDS to be applied to other communicative modes' (Machin, 2013: 348). It is MCDS's concern for critically analysing details in texts that give us this insight. We finish off the book by summarizing two areas this book has examined in detail. These are: (1) what tools have we used and found useful in analysing digital popular culture; and (2) what have we learned about the political potential of digital popular culture?

HOW DO WE ANALYSE POLITICS IN DIGITAL POPULAR CULTURE?

This book has proposed and tested an approach that considers what politics are articulated in digital popular culture and how this is achieved. The approach is one that embraces the key principles of MCDS. That is, our approach sees communication as a multimodal social practice where each mode plays a part both individually and in tandem with other modes, to articulate political discourses. Modes in our analysis are broadly categorized as lexica, visuals and (musical) sounds. Our position as analysts is to critically analyse texts in context to reveal 'what view of the world is being communicated through semiotic resources' (Abousnnouga and Machin, 2010: 139). Through our analysis, ideological discourses are revealed, such as what kinds of social relations of power, inequalities, identities and interests are perpetuated, generated, or legitimated in texts both explicitly and implicitly. So, our approach is critical in the sense that our analysis reveals communicative instances of social inequality and the abuse of power.

Our approach is well suited to analysing digital popular culture. Texts in the digital, for the most part, take advantage of the affordances offered by technologies and their multimodal capabilities. Also, digital popular culture articulates ideological discourses both explicitly and implicitly. MCDS is a useful approach to reveal these.

The approach we have examined and then used in each chapter can be viewed as a number of tools in an analytical toolkit used to reveal political discourses in digital popular culture. Though there are many more analytical tools within the broad MCDS approach than this book can possibly cover, our toolkit is one that has proved to be useful. We now summarize what these tools are.

In Chapter 4, we examined comments about music videos on YouTube by analysing the lexical representation of social actors. Through a wide range of texts, this set of tools has been shown to be central in revealing discourses (Wodak et al., 1999; Bishop and Jaworski, 2003; Wodak and Weiss, 2005). In our analysis of social actors, we consider who is included and excluded and a wide range of possibilities in terms of how people are named. We also looked at grammatical strategies, such as if an actor is represented in a clause or de-emphasized, represented in a circumstance. If an actor is represented in a clause, we considered their grammatical role, represented as doing something or having something done to them.

In Chapter 5, we used another set of tools to consider the discourses articulated in memes. Here, we analysed three aspects of the visual representation of social actors. One aspect of an image we consider is how a social actor in an image is metaphorically positioned in relation to the viewer. Here, we determine if the subject is in a 'demand' or 'offer' image; the horizontal and vertical angles of interaction between subject and viewer; and the connoted social distance between viewer and subject. A second aspect of the representation of a social actor in an image is what kind of participants are represented. Here, we consider whether they are represented as individuals or groups, how they are categorized both culturally and biologically and who is included and excluded in visuals. The third aspect of a representation is what actions are represented. We examine who is active, who is passive and where agency lies. In this analysis, we also consider other composition choices including the internal 'flow' of an image, what is salient and the chosen degree of modality.

In Chapter 6, we added to our toolkit the way we can analyse the representation of social action in both lexical and visual representations. There are a number of ways into these representations and it is our approach to pick and choose those that most suit the text under scrutiny. We may consider representations in terms of Halliday's (1994) process types. Here, varying degrees of represented power can be connoted by whether a social action is represented as an action, event, state, mental, or verbal process. We may also want to distinguish between representations of actions by three broader action types: mental processes, semiotic actions and material actions. Mental processes are most associated with reactions and a lack of power. Semiotic actions are speech acts, some connoting more power than others. Material actions usually connote the most power and involve someone doing something. These can be transactive (involving two participants) or non-transactive (involving only one participant). How actions are represented can be further classified in terms of a set of dichotomies: activation/de-activation, agentialization/de-agentialization, abstraction/concretization and single-determination/overdetermination (van Leeuwen, 1995).

Chapter 7 saw us analyse music videos. We increased our toolkit by adding metaphors, the representation of place and the role of musical sounds. Metaphors are a common and ideological way to represent. Scholars have examined their roles in a wide range of communication including mainstream media, political speeches and music, to name just a few. The representation of place is another tool used by producers to connote 'the world being communicated' and used to connote 'social relations and trends, including identity, ethnicity, attachment to place, cultural economies, social activism, and politics' (Johansson and Bell, 2009: 2; Machin, 2010: 92).

Scholars have examined the role of musical sounds in detail and have revealed their important roles in meaning making (Way, 2018a). Our approach takes into account a range of scholars, both semioticians and musicologists. For convenience, we summarize these ideas in a list of 'sound domains' identified by van Leeuwen (1999). These domains are (1) perspective in terms of either a metaphoric social distance or a hierarchy created by the 'closeness' of sounds; (2) the manipulation of time; (3) interacting sounds both sequentially and simultaneously; (4) six aspects of melody; (5) six aspects of voice quality and timbre; and (6) modality of sounds connoted by manipulating sounds to suggest naturalness or not.

A final set of tools we added to our analytical toolkit in Chapter 8 was considering texts as recontextualizations of social practices. Our case study was the recontextualization of the social practices of politicians and environmentalists in a satirical parody. Social practices are made up of activities, participants, performance indicators, times, places, tools and materials, dress and grooming, and eligibility conditions. How these are transformed into a recontextualization involves selective appropriation, relocation, refocusing and relating to other discourses (Bernstein, 1996). In our approach, we analyse how social practices are transformed in terms of what is deleted, how practices are rearranged, what linguistic substitute is used for the people, actions, issues, etc. of a practice and what is added, such as opinions, feelings and judgements.

WHAT ARE THE POLITICS ARTICULATED IN DIGITAL POPULAR CULTURE?

In the Introduction and then again in Chapter 2, we considered what some highly influential scholars and schools of thought historically believed were relations between popular culture and politics. These scholars and schools of thought have come up with very different and sometimes contradictory conclusions. Even within particular schools, such as Marxist approaches to studying popular culture, they cannot agree on how popular culture works politically. For instance, the Frankfurt School believes the cultural industry serves listeners standardized fare with unique selling points. This promotes consumption that is always passive, and endlessly repetitive, confirming the world as it is, a kind of 'social cement' thereby supporting an unfair status quo. In contrast, Gramscian studies of popular culture see people empowered as active, creating meanings from commodities offered to them by the cultural industries. Meanings are always the result of negotiations between dominant and subordinate groups. Popular culture is a negotiated mix of intentions and counterintentions, both from above and below, both commercial and authentic, a shifting balance of forces between resistance and incorporation. The point to be made here is, despite there being a range of views on relations between popular culture and politics, pretty much all see there being political potential in popular culture. Our approach is situated within this wide area of research.

Our approach also takes on board observations about relations between politics and the digital made by current scholars. Like the area outlined above, this too is a broad field of study concerned with a wide range of aspects of the digital, from the World Wide Web to social media and Web 2.0. Again, we found an array of opinions, some far more pessimistic than others. There is a large amount of scepticism in terms of 'slacktivism', 'technical determinism', 'filter bubbles' and our preference for entertainment and gossip over information. We agree with many of these positions. However, what many of them omit is where our study is located: the exact junction where digital entertainment is political. It is here where, we believe, digital popular culture can play a role in politics by articulating political discourses in a way that is entertaining.

Our case studies illustrate just how digital popular culture can be political. When we examine comments on YouTube, we find they hint at a range of complex issues but are never fully articulated. Rather than discussing the politics of actual events, such as the Gezi Park protests or the politics represented in videos about Gezi Park, we find comments frame events around a set of personal interests and shifting notions of a legitimate Turkish nationalism, at the mercy of self-interested elites. These comments lean on populist and nationalist discourses where there is an easy and trustworthy mass public consensus and there are ignorant, self-interested elites. Comments are about personalized political views that categorize people in terms of what it is to be a patriot and who fits into this category and who does not. Though far from ideal, some of these views are ones that are stifled in mainstream media.

Memes about Donald Trump articulate discourses of power. However, whether pro- or anti-Trump, the power represented in memes is not about any real tangible power or actions like cancelling Obamacare, building a wall, closing the borders to Muslims or curtailing criticisms in the press. These represent Trump with great power, though symbolic and/or metaphoric. All the same, memes are far from innocuous. We find many of these also lean on discourses of nationalism, racism and authoritarianism, discourses many of its audience would admire.

Our examination of anti-Brexit GIFs and mash-ups reveal a gross simplification of issues, events and people represented in an entertaining manner. Advantages and disadvantages of Britain leaving the European Union are not articulated. Instead, a populist discourse is articulated where the elite are represented as out of touch, despotic and opposed to 'the people' who are correct, united and victims. Our analysis of music videos (a mash-up and a cypher) reveals how musical sounds can not only emphasize discourses articulated in other modes, but also connote slightly different ones as well. In the mash-up, musical sounds connote a further simplification of Brexit seen in the lyrics and images. Sounds emphasize the idea that the elite are inauthentic, bad, emotionless and unhuman, not like us 'the people'. The three modes work together to articulate populist discourses. In the cypher attack, dominant discourses we find delegitimize Trump. He is represented as demasculinized, sneaky and weak. Eminem represents himself as angry, powerful and an authentic leader of the people. In fact, these discourses are common throughout much popular music that is deemed political (Way, 2018a). Finally, in our analysis of satirical parodies, we find a simplification of complex issues surrounding the global climate crisis. This results in representing binary opposites to legitimize protest and delegitimize politicians.

MEME-SIZED CONCLUSION ON DIGITAL POPULAR CULTURE AND POLITICS

What our multiple analyses of digital popular culture reveal is indeed these can be critical of those in power. Digital popular culture does not argue in logical easy-to-follow prose. But who wants to listen to and/or watch something like that? Who wants to listen to politicians or their opponents read out their manifestos and policies when we can scroll through our digital feeds, have a chuckle at the expense of a politician and then move on? Digital popular culture offers an affective entertaining critique. We are offered bite-sized, simplified representations of complex issues, events, practices and people. Politics are vague, abstract and lack any particulars and details. Much of this articulates popular and populist sentiments. In most instances, we find discourses of legitimacy and authenticity, usually of the producer and his/her ideas and delegitimacy of views that are different.

Much of what we experience digitally agrees with our own beliefs due to how our feeds are tailored to our interests and values. But also, some of this challenges our notions. Outlying views, whether we agree with them or not, are important. Many of these are not easily found in mainstream media in western democracies, especially media to the right of the political spectrum. In more oppressive regimes, such as Turkey, Hungary and Russia, these non-mainstream voices take on even more relevance.

A FINAL WORD ON OUR APPROACH

This book is not an exhaustive description of all possible ways we can analyse digital popular culture using MCDS. This would be an almost impossible task. MCDS is a large and loose collection of tools in a bottomless toolkit. Scholars from a wide range of disciplines dip into MCDS, with their own strengths, knowledge, specialities and experiences. For example, I have been particularly interested in popular music, protest and politics. Others may come from an interest in the analysis of news or political speeches. Though there is a wide range of approaches, what most of us have in common is a desire to critically consider the discourses of power articulated in texts by analysing texts in their contexts. The approach we have outlined in this book is a culmination of what I have used and what I have found to be successful in unearthing discourses of power in texts that propose to be political. Equipped with these tools, you are able to add to an ever-growing body of critical work – work that exposes the use and abuse of communication to articulate discourses of inequality and power to the detriment of others.

SUGGESTED READING

Abousnnouga, G. and Machin, D. (2010) Analyzing the language of war monuments. *Visual Communication*, 9(2): 131–149.

This article uses MCDS in a very innovative way to consider the ideological discourses articulated in war monuments around Britain. The author's use of MCDS informed by other disciplines demonstrates how this approach can be employed by us in a wide variety of situations.

Halliday, M.A.K. (1994) *An Introduction to Functional Grammar* (2nd edn). London: Edward Arnold.

This book contains the foundations for many of us who use CDA and/or MCDS. It is a great reference book to dip in and out of. Though Halliday focused his studies on linguistics, many of his systemic functional linguistics ideas have found their way into the approach we use here.

Machin, D. (2013) What is multimodal critical discourse studies? *Critical Discourse Studies*, 10(4): 347–355.

Much multimodal analysis is not critical. In this article, Machin sets out a solid argument for why we should analyse texts multimodally and critically. This is the approach we have used in this book.

REFERENCES

Abousnnouga, G. and Machin, D. (2010) Analyzing the language of war monuments. *Visual Communication*, 9(2): 131–149.

About BuzzFeed (2019) https://www.buzzfeed.com/about

About us (2020) Extinction Rebellion. https://rebellion.earth/the-truth/about-us/

Abrams, M.H. (1999) *A Glossary of Literary Terms* (7th edn). Fort Worth, TX: Harcourt Brace.

Adorno, T. (1941) On popular music. *Studies in Philosophy and Social Science*. New York: Institute of Social Research. pp. 17–48. http://www.icce.rug.nl/~soundscapes/DATABASES/SWA/On_popular_music_1.shtml

Adorno, T. (1991) *The Culture Industry: Selected Essays on Mass Culture*. London: Routledge.

Allbeson, T. and Allan, S. (2019) The war of images in the age of Trump, in C. Happer, A. Hoskins and W. Merrin (eds), *Trump's Media War*. London: Palgrave Macmillan. pp. 69–84.

Althusser, L. (1970) Ideology and ideological state apparatuses (notes towards an investigation). *La Pensée*. https://www.marxists.org/reference/archive/althusser/1970/ideology.htm

Althusser, L. (2005) Marxism and humanism, in *For Marx*. London and New York: Verso. pp. 221–247.

Amnesty International (2013) *Gezi Park Protests: Brutal Denial of the Right to Peaceful Assembly in Turkey*. http://www.amnesty.org.uk/news_details. asp?NewsID=20991

Anderson, B. (1991) *Imagined Communities: Reflections on the Origin and Spread of Nationalism*. London: Verso.

Andrejevic, M. (2013) Estranged free labour, in T. Sholtz (ed.), *Digital Labour: The Internet as Playground and Factory*. New York: Routledge. pp. 149–164.

Androutsopoulos, J. (2010) Multilingualism, ethnicity and genre in Germany's migrant Hip Hop, in M. Terkourafi (ed.), *Languages of Global Hip Hop*. London: Continuum. pp. 19–43.

Arnold, G., Cookney, D., Fairclough, K. and Goddard, M. (2017) Introduction: the persistence of the music video form from MTV to twenty-first-century social media, in G. Arnold, D. Cookney, K. Fairclough and M. Goddard (eds), *Music/Video: Histories, Aesthetics, Media*. New York and London: Bloomsbury. pp. 1–19.

Arnold, M. (1960) *Culture and Anarchy*. London: Cambridge University Press.

Ashdown, P. (2017) Brexit is a monumental act of self-harm which will bewilder historians. *Independent*. https://www.independent.co.uk/voices/article-50-brexit-theresa-may-eu-negotiations-paddy-ashdown-monumental-self-harm-bewilder-historians-a7656306.html

Attardo, S. (1994) *Linguistic Theories of Humor*. Berlin and New York: Mouton de Gruyter.

Auslander, P. (1999) *Liveness: Performance in a Mediatized Culture*. New York: Routledge.

Bakhtin, M. (1984) *Problems of Dostoevsky's Poetics*. Minneapolis: University of Minnesota Press.

Barbosa Caro, E. and Ramírez Suavita, J. (2019) Paramilitarism and music in Colombia: an analysis of the corridos paracos. *Journal of Language and Politics*, 18(4): 541–559.

Barton, D. and Lee, C. (2013) *Language Online: Investigating Digital Texts and Practices*. Abingdon: Routledge.

Barthes, R. (1957) *Mythologies*. Paris: Les Lettres Nouvelles.

Baumgartner, J. and Morris, J.S. (2006) The Daily Show effect: candidate evaluations, efficacy, and American youth. *American Politics Research*, 34: 341–367.

Baym, G. (2005) The Daily Show: discursive integration and the reinvention of political journalism. *Political Communication*, 22(3): 259–276.

Bennett, C. (2018) Inside Jacob Rees-Mogg. *Tatler*. https://www.tatler.com/article/jacob-rees-mogg-trivia-facts

Bennett, T. (1980) Popular culture: a teaching object. *Screen Education*, 34: 17–29.

Bergson, H. (1956) Laughter, in G. Meredith (ed.), *Comedy*. New York: Doubleday Anchor Books. pp. 3–61.

Bernstein, B. (1990) *Class, Codes and Control: The Structuring of Pedagogical Discourse*. London and New York: Routledge.

Bernstein, B. (1996) Pedagogy, symbolic control and identity. *British Journal of Sociology of Education*, 18(1): 119–124.

Billig, M. (1995) *Banal Nationalism*. London: SAGE.

Bishop, H. and Jaworski, A. (2003) We beat 'em: nationalism and the hegemony of homogeneity in the British press reportage of Germany versus England during Euro 2000. *Discourse and Society*, 14(3): 243–271.

Bishop, J. (2013) The effect of de-individuation of the internet troller on criminal procedure implementation: an interview with a hater. *International Journal of Cyber Criminology*, 7(1): 28–48.

Boardley, J. (2015) The first illustrated books. *I Love Typography*. https://ilovetypography.com/2015/11/10/the-first-illustrated-books/

Bouvier, G. (2017) Discourse in clothing: the social semiotics of modesty and chic in hijab fashion. *Gender and Language*, 10(3): 364–385.

Bou-Franch, P. and Garcés-Conejos Blitvich, P. (2014) The pragmatics of textual participation in the social media. *The Journal of Pragmatics*, 73: 1–18.

boyd, d. (2008) Can social media sites enable political action? *International Journal of Media and Cultural Politics*, 4(2): 241–244.

Brewer, P.R. and Marquardt, E. (2007) Mock news and democracy: analyzing The Daily Show. *Atlantic Journal of Communication*, 15(4): 249–267.

Brewer, P., Young, D. and Morreale, M. (2013) The impact of real news about 'fake news': intertextual processes and political satire. *International Journal of Public Opinion Research*, 25(3): 323–343.

Burgess, J. and Green, J. (2009) *YouTube: Online Video and Participatory Culture*. Cambridge: Polity Press.

Caldas-Coulthard, C.R. (1994) On reporting reporting: the representation of speech in factual and factional narratives, in M. Coulthard (ed.), *Advances in Written Text Analysis*. London: Routledge Press. pp. 295–308.

Calhoun, K. (2019) Vine racial comedy as anti-hegemonic humor: linguistic performance and generic innovation. *Journal of Linguistic Anthropology*, 29(1): 27–49.

Campbell, J. (2018) Q & A: the Irish border Brexit backstop. BBC. https://www.bbc.co.uk/news/uk-northern-ireland-politics-44615404

Chen, M. and Flowerdew, J. (2019) Discriminatory discursive strategies in online comments on YouTube videos on the Hong Kong Umbrella Movement by Mainland and Hong Kong Chinese. *Discourse and Society* 30(6): 549–572.

Classic tracks: Pulp 'Common People' (2013) *Sound on Sound*. https://www.soundonsound.com/people/classic-tracks-pulp-common-people

Clottes, S. (2019) Cave Art. *Encyclopeadia Britannica*. https://www.britannica.com/art/cave-painting

Coffey, B. and Woolworth, S. (2004) Destroy the scum, and then neuter their families: the web forum as a vehicle for community discourse? *Social Science Journal*, 41(1): 1–14.

Colleoni, E. (2013) *Beyond the differences: the use of empty signifiers as organizing device in the #occupy movement*. Paper presented at the workshop Material Participation: Technology, the Environment and Everyday Publics. University of Milan.

Comedy interview: Tom Walker on bringing his TV news alter ego Jonathan Pie to Scotland (2018) *The Scotsman*. https://www.scotsman.com/arts-and-culture/theatre-and-stage/comedy-interview-tom-walker-bringing-his-tv-news-alter-ego-jonathan-pie-scotland-1428834

Common People by Pulp (2019) *Song facts*. https://www.songfacts.com/facts/pulp/common-people

Connell, J. and Gibson C. (2003) *Sound Tracks: Popular Music, Identity, and Place*. London: Routledge.

Connick, T. (2017) Eminem slams Donald Trump in BET awards freestyle. *NME*. https://www.nme.com/news/music/eminem-slams-donald-trump-bet-awards-freestyle-2148945

Cooke, D. (1959) *The Language of Music*. Oxford: Clarendon Press.

Cook, N. (1990) *Music, Imagination and Culture*. Oxford: Clarendon Press.

Cook, N. (1998) *Music: A Very Short Introduction*. Oxford: Oxford University Press.

Coronavirus: Trump says ... (2020) Coronavirus: Trump says US in good shape to meet 'peak'. BBC. https://www.bbc.co.uk/news/world-us-canada-52101321

Cowie, S. (2020) Deny and defy: Bolsonaro's approach to the coronavirus in Brazil. *Aljazeera*. https://www.aljazeera.com/indepth/features/deny-defy-bolsonaro-approach-coronavirus-brazil-200330181645501.html

Crusades (2019) *History*. https://www.history.com/topics/middle-ages/crusades

Dawkins, R. (1976) *The Selfish Gene*. Oxford: Oxford University Press.

De Cleen, B. and Carpentier, N. (2010) Contesting the populist claim on 'the People' through popular culture: the 0110 concerts versus the Vlaams Belang. *Social Semiotics*, 20(2): 175–196.

Dean, J. (2010b) *Blog Theory*. Cambridge: Polity Press.

De Cristofaro, E. (2018) *Memes are Taking the Alt-Right's Message of Hate Mainstream*. Information Security Research and Education, University College London: Bentham's Gaze. https://www.benthamsgaze.org/2018/12/13/memes-are-taking-the-alt-rights-message-of-hate-mainstream/

Denisova, A. (2017) Parody microbloggers as chroniclers and commentators on Russian political reality. *Demokratizatsiya: The Journal of Post-Soviet Democratization*, 25(1): 23–41.

Denisova, A. (2019) *Internet Memes and Society: Social, Cultural, and Political Contexts*. New York and London: Routledge.

D'Urso, J. (2018) Who spent what on Facebook during 2017 election campaign? BBC. https://www.bbc.co.uk/news/uk-politics-43487301

Eisner, W. (1985) *Comics and Sequential Art*. Florida: Poor House Press.

El Khachab, C. (2016) Living in darkness: internet humour and the politics of Egypt's electricity infrastructure. *Anthropology Today*, 32(4): 21–24.

Esralew, S. and Young, D. (2012) The influence of parodies on mental models: exploring the Tina Fey–Sarah Palin phenomenon. *Communication Quarterly*, 60(3): 338–352.

Esteves, V. and Meikle, G. (2015) 'Look @ this fukken doge': internet memes and remix cultures, in C. Atton (ed.), *The Routledge Companion to Alternative and Community Media*. New York: Routledge. pp. 561–570.

Eyerman, R. and Jamison, A. (1998) *Music and Social Movements: Mobilising Traditions in the Twentieth Century*. Cambridge: Cambridge University Press.

Extinction Rebellion are diverting police from stopping knife crime, warns Sadiq Khan (2019) *LBC 'Speak to Sadiq'*. https://www.lbc.co.uk/radio/special-shows/speak-sadiq/extinction-rebellion-diverting-police-knife-crime/

Extinction Rebellion rush-hour protest sparks clash on London Underground (2019) *Guardian*. https://www.theguardian.com/environment/2019/oct/17/extinction-rebellion-activists-london-underground

Fairclough, N. (1989) *Language and Power*. Harlow: Pearson Education.

Fairclough, N. (1995a) *Critical Discourse Analysis: The Critical Study of Language*. London: Longman.

Fairclough, N. (1995b) *Media Discourse*. London: Edward Arnold.

Fairclough, N. (2003) *Analyzing Discourse: Textual Analysis for Social Research*. London: Routledge.

Feinberg, L. (1967) *Introduction to Satire*. Ames: Iowa State University Press.

Fiske, J. (1989) *Understanding Popular Culture*. London: Routledge.

Flowerdew, J. and Leong, S. (2007) Metaphors in the discursive construction of patriotism: the case of Hong Kong's constitutional reform debate. *Discourse and Society*, 18(3): 273–294.

Fonagy, I. and Magdics, K. (1972) Emotional patterns in intonation and music, in D.L. Bolinger (ed.), *Intonation*. Harmondsworth: Penguin.

Forman, M. (2002) *The Hood Comes First: Race, Space, and Place in Rap and Hip-Hop*. Middletown: Wesleyan University Press.

Foucault, M. (1979) *Discipline and Punishment*. Harmondsworth: Penguin.

Foucault, M. (1989) *The Archeology of Knowledge*. London: Routledge.

Fraley, T. (2009) 'I got a natural skill …': hip-hop, authenticity, and whiteness. *Howard Journal of Communications*, 20(1): 37–54.

Frith, S. (1981) *Sound Effects: Youth, Leisure and the Politics of Rock'n'roll*. New York: Pantheon.

Frith, S. (1988) *Music for Pleasure: Essays in the Sociology of Pop*. Cambridge: Polity Press.

Frith, S. (1996) *Performing Rites: On the Value of Popular Music*. Cambridge, MA: Harvard University Press.

Giesea, J. (2015) *Hacking Hearts and Minds: How Mimetic Warfare is Transforming Cyberwar*. https://www.act.nato.int/images/stories/media/doclibrary/open201706-memetic2.pdf

Gilbert, J.R. (2004) *Performing Marginality: Humor, Gender, and Cultural Critique*. Michigan: Wayne State University Press.

Gitelman, L. (2013) *Raw Data is an Oxymoron*. Cambridge, MA: MIT Press.

Glasser, A. (2017) Politicians are addicted to data like it's campaign cash. *Slate.* https://slate.com/technology/2017/10/politicians-are-addicted-to-big-data-like-its-campaign-cash.html

Goodwin, A. (1993) *Dancing in the Distraction Factory: Music Television and Popular Culture.* London: Routledge.

Gramsci, A. (1971) *Selection from Prison Notebooks.* London: Lawrence and Wishart.

Gray, J., Jones, J. and Thompson, E. (2009) *Satire TV: Politics and Comedy in the Post-Network Era.* New York: New York University Press.

Griffin, Dustin (1994) *Satire: A Critical Reintroduction.* Lexington: University Press of Kentucky.

Grossberg, L. (1992) *We Gotta Get Out of This Place: Popular Conservatism and Postmodern Culture.* New York: Routledge.

Guess, A., Nyhan, B. and Reifler, J. (2018) *Selective Exposure to Misinformation: Evidence from the Consumption of Fake News during the 2016 US Presidential Campaign.* Brussels: European Research Council.

Hall, S. (1982) The rediscovery of ideology: the return of the repressed in media studies, in J. Wollacott, M. Gurevitch, J. Curran and T. Bennett (eds), *Culture, Society and the Media.* London: Routledge. pp. 52–86.

Halliday, M.A.K. (1994) *An Introduction to Functional Grammar* (2nd edn). London: Edward Arnold.

Happer, C., Hoskins, A. and Merrin, W. (2019) Weaponising reality: an introduction to Trump's war on the media, in C. Happer, A. Hoskins and W. Merrin (eds), *Trump's Media War.* London: Palgrave Macmillan. pp. 3–22.

Hargittai, E. (2008) The digital reproduction in inequality, in D. Grusky (ed.), *Social Stratification.* Boulder, CO: Westview Press. pp. 936–944.

Harman, A., Milner, A. and Mellers, W. (1962) *Man and His Music: The Story of Musical Experience in the West.* Oxford: Oxford University Press.

Hartley, J. (1982) *Understanding News.* London: Routledge.

Hassa, S. (2010) Kiff my zikmu: symbolic dimensions of Arabic, English and Verlan in French rap texts, in M. Terkourafi (ed.), *Languages of Global Hip Hop.* London: Continuum. pp. 44–66.

Hebdige, D. (1979) *Subculture: The Meaning of Style.* Suffolk: Methuen.

Hern, A. (2019) Tim Berners-Lee on 30 years of the world wide web: we can get the web we want. *Guardian.* https://www.theguardian.com/technology/2019/mar/12/tim-berners-lee-on-30-years-of-the-web-if-we-dream-a-little-we-can-get-the-web-we-want

Hesmondhalgh, D. and Negus, K. (2002) *Popular Music Studies.* London: Arnold.

Hess, J.S. (2010) From American form to Greek performance: the global hip-hop poetics and politics of the Imiskoumbria, in M. Terkourafi (ed.), *Languages of Global Hip Hop.* London: Continuum. pp. 162–193.

Hibbett, R. (2005) What is indie rock? *Popular Music and Society*, 28(1): 55–77.

Hobsbawm, E.J. (1990) *Nations and Nationalism since 1780: Programme, Myth, Reality*. Cambridge: Cambridge University Press.

Hoffman, L.H. and Thomson, T.L. (2009) The effect of television viewing on adolescents' civic participation: political efficacy as a mediating mechanism. *Journal of Broadcasting and Electronic Media*, 53: 3–21.

Hoffman, L.H. and Young, D.G. (2011) Satire, punch lines, and the nightly news: untangling media effects on political participation. *Communication Research Reports*, 28(2): 159–168.

Holbert, R.L. (2005) A typology for the study of entertainment television and politics. *American Behavioral Scientist*, 49: 436–453.

Hollander, B.A. (2005) Late-night learning: do entertainment programs increase political campaign knowledge for young viewers? *Journal of Broadcasting and Electronic Media*, 49: 402–415.

Howard, P.N. and Hussain, M. (2013) *Democracy's Fourth Wave? Digital Media and the Arab Spring*. New York: Oxford University Press.

Işık, G. (2013) Yeni toplumsal hareketler ve sanal gerçeklik boyutunda gezi parkı eylemleri. *Seçukİletişim*, 8(1): 19–33.

Ito, M. (2009) *Engineering Play: A Cultural History of Children's Software*. Cambridge, MA: MIT Press.

Ito, M., Baumer, S., Bittanti, M., boyd, d., Cody, R., Herr, B., Horst, H.A., Lange, P.G., Mahendran, D., Martinez, K., Pascoe, C.J., Perkel, D., Robinson, L., Sims, C. and Tripp, L. (2010) *Hanging Out, Messing Around, Geeking Out: Kids Living and Learning with New Media*. Cambridge, MA: MIT Press.

Jackson, J. (2017) Eli Pariser: activist whose filter bubble warnings presaged Trump and Brexit. *Guardian*. https://www.theguardian.com/media/2017/jan/08/eli-pariser-activist-whose-filter-bubble-warnings-presaged-trump-and-brexit

Jenkins, H. (2009) *Confronting the Challenges of Participatory Culture: Media Education for the 21st Century*. Cambridge, MA: MIT Press.

Johansson, O. and Bell, T. (2009) Introduction, in O. Johansson and T. Bell (eds), *Sound, Society and the Geography of Popular Music*. Farnham: Ashgate. pp. 1–6.

Jones, R.H., Chik, A. and Hafner, C. (eds) (2015) *Discourse and Digital Practices: Doing Discourse Analysis in the Digital Age*. London: Routledge.

Keen, A. (2007) *The Cult of the Amateur*. New York: Doubleday.

Keppler, N. (2018) Pulp's Common People – railing against class tourism. *Financial Times*. https://ig.ft.com/life-of-a-song/common-people.html

KhosraviNik, M. (2017) Social media critical discourse studies (SM-CDS), in J. Flowerdew and J. Richardson (eds), *Handbook of Critical Discourse Studies*. London: Routledge. pp. 582–596.

Kitschelt, H.P. (1986) Political opportunity structures and political protest: anti-nuclear movements in four democracies. *British Journal of Political Science*, 16(01): 57–85.

Kligler-Vilenchik, N. and Thorson, K. (2015) Good citizen as a frame contest: Kony2012, memes and critiques of the networked citizen. *New Media and Society*, 8(9): 1–19.

Korczynski, M. (2014) *Songs of the Factory: Pop Music, Culture and Resistance*. New York: Cornell University Press.

Krasodomski-Jones, A. (2016) How politicians are learning from Social Media'. *ITNOW*. https://academic.oup.com/itnow/article-pdf/58/4/60/8091068/bww116.pdf

Kress, G. (1985) *Linguistic Processes in Sociocultural Practice*. Victoria, Australia: Deakin University Press.

Kress, G. and Hodge, R. (1979) *Language as Ideology*. London: Routledge.

Kress, G. and van Leeuwen, T. (1996) *Reading Images: The Grammar of Visual Design*. London: Routledge.

Kress, G. and van Leeuwen, T. (2001) *Multimodal Discourse: The Modes and Media of Contemporary Communication*. London: Arnold.

Krzyżanowski, M. (2016) Recontextualization of neoliberalism and the increasingly conceptual nature of discourse: challenges for critical discourse studies. *Discourse and Society*, 27(3): 308–321.

Krzyżanowski, M. (2020) Normalization and the discursive construction of 'new' norms and 'new' normality: discourse in/and the paradoxes of populism and neoliberalism. *Social Semiotics*, 30.

Krzyżanowski, M. and Forchtner, B. (2016) Theories and concepts in critical discourse studies: facing challenges, moving beyond foundations. *Discourse and Society*, 27(3): 253–261.

Laclau, E. (2005) *On Populist Reason*. London: Verso.

Laclau, E. and Mouffe, C. (2001) *Hegemony and Socialist Strategy*. London: Verso.

Lakoff, G. and Johnson, M. (1980) *Metaphors We Live By*. London: University of Chicago.

LaMarre, H.L., Landreville, K.D. and Beam, M.A. (2009) The irony of satire: political ideology and the motivation to see what you want to see in the Colbert Report. *International Journal of Press/Politics*, 14, 212–231.

LaMarre, H.L., Landreville, K.D., Young, D. and Gilkerson, N. (2014) Humor works in funny ways: examining satirical tone as a key determinant in political humor message processing. *Mass Communication and Society*, 17(3): 400–423.

Lange, P. (2007) Publicly private and privately public: social networking on YouTube. *Journal of Computer-Mediated Communication*, 13(1): 361–380.

Lange, P. (2014) Commenting on YouTube rants: perceptions of inappropriateness or civic engagement? *Journal of Pragmatics*, 73: 53–65.

Lange, P. (2018) Informal learning on YouTube. *The International Encyclopedia of Media Literacy*. https://onlinelibrary.wiley.com/doi/pdf/10.1002/9781118978238.ieml0090

Lavoie, S. (2018) Modern photography is changing how we remember our lives. *OneZero*. https://onezero.medium.com/modern-photography-is-changing-how-we-remember-our-lives-4b59adab4a2e

Leavis, F.R. and Thompson, B. (1977) *Culture and Environment*. Westport, CT: Greenwood Press.

Lee, F. (2010) Globalizing keepin' it real: South Korean hip-hop playas, in M. Terkourafi (ed.), *Languages of Global Hip Hop*. London: Continuum. pp. 139–161.

Lees, M. (2016) What Gamergate should have taught us about the 'alt-right'. *Guardian*. https://www.theguardian.com/technology/2016/dec/01/gamergate-alt-right-hate-trump

Leppanen, S., Westinen, E. and Kytola, S. (eds) (2017) Introduction, in *Social Media Discourse, (Dis)identification and Diversities*. New York: Routledge. pp. 1–35.

Lindgren, S. (2010) At the nexus of destruction and creation: pirate and anti-pirate discourse in Swedish online media, in U. Dai (ed.), *New Media and Interactivity [NMIC2010 proceedings]*. Istanbul: Marmara University. pp. 229–236.

Lomax, A. (1968) *Folk Song Style and Culture*. London: Transaction.

Lorraine, L. (2006) Music and national culture: pop music and resistance in Brazil. *Portuguese Cultural Studies*, 0: 36–44.

Machin, D. (2007) *Introduction to Multimodal Analysis*. London: Hodder Education.

Machin, D. (2010) *Analyzing Popular Music*. London: SAGE.

Machin, D. (2013) What is multimodal critical discourse studies? *Critical Discourse Studies*, 10(4): 347–355.

Machin, D. and Mayr, A. (2012) *How to Do Critical Discourse Analysis: A Multimodal Introduction*. London: SAGE.

Machin, D. and Richardson, J.E. (2012) Discourses of unity and purpose in the sounds of fascist music: a multimodal approach. *Critical Discourse Studies*, 9(4): 329–345.

Machin, D. and van Leeuwen, T. (2005) Computer games as political discourse: the case of Black Hawk Down. *Journal of Language and Politics*, 4(1): 119–141.

Machin, D. and van Leeuwen, T. (2016) Multimodality, politics and ideology. *Journal of Language and Politics* 15(3): 243–258.

Madsen, A. (2016) Beyond the bubble: three empirical reasons to re-conceptualize online visibility. *Journal of Media and Communication Research*, 31(59): 6–27.

Makovicky, N., Tremon, A. and Zanonai, S. (2019) *Slogans: Subjection, Subversion, and the Politics of Neoliberalism*. London: Routledge.

Maloy, L. (2010) 'Stayin' alive in da club': the illegality and hyperreality of mashups. *Journal of the International Association for the Study of Popular Music*, 1(2): 1–20.

Manghani, S. (2017) The pleasures of (music) video, in G. Arnold, D. Cookney, K. Fairclough and M. Goddard (eds), *Music/Video: Histories, Aesthetics, Media*. New York and London: Bloomsbury. pp. 21–40.

Marres, N. (2012) The redistribution of methods: on intervention in digital social research, broadly conceived. *The Sociological Review*, 60(1): 139–165.

Mason, R. (2019) Hammond 'terrified' by Rees-Mogg claim of no-deal Brexit boost. *Guardian*. https://www.theguardian.com/politics/2019/jul/17/philip-hammond-terrified-by-jacob-rees-mogg-claim-of-no-deal-brexit-boost

Maximum Media (2019) https://www.maximummedia.ie/

McKerrell, S. (2012) Hearing sectarianism: understanding Scottish sectarianism as song. *Critical Discourse Studies*, 9(4): 1–12.

McKerrell, S. (2015) Social distance and the multimodal construction of the other in sectarian song. *Social Semiotics*, 25(5): 1–19.

McKerrell, S. and Way, L. (2017) Understanding music as multimodal discourse, in L. Way and S. McKerrell (eds), *Music as Multimodal Discourse: Media, Power and Protest*. London and New York: Bloomsbury. pp 1–20.

Meikle, G. (2014) Social media, visibility and activism: the Kony 2012 campaign, in M. Ratto and M. Boler (eds), *DIY Citizenship: Critical Making and Social Media*. Cambridge, MA: MIT Press.

Merrin, W. (2019) President Troll: Trump, 4Chan and memetic warfare, in C. Happer, A. Hoskins and W. Merrin (eds), *Trump's Media War*. London: Palgrave Macmillan. pp. 201–226.

Milner, R.M. (2012) The world made meme: discourse and identity in participatory media. PhD thesis. University of Kansas.

Milner, R.M. (2016) *The World Made Meme: Public Conversations and Participatory Media*. Cambridge, MA: MIT Press.

Milner, R.M. (2018) Media lingua franca: fixity, novelty, and vernacular creativity in internet memes. *AoIR Selected Papers of Internet Research*, 3. https://journals.uic.edu/ojs/index.php/spir/article/view/8725

Milton, J. (2017) Eminem's fiercest political moments. *NME*. https://www.nme.com/blogs/nme-blogs/eminems-shocking-political-moments-trump-bush-2149005

Molek-Kozakowska, K. (2013) The late night TV show as a strategic genre, in P. Cap and U. Okulska (eds), *Analyzing Genres in Political Communication: Theory and Practice*. Amsterdam: John Benjamins. pp. 321–344.

Moore, A. (2002) Authenticity as authentication. *Popular Music*, 21(2): 209–223.

Moore, A. (2013) *Song Means: Analyzing and Interpreting Recorded Popular Song*. Farnham: Ashgate.

Morozov, E. (2009) The brave new world of slacktivism. *Foreign Policy*. http://neteffect.foreignpolicy.com/posts/2009/05/19/the_brave_new_world_of_slacktivism

Mottier, V. (2008) Metaphors, mini-narratives and Foucauldian discourse theory, in T. Carver and J. Pikalo (eds), *Political Language and Metaphor*. London: Routledge. pp. 182–194.

Nabi, R.L., Moyer-Guse, E. and Byrne, S. (2007) All joking aside: a serious investigation into the persuasive effect of funny social issue messages. *Communication Monographs*, 74: 29–54.

Norris, P. and Inglehart, R. (2019) *Cultural Backlash: Trump, Brexit and Authoritarian Populism*. Cambridge: Cambridge University Press.

Ord, M. (2017) Song, sonic metaphor, and countercultural discourse in British folk-rock recordings, in L. Way and S. McKerrell (eds), *Music as Multimodal Discourse: Media, Power and Protest*. London and New York: Bloomsbury. pp. 201–222.

Ord, M. (2019) From here: the multimodal construction of place in English folk field recordings. *Journal of Language and Politics*, 18(4): 598–616.

Papacharissi, Z. (2015) Affective publics and structures of storytelling: sentiment, events and mediality. *Information, Communication and Society*, 19(3): 307–324.

Pariser, E. (2012) *The Filter Bubble: How the New Personalized Web is Changing What We Read and How We Think*. London: Penguin Random House.

Pearce, K. and Hajizada, A. (2014) No laughing matter. Humor as a means of dissent in the digital era: the case of authoritarian Azerbaijan. *Demokratizatsiya*, 22: 67–85. http://demokratizatsiya.pub/archives/22_1_B158221228502786.pdf

Peddie, I. (2011) *Popular Music and Human Rights. Volume 2: World Music*. Farnham: Ashgate.

Phillips, W. (2009) Why so socialist? *Unmasking the Joker*. http://henryjenkins.org/blog/2009/08/unmasking_the_joker.html

Polk, J., Young, D. and Holbert, R.L. (2009) Humor complexity and political influence: an elaboration likelihood approach to the effects of humor type in The Daily Show with Jon Stewart. *Atlantic Journal of Communication*, 17(4): 202–219.

Power, M., Dillane, A. and Devereux, E. (2012) A push and a shove and the land is ours: Morrissey's counter-hegemonic stance(s) on social class. *Critical Discourse Studies*, 9(4): 375–392.

Prosser, M. (2006) Memetics – A growth industry in US military operations. Master's thesis. https://apps.dtic.mil/dtic/tr/fulltext/u2/a507172.pdf

Pybus, J. (2019) Trump, the first Facebook president: why politicians need our data too, in C. Happer, A. Hoskins and W. Merrin (eds), *Trump's Media War*. London: Palgrave Macmillan. pp. 227–240.

Quinn, B. (2018) Jacob Rees-Mogg's investment firm launches second Irish fund. *Guardian*. https://www.theguardian.com/politics/2018/jul/22/jacob-rees-mogg-second-irish-fund-scm

Rawlinson, K. (2019) Extinction Rebellion: Johnson calls climate crisis activists 'uncooperative crusties'. *Guardian*. https://www.theguardian.com/politics/2019/oct/07/uncooperative-crusties-boris-johnson-attacks-extinction-rebellion-activists

Richardson, J.E. (2007) *Analyzing Newspapers: An Approach from Critical Discourse Analysis*. London: Palgrave Macmillan.

Roderick, I. (2013) Representing robots as living labour in advertisements: the new discourse of worker–employer power relations. *Critical Discourse Studies*, 10(4): 392–405.

Santa Ana, O. (2009) Did you call in Mexican? The racial politics of Jay Leno immigrant jokes. *Language in Society*, 38(1): 23–45.

Schafer, R.M. (1977) *The Tuning of the World*. Michigan: Knopf.

Schreckinger, B. (2017) World War meme: how a group of anonymous keyboard commandos conquered the internet for Donald Trump – and plans to deliver Europe to the far right. *Politico Magazine*. https://www.politico.com/magazine/story/2017/03/memes-4chan-trump-supporters-trolls-internet-214856

Scollon, R. (2001) *Mediated Discourse: The Nexus of Practice*. London: Routledge.

Scott, T. (2007) Analyzing political conversation on the Howard Dean candidate blog, in M. Tremayne (ed.), *Blogging, Citizenship and the Future of Media*. New York: Routledge.

Seargeant, P. and Tagg, C. (eds) (2014) *The Language of Social Media: Identity and Community on the Internet*. London: Palgrave Macmillan.

Shaw, M. (2019) Vote Leave relied on racism. Brexit: The Uncivil War disguised that ugly truth. *Guardian*. https://www.theguardian.com/commentisfree/2019/jan/08/vote-leave-racism-brexit-uncivil-war-channel-4

Shifman, L. (2011) An anatomy of a YouTube meme. *New Media and Society*, 14(2): 187–203.

Shifman, L. (2013) Memes in a digital world: reconciling with a conceptual troublemaker. *Journal of Computer-Mediated Communication*, 18: 362–377.

Shuker, R. (2001) *Understanding Popular Music* (2nd edn). London: Routledge.

Songfacts (2017) The Storm by Eminem. *Songfacts*. https://www.songfacts.com/facts/eminem/the-storm

Southern, L. (2016) Lad-lite publisher JOE Media rings in 2016 by doubling its UK team. *DigidayUK*. https://digiday.com/uk/joe-media-kicks-off-2016-doubling-uk-team/

Storey, J. (2006) *Cultural Theory and Popular Culture: An Introduction* (4th edn). Harlow: Pearson.

Street, J. (1988) *Rebel Rock: The Politics of Popular Music*. Oxford: Basil Blackwood.

Street, J. (2013) The sound of geopolitics: popular music and political rights. *Popular Communication: The International Journal of Media and Culture*, 11(1): 47–57.

Stylianou, E. (2010) Keeping it native (?): the conflicts and contradictions of Cypriot hip hop, in M. Terkourafi (ed.), *Languages of Global Hip Hop*. London: Continuum. pp. 194–222.

Suler, J. (2005) The online disinhibation effect. *International Journal of Applied Psychoanalytical Studies*, 2(2): 184–188.

Tagg, P. (1984) Understanding musical time sense: concepts, sketches and consequences. http://www.tagg.org/articles/xpdfs/timesens.pdf

Tagg, P. (1990) Music in mass media studies: reading sounds for example, in K. Roe and U. Carlsson (eds), *Popular Music Research*. Sweden: Nordicom.

Tagg, P. (2012) *Music's Meanings: A Modern Musicology for Non-Musos*. New York: Mass Media Music Scholars' Press.

Tarrow, S. (1994) *Power in Movement: Social Movements, Collective Action and Politics*. Cambridge: Cambridge University Press.

Terkourafi, M. (2010) *Languages of Global Hip Hop*. London: Continuum.

This Monday – the International Rebellion continues in more than 60 cities around the world (2019) *Extinction Rebellion*. https://rebellion.earth/2019/10/04/this-monday-the-international-rebellion-continues-in-more-than-60-cities-around-the-world/

The making of ... Pulp's Common People (2014) *Uncut*. https://www.uncut.co.uk/features/the-making-of-pulp-s-common-people-8632

Trevor-Roper, H. (1993) 'The invention of tradition: the Highland tradition of Scotland' in E. Hobsbawm and T. Ranger (eds), *The Invention of Tradition*. Cambridge: Cambridge University Press.

Tucker, J. (2011) *It's a Jetson's World: Private Miracles and Public Crimes.* Alabama: Mises Institute. https://mises-media.s3.amazonaws.com/Its%20 a%20Jetsons%20World%20Private%20Miracles%20and%20Public%20 Crimes_2.pdf

UK Parliament declares climate change emergency (2019) *BBC.* https://www. bbc.co.uk/news/uk-politics-48126677

van Dijk, T.A. (1991) *Racism and the Press.* London: Routledge.

van Dijk, T. (1993) Principles of critical discourse analysis. *Discourse and Society,* 4(2): 249–283.

van Leeuwen, T. (1993a) Genre and field in critical discourse analysis: a synopsis. *Discourse and Society,* 4(2): 193–223.

van Leeuwen, T. (1993b) Language and representation – The recontextualization of participants, activities and reactions. Unpublished PhD thesis. University of Sydney.

van Leeuwen, T. (1995) Representing social action. *Discourse and Society,* 6(1): 81–106.

van Leeuwen, T. (1996) The representation of social actors, in C. Caldas-Coulthard and M. Coulthard (eds), *Texts and Practices: Readings in Critical Discourse Analysis.* London: Routledge. pp. 32–70.

van Leeuwen, T. (1999) *Speech, Music, Sound.* London: Macmillan Press.

van Leeuwen, T. (2005) *Introducing Social Semiotics.* London: Routledge.

van Leeuwen, T. (2008) *Discourse and Practice: New Tools for Critical Discourse Analysis.* New York: Oxford University Press.

van Leeuwen, T. (2017) Sonic logos, in L. Way and S. McKerrell (eds), *Music as Multimodal Discourse: Media, Power and Protest.* London and New York: Bloomsbury. pp. 119–134.

van Leeuwen, T. and Wodak, R. (1999) Legitimizing immigration: a discourse historical approach. *Discourse Studies,* 1(1): 83–118.

Vatikiotis, P. (2014) New media, democracy, participation and the political. *Interactions: Studies in Communication and Culture,* 5(3): 293–307.

Veloso, F. and Bateman, J. (2013) The multimodal construction of acceptability: Marvel's Civil War comic books and the PATRIOT Act. *Critical Discourse Studies,* 10(4): 427–443.

Von Hippel, E. (2005) *Democratising Innovation.* Cambridge, MA: MIT Press.

Wallis, C. (2011) New media practices in China: youth patterns, processes, and politics. *International Journal of Communication,* 5: 406–436. https://ijoc.org/ index.php/ijoc/article/viewFile/698/530

Walser, R. (1995) Rhythm, rhyme, and rhetoric in the music of Public Enemy. *Ethnomusicology,* 39(2): 193–217.

Way, L. (2010) How Turkish Cypriot radio news works against a Cyprus solution: the opening of the Lokmacı/Ledra street border crossing. *Global Media Journal: Mediterranean Edition*, 5(1/2): 29–39.

Way, L. (2011) The local news media impeding solutions to the Cyprus conflict: competing discourses of nationalism in Turkish Cypriot radio news. *Social Semiotics*, 21(1): 15–31.

Way, L. (2013) *Self-Serving National Ideologies: A Critical Discourse Analysis of Turkish Cypriot Radio News*. Saarbrücken, Germany: Scholars Press.

Way, L. (2015) YouTube as a site of debate through populist politics: the case of a Turkish protest pop video. *Journal of Multicultural Discourse*, 10(2): 180–196.

Way, L. (2016) Protest music, populism, politics and authenticity: the limits and potential of popular music's articulation of subversive politics. *Journal of Language and Politics*, 15(4): 422–446.

Way, L. (2018a) *Popular Music and Multimodal Critical Discourse Studies: Ideology, Control and Resistance in Turkey since 2002*. London: Bloomsbury.

Way, L. (2018b) Turkish newspapers and how they use Brexit for domestic political gain, in Ridge-Newman, A. (ed.) *EU Referendum and the Media: National And International Perspectives*. London and New York: Palgrave Macmillan. pp. 281–294.

Way, L. (2019a) Discourse, music and political communication: towards a critical approach. *Journal of Language and Politics*, 18(4): 475–490.

Way, L. (2019b) Music video as party political communication: opportunities and limits. *Journal of Language and Politics*, 18(4): 579–597.

Way, L. and McKerrell, S. (eds) (2017) *Music as Multimodal Discourse: Music, Power and Protest*. London and New York: Bloomsbury.

Webb, N. (2015) JOE.ie boss McGarry plots €20m move on UK market. *Independent. ie*. www.independent.ie/business/irish/joe-ie-boss-mcgarry-plots-20m-move-on-uk-market-31283349.html

Why video is exploding on social media in 2019 (2019) *Wyzowl*. https://www.wyzowl.com/video-social-media-2019/

Wiggins, B.E. (2019) *The Discursive Power of Memes in Digital Culture: Ideology, Semiotics, and Intertextuality*. New York and London: Routledge.

Wilford, G. (2017) Jacob Rees-Mogg is earning millions from his investment company, accounts reveal. *Independent*. https://www.independent.co.uk/news/uk/politics/jacob-rees-mogg-conservative-mp-north-east-somerset-capital-management-investment-firm-belgravia-a7902951.html

Williams, R. (1963) *Culture and Society*. Harmondsworth: Penguin.

Williams R. (1988) *Key Words*. London: Fontana Press.

Wodak, R. (2001) What CDA is about: a summary of its history, important concepts and its development, in R. Wodak and M. Meyer (eds), *Methods of Critical Discourse Analysis*. London: SAGE. pp. 1–13.

Wodak, R. and Forchtner, B. (2014) Embattled Vienna 1683–2010: right-wing populism, collective memory and the fictionalisation of politics. *Visual Communication*, 13(2): 231–255.

Wodak, R. and Weiss, G. (2005) Analyzing European Union discourses: theories and applications, in R. Wodak and P. Chilton (eds), *A New Agenda in (Critical) Discourse Analysis: Theory, Methodology and Interdisciplinarity*. Amsterdam: John Benjamins. pp. 121–36.

Wodak, R., de Cillia, R., Reisigl, M. and Leibhart, K. (1999) *The Discursive Construction of National Identity*. Edinburgh: Edinburgh University Press.

Wright, W. (1975) *Six Guns and Society: A Structural Study of the Western*. Ewing: University of California Press.

YouTube by numbers (2019) *YouTube for Press*. https://www.youtube.com/yt/about/press/

Young, D. (2008) The privileged role of the late-night joke: exploring humor's role in disrupting argument scrutiny. *Media Psychology*, 11(1): 119–142.

Young, D.G. and Tisinger, R. (2006) Dispelling late-night myths: news consumption among late-night comedy viewers and the predictors of exposure to various late-night shows. *Harvard International Journal of Press/Politics*, 11(3): 113–134.

Zappettini, F. and Krzyżanowski, M. (2019) 'Brexit' in media and political discourses: from national populist imaginary to cross-national social and political crisis. *Critical Discourse Studies*, 16(4): 381–388.

Zbikowski, L. (2015) Words, music, and meaning, in P.A. Brandt and J.R. do Carmo Jr (eds), *Semiotic de la musique*. Liège: Presses universitaires de Liège–Sciences humaines. pp. 143–164.

Zhang, Y. and O'Halloran, K. (2012) The gate of the gateway: a hypermodal approach to university homepages. *Semiotica*, 190–1(4): 203–225.

INDEX